Johnny
Appleseed

MAN AND MYTH

by Robert Price

GLOUCESTER, MASS.

PETER SMITH

1967

This earliest drawing of John Chapman appeared as a frontispiece in H. S. Knapp's History of the Pioneer and Modern Times of Ashland County, Ohio, *1863. Said to have been drawn in the 1850's by a student of Oberlin College who had known Chapman, it corresponds to the verbal description furnished to Henry Howe in 1845 by Miss Rosella Rice of Perrysville. A later artist changed the strange headgear to a normally brimmed hat and the result became the standard picture of Johnny Appleseed now engraved in American folklore.*

JOHNNY APPLESEED: EARLIEST DRAWING

ACKNOWLEDGMENTS

THE author is grateful to the writers and publishers listed below for permission to quote specific passages from the works named: Appleton-Century-Crofts, "The Apple-Barrel of Johnny Appleseed," from *Going to the Sun*, by Vachel Lindsay; Frances Frost and the publishers, "American Ghost," *New York Herald Tribune*, August 21, 1943; The Macmillan Company, "In Praise of Johnny Appleseed," from *Johnny Appleseed and Other Poems*, by Vachel Lindsay; Rinehart and Company, "Johnny Appleseed," from *A Book of Americans*, copyright, 1933, by Rosemary and Stephen Vincent Benét.

CONTENTS

ILLUSTRATIONS

SPOT DRAWINGS BY H. LAWRENCE HOFFMAN

FOREWORD

THE SEARCH began along Mootz Run in Licking County, Ohio, one summer day in 1930. Doc Cash had been tracing the site of an early grist mill, completed there in 1818, and Tom Parry, who had lived much of his life in the cottage just beyond the covered bridge, was pointing out the evidences of buildings that had once been part of an early ghost town around the mill. Then Tom said, "And right up there is where Johnny Appleseed planted a nursery." He pointed to a spot near the stream. "That's what old Mr. Hawley said when he was back here on a visit about the time I moved into the neighborhood. He remembered some of the trees and said there'd been a brush fence around the spot."

The Hawley family had come to the township with the pioneer generation before the 1830's. They could have known if John Chapman, who was roaming at least some of these tributaries of the Licking River between 1803 and 1820, had nurtured a planting here. Could any evidence be found to support the local tradition? Unfortunately, I soon discovered, nobody had ever given the few facts and the multitudinous fancies concerning Johnny a critical sifting. So I set out to do the task, and now nearly a quarter century afterward, though the long trail that has taken me thousands of miles back and forth across much of Eastern America never got back to a point certifiably nearer than twenty-five miles of the Mootz Run starting-place, it has been a richly interesting journey.

No one had dreamed, when the search began, to what extent it must be a quest for both a man and a myth, or that during the particular decades of my trailing, the strange appleseed planter would leap into an amazing public popularity to become one of America's half dozen favorite folk heroes. If John Chapman, when he died near Fort Wayne in 1845, had merely lain down to the long rest like ordinary men, then the history of his labors—though remarkable— could have been told quickly and simply, for the old Yankee tree peddler had taken little care to leave himself in the records.

Instead, because even in his dying John could not be commonplace, he stepped spryly out of the flesh that snowy March day, straightened his mushpot hat, girt up his coffee-sack shirt, eased his bare feet in celestial sunshine and started off to longer travels and greater labors than he had ever known before. He had walked more miles than any other recorded borderer of his generation—now he belonged to the American trails and rivers forever. He had strewn appleseeds over much of the land between the Allegheny and the Mississippi—now he would become the mythical planter of all first orchards from the Atlantic to the Pacific. And when American horticulture had been well established, he would turn his hand, during the next hundred years, to anything else that would make the land fruitful and beautiful.

He had been a hero on the Indian border and a kindly, humanitarian Christian missionary who had left folk talk like his seeds growing wherever he had gone. In the Middle Western wilderness, he had helped make straight the paths for the march of American democracy. Now that these paths overlaced a continent, he would become a symbol of a nation's philosophy setting an example of faith and industry and common neighborliness among all races and levels of men and—to use Vachel Lindsay's metaphor—even conjure an apple barrel out of the sun from which the Rambos and Baldwins of democracy might go rolling around the world.

Now that John Chapman's real story is ready to present for the first time, I must acknowledge much aid during the search for it, for the Johnny Appleseed path has had a strong lure for a host of people and some of them have helped me greatly whether by their inspiration or pleasant fellowship or plain hard work.

To the late Hamlin Garland and Edgar Lee Masters, and to Carl Sandburg and Louis Bromfield—all men of the broad view who have spent many years learning the American story —I owe much for words of encouragement, enthusiasm and advice at various times during the past twenty-four years. The thought that they had seen potential value in my project helped me through some very discouraging moments.

Both earlier and present-day writers about John Chapman have been legion and many of them have been acknowledged in the present volume. Two stand out, however, for the special magnitude of their work. The first is Mr. Robert C. Harris, Fort Wayne scholar and educator, whose long researches and enthusiastic interest as secretary of the public-spirited Fort Wayne Johnny Appleseed Commission have not only uncovered much archive data relating to Chapman's last years but have helped create in Fort Wayne one of America's finest memorials to the pioneer nurseryman. The second is Miss Florence Wheeler, public librarian of Leominster, Massachusetts, whose genealogical researches over a period of several years finally revealed the identity of the Chapman family connections and traced both the paternal and maternal lines to the first forebears in New England.

Although, too, this study owes a great debt to dozens of libraries and librarians from coast to coast, I must especially acknowledge the multitudinous services of Dr. Harlow Lindley and Miss Helen Mills, former secretary and assistant librarian respectively, along with their associates, of the Ohio Archaeological and Historical Society. Dr. Howard Peckham and the staff of the Indiana State Historical Society and the librarians of the Indiana State Library have served with equal generosity in the Hoosier state's great historical collections. The enormous accumulation of additional small debts can only be suggested by the present bibliography and notes; by my *John Chapman: A Bibliography* . . . published in 1944; and by the hundreds of persons whose letters rest in my files or whose helpful converse is pleasant memory.

The final researches for this study were made possible by a year's grant-in-aid from the Library of Congress beginning in September, 1945. Since the labor could not have been completed without this year of investigation, special thanks are due to the Rockefeller Foundation that supplied the funds, to Dr. Luther H. Evans, then Librarian of Congress who administered them, and to President J. Gordon Howard and Dean Paul B. Anderson of Otterbein College who arranged my year's leave from teaching duties.

My wife, Hazel H. Price, who has shared this long search for John Chapman's reality, has been my most valued assistant and critic.

There are certain peculiar penalties that devolve upon the researcher who serves too long in a public quest, especially if his object has such powers as Johnny Appleseed's to pull swarms of "enthusiasts" into the trail. Since 1939 I have been publishing more or less regularly the results of my labors, only to discover that in the large annual output of magazine and newspaper features, poems, radio programs and children's books which Johnny inevitably inspires, my long-sought facts (and often my very words!) are beginning to come back to me in an ever-changing variety of new, quaint or curious, naively original or startlingly imaginative misconceptions and fancyings. A mere researcher stands helpless before this superior power. But not hopeless, for he knows that when a folk tale attains the status of a myth and embodies a cherished ideal of the people, then its true worth no longer lies merely in the dead facts that may have inspired it but in the new, living and creating force that it has become in the present.

ROBERT PRICE

Otterbein College
January 1, 1954

PART ONE

ABOUT THE TIME of the survey of the lands in the United States military district, northwest of the river Ohio, preparatory to their location by those holding the warrants which had been issued by the government to the soldiers of the revolutionary war, for services during that war, there came to the valley of the Muskingum and its tributaries, the Tuscarawas, Walhonding, Mohican, &c., a man whose real name, if ever known, is not now remembered by the oldest inhabitants here, but who was commonly known and called all over the country by the name of Johnny Appleseed.

This man had imbibed so remarkable a passion for the rearing and cultivation of apple trees from the seed, and pursued it with so much zeal and perseverance, as to cause him to be regarded by the few settlers, just then beginning to make their appearance in the country, with a degree of almost superstitious admiration.

Immediately upon his advent, he commenced the raising

Into the Old Northwest

of apple trees from the seed, at a time when there were not, perhaps, fifty white men within the forty miles square. He would clear a few rods of ground in some open part of the forest, girdle the trees standing upon it, surround it with a brush fence, and plant his apple seeds. This done, he would go off some twenty miles or so, select another favorable spot, and again go through the same operation. In this way, without family and without connection, he rambled from place to place, and employed his time, I may say his life.

When the settlers began to flock in and open their "clearings", old Appleseed was ready for them with his young trees; and it was not his fault if everyone of them had not an orchard planted out and growing without delay.

Hovey's Magazine of Horticulture, April, 1846

> *And he ran with the rabbit and slept with the stream,*
> *And so for us he made great medicine,*
> *And so for us he made great medicine,*
> *And so for us he made great medicine,*
> *In the days of President Washington.*

VACHEL LINDSAY, "In Praise of Johnny Appleseed"

1

A TRAIL FROM NEW ENGLAND

WHATEVER else John Chapman may have been in fact or fancy, there is no doubt that he was as thoroughgoing an example of good old-fashioned American individualism as ever chopped out a clearing. There isn't much a biographer can do, accordingly, but let him bow into his own story in his own vigorously independent way. A host of other colorful tales to the contrary, it is a fact that there is just one account, approaching reliable record, of the famous pioneer nurseryman's entry into the Middle West.[1] According to it, Johnny Appleseed walked into the American story one mid-autumn day in 1797, not vision-eyed among the orchards of the Potomac or riding triumphantly into Pittsburgh on the front seat of a conestoga wagon, but plodding along somewhere atop the Allegheny plateau in northern Pennsylvania and just about to be bogged down in a November snowfall.

The setting is spectacular enough for the stage entrance of any American folk hero. About halfway across Pennsylvania, just below the New York line, the Allegheny plateau rears up into a cap of high, broad ridges that send the general elevation to over 2,500 feet. An eagle soaring high on a clear day can look down on headwaters that rise within only short distances of each other and then rush out of the tangle of gorges and valleys north to the Genesee and the Great Lakes, east to the Susquehanna and the Atlantic, and west to the Allegheny and the Gulf of Mexico. It is a spot geographically dramatic even today, and in 1797 it was a primeval wilderness completely unspoiled by settlement and scarcely touched even by a surveyor's chain.

In late October or early November of that year, says this first of the Johnny Appleseed stories, twenty-three-year-old John Chapman was making a long journey alone and afoot across this plateau. His course can be plotted easily on a map by inscribing a shallow curve from the Wilkes-Barre mining country on the Susquehanna River in eastern Pennsylvania northward up the watercourse, then west across the whole Appalachian highland, to a spot on the upper Allegheny River about twelve miles below the New York line, where the little city of Warren now lies.

The east end of this curve in 1797 rested in the Wyoming Valley, a busy farming community, that was still fresh in fame because of the most gruesome Indian massacre committed during the recent Revolutionary war years. In this particular autumn it was enjoying a vigorous economic boom after a long series of shameful land feuds and had been attracting considerable attention from Easterners, particularly settlers from the Connecticut Valley.

The middle of this curve, after it left the old trail up the Susquehanna, extended westerly through leagues of mountain wilderness. And the west tip on the other side of the plateau rested in the vast forests of the upper Allegheny in northwestern Pennsylvania. The precise spot of termination seems to have been the single log structure that was the blockhouse headquarters of the Holland Land Company.

Having heard favorable reports of the Allegheny country, says the tale, young John Chapman, who had been sojourning in the Wyoming Valley, started making the trip over the mountains sometime in November of 1797. The weather was pleasant during the first few days up the broad Susquehanna and continued so as he pushed on west into the heavy forests that covered the mountains of what is now the counties of Bradford, Tioga, and Potter.

Then suddenly there was a furious onslaught of winter. Snow fell till it piled up three feet on the level, and young John was caught a hundred miles from his starting place without adequate protection or supplies. He had seemingly packed along only the woodsman's usual equipment—a rifle, a tomahawk, and just enough provisions in his knapsack to make the trip unhindered. Besides, he was barefooted. (Those bare feet were to plod through many a later yarn.)

Charles Peirce in Philadelphia, who kept a now very precious diary of Pennsylvania weather that fall, recorded that all during the first weeks of November eastern Pennsylvania was enjoying a spell of delightfully pleasant Indian summer mildness; then suddenly there was a severe attack of early winter.[2] In Philadelphia more than three times the normal amount of snow descended during November, and some four and a half inches of rain, most of it falling in the latter weeks of the month. Potter County, a hundred miles farther north and high in elevation, has a reputation for overwhelming snows that pile deep in the valleys and stay for weeks.

John Chapman, when the rigorous winter overtook him miles west of the last cabins on the Tioga, had not reckoned on weather like this.

He did the sensible thing when the snow struck—chose a sheltered camp site and settled down to size up his predicament. As a first measure, he tore off the short skirt of his blanket coat and bound the strips tightly around his feet and ankles to serve the double purpose of shoes and stockings. (In later years, those feet would come in for far less commiseration!) Then, however, there was the difficulty of wading through the wet, knee-deep snow. He needed snowshoes, and these beautiful Pennsylvania slopes did not grow seasoned hickory bows or moosehide laces.

They did produce, however, great groves of patriarchal beech trees with long drooping ash-colored branches that bore sprays of light, flexible, thick-set horizontally spreading twigs. And John, who somewhere in his twenty-three years had come by a considerable store of knowledge about getting on in a hand-to-hand struggle with primeval nature, cut a quantity of these, heated them by his fire till they became pliable, then by deft bending and weaving was able to shape them into a pair of serviceable snowshoes. These he fastened to his feet with moosewood bark, and continuing his journey without further serious trouble, he arrived at the site of the future city of Warren sometime about the first of December.

In his knapsack, the tale concludes, John was packing along a small quantity of appleseeds. The next spring he selected a spot on the Big Brokenstraw, that flows into the Allegheny from the west, six miles below Warren, and sowed the seed for an apple nursery. This was the first, whether of history or of tradition, in that long network of famous appleseed plantings that would stretch far into the forests of the Old Northwest and even farther into the lush wonderland of American fancies.

2

Johnny Appleseed enthusiasts have long told a bit differently of his first tree planting. They especially like a colorful version that brings him to Pittsburgh, the "Gateway to the West," late in the 1780's or early in the '90's, usually riding in the front seat of a covered wagon. They give him several years of unusual and rather childish residence at the confluence of the Allegheny and the Monongahela while he serves as a strange young missionary carrying on a travelers' aid station for the overland migrants going down river into the Ohio country. Then, when his vision is ripe, they send him and his seeds on into the Northwest Territory, ahead of the main column of settlers, to prepare the wilderness for the march of democracy. This fanciful reconstruction, now firmly established through endless tellings in rhyme and children's tale, novel and screen play (Walt Disney's *Melody Time* gave it a crowning glory), has the charm of quaintness and sentiment; but it does make its hero appear a trifle undernourished both physically and mentally and tends to make him too pretty-pretty for comfort. The real John Chapman was neither weak nor pretty.

On the other hand, the Allegheny snowstorm version of John Chapman's coming to the West, whatever its historical value, was set down about 1853 by Judge Lansing Wetmore, respected early chronicler of Warren County, Pennsylvania. The judge had come into the Brokenstraw neighborhood in 1815, at the age of twenty-three, when the memory of John Chapman and his trees was still green in the county. He had heard the tale from the families who had started their pioneer orchards from the Chapman seedlings, and he himself remembered the remains of the nursery. "The waters have long since washed away a portion of the ground," he said, "and took some of his trees to a bar below, which is still known as Apple-tree Bar. This nursery furnished the trees for most of the old orchards on the Brokenstraw."

The story was written out years afterward, of course, merely as he remembered it, and doubtless it had picked up a few variations and grace notes since John himself first related his adventure to Allegheny settlers. John's yarns from his lonely wilderness journeys would in time be scattered over much of the country that stretches between the Allegheny and the Wabash, and people would never quite agree as to the details. But this tale has much to back it up, and the Judge was certainly not spinning it out of fancy merely to extend a popular legend to his own neighborhood as so many later chroniclers would do for Johnny Appleseed in Ohio, Indiana, Missouri, and elsewhere. Apparently, Wetmore had not yet even heard of the grotesque nickname, "Johnny Appleseed," that in 1853 was chiefly known locally and farther west. Or if he had, he gave no sign in his account that he associated it with the youth who, in the pioneer lore of Warren County, had planted along the Brokenstraw. The Judge's historical writing seems to have kept honestly to community tradition.

Of John's origins, or of where he had gone, the Judge, who did not hesitate to put down all he had heard, appears to have been ignorant. He concluded his tale merely by saying of John that "the demand for fruit trees being limited, and unable to obtain a livelihood by his favorite pursuit, he went to Franklin, where he established another nursery. Subsequently he removed to Indiana."

It is precisely in Franklin, Pennsylvania, some fifty miles down the Allegheny from Warren, that documentable records can first tack a certifiable footnote or two onto John Chapman's elusive early doings in the Middle West.

3

In the meantime, there is little wonder that the first Brokenstraw cabin dwellers who saw John Chapman in the years just before and after 1800 found out very little about their appleman's origins, for people who came to know him all the rest of his life learned little more. After he died in 1845, the records of his life disappeared so completely for a time that the grizzled planter who had begun to wander through so much fantastic local lore seemed often more like a phantom sprung from the moon or from an ancient sycamore along the Muskingum or the Kokosing than someone begotten of the flesh. Many fertile imaginations went to work on his story, though, and fancied lineages and youthful adventures have been springing up for him ever since with the vigor of brambles along a rail fence or junipers in a New England pasture.

It was not until 1935 that his birth and family connections were trailed again to the right place, in Leominster, Massachusetts, and his solid Yankee background partially restored.[3] Leominster now even points out the traditional Chapman homesite, marked by a lonely cellar hole in the south slope of the Nashua River below the city. There the Massachusetts Fruit Growers Association in 1940 put up a little granite monument with a bronze inscription reading: "He planted seeds that others might enjoy fruit." But the civil authorities of today's humming mill city usually have the bronze plaque in storage to protect it from vandals. New England has changed much since the quiet farming back-country days of 1774.

Somewhere here in Leominster, the records of the First Congregational Church clearly show, John Chapman was born on September 26, 1774—not in the moon of appleblossoms as the folk tales insist, but in apple-picking time.[4] To be sure, the apple crop may have been particularly abundant in Massachusetts that fall. Or the sumac may have flamed with special brilliance across the Worcester County countryside. And at the moment of John's advent, a rainbow may indeed have startled the crows of Leominster by leaping across the valley from the summit of old South Monoosnock Hill (where an early resident once caught a glimpse of the Great Carbuncle itself). All this may have happened—the records do not say.

John's father, Nathaniel Chapman, a local farmer and carpenter, had come from Topsfield, according to the genealogy ingeniously established in 1939 by Miss Florence Wheeler, Leominster librarian. It can be traced through five substantial generations to an Edward Chapman, farmer and miller, who came supposedly from Shropshire, landed in Boston in 1639, and settled in Ipswich as early as 1642.[5] When he died in 1678, he left among other bequests to his second wife, "ten good bearing fruit trees near the end of the house." Orcharding was in the family early.

He had married Elizabeth, the daughter of James Simons (also spelled Simonds or Symonds), one of Leominster's first settlers and a stalwart man. James was descended from a William Simons who had arrived in Boston on the *Planter* in 1635 and settled in nearby Woburn about 1644. He had come from Woburn to the Nashua Valley backlands shortly after his marriage in May, 1740—his first child was born there the following August. There he built one of the first frame houses, a simple, unadorned one, solid enough to stand for a

hundred and fifty years.[6] He took an interest in publi[c]
and when the local minister in 1758 went modern and
ported the "New Light" doctrines of revelation and conve[r]
sion as opposed to the older Calvinistic authoritarianism, he
went along with the liberal view in the congregational split
that followed. Elizabeth Simons Chapman was his fifth child.

There was intelligence and perhaps a bit of fantasy in the
Simons line. One of Elizabeth's first cousins, in fact, was none
other than the famous and notorious "Count Rumford." Benjamin Thompson of Woburn, son of James's sister, had for-
saken the colonial cause during the war for independence and
fled to England, where he won the favor of King George III,
was given high positions of state, and finally knighted. He
went eventually into the service of the Elector Palatine of
Bavaria; there he became minister of war and chief of the
regency, and was made a count. In addition, he was a scientist
who performed experiments with gunpowder, heat transmis-
sion, and moisture absorption that took his renown into every
learned society in Europe. His writings could be read in several languages. When Benjamin Thompson—Count Rumford,
Count of the Holy Roman Empire, Fellow of the Royal
Society, etc., etc.—died in 1814, possessed of a vast fortune
and decorated by half a dozen nations, his cousin John Chapman—"Appleseed John," "Johnny Appleseed"—was planting
trees and folk fancies across a large portion of Middle Western America. There was something to reckon with in this
Simons blood.

Little is known now about the Chapman household in
Leominster. When John was born, there was one older child,
Elizabeth, four years his senior. The mother appears to have
been frail in health. The home was of the humblest and, if
Leominster tradition is correct, it stood on rented land be-

n Johnson of Woburn, whose wife was a
h Simons Chapman.[7] Nathaniel Chapman
/ned any land either in Leominster or any-
fact of history, though, is sure: five days
born, the Worcester County convention, in
miles away, had voted for a complete reor-
e district militia. All officers of the British
Crown had ... carefully eliminated, and since relations between the colonists and the mother country were growing
hourly more unruly, every town in the county had been in-
structed to enlist one third of all privates between the ages of
sixteen and sixty years "to be ready to act at a minute's
warning."

Nathaniel Chapman was one of these original "Minute
Men" and, the next April, was in one of the three Leominster
companies that set out to Lexington. Though the Leominster
troops did not arrive in time to take part in the famous skir-
mishes in Concord or along the line of the Redcoats' retreat, he
was one of those who enlisted immediately as a part of Colonel Asa Whitcomb's Twenty-third Regiment of Foot and
went into camp shortly thereafter in Cambridge. He apparently fought in the Battle of Bunker Hill in June, 1775, and a
year later was with Washington's army in New York.[8]

He was probably not with his young wife, Elizabeth
Simons Chapman, when she died in July, 1776, in Leominster.

Time has saved just one personal memento of John Chapman's mother. It is a letter written by her on June 3, 1776, to
her husband, then in Captain Pollard's Company of Carpenters, with Washington in New York.[9] The message is brief,
brave, pathetic—it tells all that can be known now of the ordeal through which Elizabeth was passing.

No word had come from her husband for many weeks,

possibly not since the army had set out for New York. Within the past two days, however, the sick wife had received two letters, one on Friday, another on "Sabbathday evening." Now, on Monday, she was hastening to answer so that Mr. Mullins might carry the letter.

She felt that she must inform Nathaniel of her serious plight; yet she would not alarm him unduly, for he had worries enough of his own. Still, if he were only with her in person, the awful fears would soften. Even though couched with so much moderation and restraint the letter is pathetically pleading.

Loving Husband, it begins.

These lines come with my affectionate regards to you hoping they will find you in health, tho I still continue in a very weak and low condition. I am no better than I was when you left me but rather worse, and I should be very glad if you could come and see me for I want to see you.

Our children are both well thro the Divine goodness.

Elizabeth was nearly six now—John not yet turned two.

I have received but two letters from you since you went away—neither knew where you was till last Friday I had one and Sabathday evening after, another, and I rejoice to hear that you are well and I pray you may thus continue and in God's due time be returned in safety. I send this letter by Mr. Mullins and I hope it will reach you and I should be glad if you would send me a letter back by him.

I have wrote that I should be glad you could come to see me if you could, but if you cannot, I desire you should make yourself as easy as possible for I am under the care of a kind Providence who is able to do more for me than I can ask or think and I desire humbly to submit to His Holy Will with patience and resignation, patiently to bear what he shall see fitt to lay upon me. My cough is something abated, but I think I grow weaker. I desire your prayers for me that I may be prepared for the will of God that I may so improve my remainder of life that I may answer the great end for which I was made, that I might glorify God here and finally come to the enjoyment of Him in a world of glory, thro the merits of Jesus Christ.

Remember, I beseech you, that you are a mortall and that you must submit to death sooner or later and consider that we are always in danger of our spiritual enemy. Be, therefore, on your guard continually, and live in a daily preparation for death—and so I must bid you farewell and if it should be so ordered that I should not see you again, I hope we shall both be as happy as to spend an eternity of happiness together in the coming world which is my desire and prayer.

So I conclude by subscribing myself, your

Ever loving and affectionate wife

Elizabeth Chapman

There were two postcripts:

Brother Zebedee is well and is in Boston.[10] Father's family is all as well as common. Mr. Johnson's family is well. The Widow Smith's and Joshua Peirce's folks are all well, and all our friends are as well as usual.

The other:

I have not bought a cow for they are very scarce and dear and I think I can do without, and I would not have you uneasy about it or about any money for I have as much as I need for the present.

The letter was addressed to:

> *Mr. Nathaniel Chapman in New York in Capt. Pollard's Company of Carpenters. The favor by Mr. Mullins.*

By the time this letter could have reached Nathaniel, the army in New York was anxiously engaged in the construction of entrenchments against an inevitable attack. By June 10, the British fleet had left its base at Halifax and was headed south. By July 1, it was off Sandy Hook. On July 10, troops were being landed on Staten Island. Whether at any time during these weeks of critical preparation, Nathaniel was able to respond in person to his wife's pathetic appeal, we do not know. The likelihood seems small.

The concluding events are calendared in the Leominster town records.[11] On June 26, 1776, three weeks after her letter to Nathaniel, Elizabeth Chapman was delivered of her third child, a son. She died on July 18. According to family tradition the infant, who had been named Nathaniel, survived her by a couple of weeks. Their burial places are unknown today.

The two orphaned children, it is logical to suppose, were taken into the care of the Simons family in Leominster.

John Chapman's mother's last brave letter to her husband was carefully treasured, in spite of Nathaniel's long soldiering and later remarriage, and was ultimately given into the safekeeping of his oldest child, Elizabeth, among whose descendants it came to light one hundred sixty-one years later.

4

What else happened during the boyhood of John Chapman that might have started his life and thought in the direction of the strange career ahead is uncertain. He may have lived for a time in Longmeadow, south of Springfield, Massachusetts. In fact, a little marker erected in 1936 in Stebbins Park by the Springfield Garden club declares firmly: "He spent his boyhood in this pleasant valley or somewhere nearby. Here he received inspiration for his life work of spreading westward his gospel of beauty and service."

About the inspiration one cannot be sure. Any boy's inspirations are elusive, especially after a century and a half. But as for the Connecticut Valley's being the setting for John's boyhood, the Stebbins Park memorial has some probability on its side. Many years later the roving tree-peddler left distinct impressions among the farmers of Ohio and Indiana that he had come from the vicinity of Springfield. Nathaniel Chapman did, certainly, remarry and settle there after his soldiering had led him variously to Valley Forge and to the military depot in Springfield, from which he was released into permanent civilian status in September, 1780.[12] The prettied-up stories have sometimes made this father of Johnny Appleseed a hero of the Revolution. Whatever his earlier record, the journals of the Continental Congress give only the unpleasant truth that Captain Chapman along with other Springfield officers was released late in 1780 because of unsatisfactory management of the military stores. In years to come he was given neither a pension nor a land bounty for his services.

In the July previous, however, evidently foreseeing the approaching shift in his fortunes, Captain Nathaniel had begun his transition to civilian life by marrying Miss Lucy Cooley, who resided a mile and a half south of the Springfield line in Longmeadow.[13] Lucy was eighteen—the Captain thirty-four. By this union Nathaniel Chapman of Leominster had

JOHN CHAPMAN'S BIRTHPLACE

This monument, erected by the Leominster, Mass., Bi-Centennial Committee in 1940, marks the traditional site of the Chapman home in Leominster. Courtesy of the Leominster Bi-Centennial Committee.

N CHAPMAN'S BIRTH RECORD IN LEOMINSTER, ss., town records. Certified copy, courtesy of minster City Clerk.

Photograph by Miss Annie E. Emerson, 1915

ADITIONAL BOYHOOD HOME OF JOHN CHAPMAN, LONGMEADOW, MASS.

THE LONGMEADOW MEETINGHOUSE
From an engraving, 1839

THE SIMONDS HOMESTEAD, LEOMINSTER
From original drawing by Mary A. Tolman for Old Landmarks in Leominster, *1896*

allied himself with a very respectable family and certainly one of the most prolific of the Connecticut Valley.

If the Captain's oldest son, who would now have been approaching six, came down from Leominster to live here in his father's second household in Longmeadow, it was not many years before he must have begun to feel the nest crowded, for the Captain set about fathering ten more sons and daughters in about the shortest time allowable. Stories have had it that John left early, and there is every reason why he would have. The Captain was seemingly never a strong provider for his flock. "More stock than fodder," as Longmeadowans would say. The one house the Chapmans are known to have lived in, from the clues in the Federal census of 1790, was a tiny frame structure, one of the oldest in the town,[14] a couple of miles below the Springfield line, just off the main highway that followed the terrace of the river valley south along the Connecticut meadows.

If John really did grow up here, then the solid elementary schooling of Longmeadow might account for the fair copperplate script that he kept intact most of his long life and for the reading facility that ultimately led him to become the most famed peruser of Emanuel Swedenborg west of the Alleghenies. He most certainly never attended Harvard College as one tale has said.

He would have grown up in a church pattern too, though by this time in Longmeadow a merely conventional Calvinistic one that, current reports seem to indicate, had become well-nigh sterile. Though John appears to have been a religious man throughout all his years, the dry rot in the New England worship of his youth could have sent him off early in quest of a warmer and more imaginative faith such as that which he eventually found.

He would have been close here also to forest and stream. The road past the Chapman door ran directly down to the river on the one hand and into the woods on the other. By the time he was to wrestle with the elements in the Allegheny Valley, he had learned well somewhere all the ways of outdoor living. He was to have one of the finest skills in matching wits with water, for example, that the frontier ever knew. He could very easily have learned these arts along the Connecticut.

He would have heard much in Longmeadow through these years, too, about outside affairs, for the road through the town was a main thoroughfare of public traffic from Boston and Springfield to Hartford and points south. The young American nation was likewise just a husky boy trying his leg muscles and wondering which way to run. When John was ten, he must have heard talk of the Treaty of Paris and a new American boundary set somewhere in the distant west along a stream called the Mississippi. When he was twelve, a federal ordinance was being set to work shaping the future of a great public domain somewhere in those vast government holdings, to be known as the Northwest Territory. A year later a company of western Massachusetts people were establishing Marietta, the first permanent settlement in this new territory, at a spot just where a river with the musical Indian name of Muskingum joined the Ohio.

All this and much more the boy John Chapman could have learned easily enough if he grew up in the Connecticut Valley's beautiful town of Longmeadow. But exactly what he learned and where he learned it through all those impressionable years of his own and the young American nation's first life is today anybody's guess. Where, for instance, back in the now-romantic-seeming days of President Washington did he pick up his interest in the nurture of apple seedlings? Just as he was approaching his maturity, was he swept with the natural overflow of population from the debt-ridden and restless Connecticut Valley over into the new boom-country along the upper Susquehanna? And now in the fall of 1797, in the eighth month of the presidency of John Adams, had he heard of the Holland Land Company's vast offerings of cheap land in Pennsylvania's Allegheny northwest?

In spite of all the delightful imaginings by several generations of Johnny Appleseed cultists, these questions still remain unanswered. Not a single fact is known today, based upon either record or direct tradition, that will bridge the wide gap between John Chapman's certifiable origins in Leominster, Massachusetts, and his probable appearance in the upper Allegheny country of northwestern Pennsylvania in 1797.

2

HIGH ADVENTURE ON THE ALLEGHENY

IF JUDGE Wetmore's Warren County narrative reflects fact, it still leaves young Chapman pretty much of a shadow, and a shadow he persists in remaining for a number of years. A very lively one, though, and—if it is fair to attribute to a young fellow of twenty-three what people remembered of a much older man—we can imagine John as spare-built, sinewy and large-boned. He was about five feet nine inches in height and he had blue eyes. Also, whatever ideas he may have had for utilizing it, he was packed full of Yankee energy.

He had literally walked in by the backdoor to Pennsylvania's last great land rush, and he found it immediately interesting. The main push of settlement into the Allegheny wilderness was coming upstream from Pittsburgh, and in 1797 it was just beginning to move briskly for a big final sweep northward. Even so, the log house outpost of the Holland Land Company at the mouth of Conewango Creek on the upper bend of the Allegheny River was a hundred and fifty miles up from Pittsburgh and fifty miles into the wilderness beyond Franklin, the nearest town and trading point.

John would have known about Warren, though, for the town, while it had existed officially on the map only since

April, 1795, had been widely publicized throughout the East by the land promoters. It actually consisted in November, 1797, of a plat and a single log house on the north bank of the river, with Daniel McQuay, local manager for the Holland Land Company, the sole occupant. No other building was in sight, save possibly another simple log structure just outside the town bounds. All else was a magnificent untouched forest, largely of red, black, and white oak. Immediately behind, on the north, rose the precipitous sheltering ridge that gives the city of Warren its touch of rugged beauty today. In 1797 only a few individual settlers from down river had begun to penetrate the forests to the west and south.

The vast west Pennsylvania area north of Pittsburgh had been opened to white settlers as early as 1792, but the Indian troubles had held back the main advance until after "Mad Anthony" Wayne's decisive victory over the Indian tribes at Fallen Timbers in 1794. In the meantime, the backlands had been largely bought up under laws conveniently suited to line the pockets of big speculators. One group of Dutch bankers, who came to be known eventually as the Holland Land Company, laid claim to no less than five million acres in central and western New York and in northern and western Pennsylvania.

There had been just one hitch. Pennsylvania laws had allowed the taking up of land on the easiest and worst of systems, a warrant and patent plan with small down payments, that required no previous survey and promised establishment of title, provided that settlement be made within two years. Settlement involved the clearing, fencing, and cultivating of at least two acres out of every one hundred in a warrant. In addition, a house must be built, and there must be evidence of continued residence.

Previous to 1794, the Indian depredations in the Allegheny Valley had given speculators reasonable excuse for not meeting these requirements. But beginning in 1795, the commonwealth's Board of Property had decided that the two-year rule must apply firmly thereafter and that all tracts warranted would have to be settled before the end of 1797.

The Holland Land Company, caught with vast tracts, parts of which were very rough and often inaccessible, had begun the biggest settlement promotion the East had ever experienced. "Improvements" were made at strategic points, and inducements of every sort were offered to anyone who would go there and stay long enough to establish a claim—free land, free provisions, equipment on credit, assistance in building, etc. Advertisements flared in the Eastern press. Agents worked in all the populous areas of Pennsylvania and adjoining states.

Pennsylvania was to suffer long for these sins. As in most land booms, the riffraff were the quickest persuaded. The settlers that speculators urged into the Allegheny Valley just after 1795, together with the state's slipshod provisions for fixing land titles, were to create one of Pennsylvania's sorest muddles. Actually, much of the region now being promoted was wholly unsuited to farming and would remain a sort of hinterland for nearly seventy-five years until its precious deposits of oil were at last found to be of value.

By an act of 1795, the Pennsylvania legislature had established three new towns: Erie (old Fort Le Boeuf) on Lake Erie, Franklin (old Fort Venango) on the Allegheny at the mouth of French Creek; and Warren on the upper Allegheny at the mouth of the Conewango. Lots in Warren went on sale in 1796, but the spot was still too far away from the nearest trading posts to attract many newcomers. In fact, as it turned out, actual development was to wait ten years until new routes could be opened from north and east across New York.

In the meantime, young John Chapman or anyone else who wandered to the Holland Land Company's isolated wilderness-bound Warren office in the fall of 1797 found company business up here in the forest anything but pressing and Irish Dan McQuay having a generally pleasant time. McQuay, by reputation, was witty, reckless, adventurous, and frequently drunk, with a rugged sociability that was something to be appreciated up in this lonely place.

Besides, no one knew better than he the peculiar prospects of the outlying country and particularly of the valley land along Brokenstraw Creek to the west, into which the settlers undoubtedly would crowd first. He was about to move into it himself, and young John Chapman—so Judge Wetmore's account indicates—was soon with him.

Apparently John spent the winter of 1797–98 scouting up and down the Allegheny, for his name appears at least once at this time in the trading-post records of Edward Hale at Franklin fifty miles downstream from Warren.[1] But he was back on the upper river in the spring and, said Wetmore, he *"selected a spot for his nursery—for that seemed to be his primary object—near White's, on the big Brokenstraw, and sowed his seed."* [2]

Brokenstraw Creek flows into the Allegheny from the west six miles below Warren. Today, it traces a beautiful farming country, with broad fertile corn bottoms spreading out along the stream between sharply rising uplands. In pre-settlement days, the rich flats were covered every summer with tall prairie grass that broke and fell over in the autumn to suggest the Indian name Cushanadauga or Brokenstraw. Here and there were tracts of virgin pine unsurpassed in America, and on the hillsides grew great oaks, chestnuts, whitewoods, ashes, and maples.

There were only four other settlers already up the creek. John McKinney had come from Ireland in the summer of 1795 and was clearing land about five miles up. In the spring of 1796, Mathew Young, a Scotsman and bachelor, had settled a short way below McKinney, where Youngsville now stands. In 1797 Callender Irvine with his servant Black Tom was trying to establish a claim near the mouth of the creek where Irvinetown is now. And by the spring of 1798, Dan McQuay had deserted the Holland Land Company's blockhouse and had also located for himself; within ten years he would be rafting logs from these slopes all the way down the Allegheny, the Ohio, and the Mississippi to New Orleans.

John went farther upstream than any of the others, if Judge Wetmore was right, for White's Town was once a local name for a point several miles above Young's. John may have been merely "squatting" here, or he may have been temporarily in the employ of the Holland Land Company with a permanent claim in mind—no record of his exact intentions has been saved.[3] Anyhow, Judge Wetmore was sure that here was the first planting and that from here John moved down the Allegheny to Franklin.

2

Here the shadow begins to take on a good deal more substance. John had set down his stakes in the French Creek neighborhood just above the town of Franklin and about fifty miles below the Warren blockhouse. His activities were to center here through much of the time between 1797 and 1804.

This Franklin region was also in the rawest stages of first

settlement, but it was much farther along than Warren and it was one of those newly opened strategic areas, both geographically and economically, to which John's instinct was to lead him unerringly over and over again. If the upper Allegheny around Warren, through which he had come into the West, was the rear door to the Pennsylvania frontier, and Pittsburgh, nearly a hundred and fifty miles below was the front, then Franklin in Venango County was the best of all intermediate points where any one could meet the flow of new population. There was plenty of virgin land. On some of it Chapman might establish a claim for himself. And if nurserying was to be his main business, there were wilderness spots where he could plant patches of appleseeds undisturbed by deeds or leases. His nursery stock would be ready in a short time for people who would be eager to buy, and he would have customers for at least a decade to come. In the meantime he could live simply, free to go and come as he liked in the unrestrained pattern that he appeared not yet ready to abandon.

Here where French Creek comes down between high bluffs from northwestern Pennsylvania to converge with the Allegheny ninety miles above Pittsburgh, ancient trails north from Lake Erie, west and south from the Ohio, and southeast from the Kitanning had been main roads since unrecorded ages. One key town after another had risen here through various regimes—Indian villages, French Fort Machault, British Fort Venango, and finally Franklin in 1795, laid out at the mouth of French Creek. Now a land office was opened and trading posts that had long operated here at the door to the Indian country began stocking up for a larger commerce. A new life was just about to surge into the rich bottoms between the forested ridges north and west of the Allegheny.

Up French Creek, people were to remember John chiefly as an unsettled floater who labored futilely, and perhaps not overhard, to establish a land claim. Old-timers believed that he had come there at the same time as John Martin, who had settled from Maryland in 1796, and that he had moved on into Ohio after several years of unsuccessful labor and eccentric adventures.[4] Interestingly enough, the French Creekers who left stories of him seem, like Judge Wetmore, not to have known that their restless early resident was the famous Johnny Appleseed of farther West.

"John Chapman, a young man full of adventure," ran the local tradition caught by historian J. H. Newton in 1879, *"came in about the same time as the Martins did, or probably before.*

"He was one of those characters, very often found in the new country, always ready to lend a helping hand to his neighbors. He helped others more than himself.

"He took up land several times, but would soon find himself without any, by reason of some other person 'jumping' his claim."

The leading merchants in the infant town of Franklin were Edward Hale and George Power, two of the most renowned Indian traders in the trans-Appalachian country. Cash was always scarce in a frontier community, so that any one who stayed around very long and could establish credit got on record in the trading post ledgers. Edward Hale appears to have set down John Chapman's name late in 1797, and George Power seems to have carried it during the general period between 1797 and 1800.[5]

Also his name was caught in the federal census report that Hale completed for Venango County in April, 1801.[6] John was living alone, the report shows, and the recording of his name on the enumerator's unalphabetized list, close by such other well-known pioneers in Venango County as Nickerson, Martin, Sutly, and Duffield, indicates that he was located at some spot up along French Creek, several miles above the trading post.

The census listed John as between twenty-six and fifty-five—he was actually twenty-six. He was also listed under "Head of Family," but that meant neither that he was married nor that he had one of the Indian women who did not get into polite records; it was just the usual way in the early censuses of recording independent bachelors who were living in their own quarters. John presumably was established on his own claim somewhere up French Creek.

The raw state of the locality is suggested vividly in this census return of 1800. Franklin itself was still just a trading center, having acquired only ten families in the past five years (and Mrs. Mary Ann Irvine, who recalled these years in 1876, could think of only half that number who were actually living in town). Newcomers stopped just long enough to stock up, get their bearings, and strike out for a claim. In the rest of the county, the census shows only one hundred sixty-one heads of families in all the large area that stretched up French Creek and westward, and less than half that number in the rougher east portion along the Allegheny. At least sixty-four of these "heads" were single men of various ages, living on their own. Some of these lone men were doubtless trappers and traders—largely drifters. But many, as in every first-broken patch of wilderness, were ambitious young men trying to fight through that initial period of settlement, too rough for any but the hardiest of women and children, when minimum clearings must be made, a log building set up, a crop raised, and residence stuck out long enough to win the land. If a man was lucky and looked smartly to his legal rights here in Pennsylvania, he might even win four hundred acres with a pre-emption claim to a thousand more.

But existence on this lonely outer edge of civilization was the most primitive imaginable, and for single men it tended to become much like that of the Indians who still came, went, and lived in considerable numbers along French Creek. The permanent white population had come only since 1795, and most of it since 1797. Three to five years could not change much of the wilderness, and those who conquered it had first to adopt its mode of life.

John Chapman learned these ways so well that all the rest of his years he would never care to abandon them completely. When he appeared in central Ohio a few years later, people noted that he moved among the Indians freely and respected, living as they did and communicating with them readily. Up in this outer fringe of settlement in northwest Pennsylvania between 1797 and 1804, he saw the Senecas and Munsees commonly, often daily. From all the back country clear to Lake Erie, they followed the main paths down French Creek to the trading establishments in Franklin. Such names as "Young Snake," "Old Chit," "Bottle Beaver," "Twenty Canoes," "Shut the Door," and "Old Halftown" mingle with Chapman's in the trading-post books. Trinkets, hunting equipment, clothing, and liquor were the chief objects of barter, and furs in season the usual means of settling the year's accounts.

John seems never to have succeeded in gaining a deed to any land here in Pennsylvania. If, as French Creek tradition said, he failed in several attempts to establish claims, he was only one of thousands of such claimants who labored futilely here. The land laws did not give adequate protection to honest efforts of small investors, and many an older and more businesslike settler than John Chapman lost to claim-jumpers in western Pennsylvania. It was a cut-throat struggle intensified by the lack of properly surveyed and recorded bounds, by a melee of squatters and unprotected claim holders, and by the ruthless devices of the big companies to cash in on their holdings. It was the enterprising man with plenty of ready money, or with no stuffy regard for the rights of the weaker, who finally acquired the land. In a few years, dozens of worthy farmers who had put the best of their lives and precious savings into farms in western Pennsylvania would be thrust out on technicalities of title. In the bitter feuds, fences would be destroyed, buildings burned, and whole areas depopulated.

John Chapman was here during the early stages of the struggle. He certainly wanted land, but he just as surely had little cash and may already have developed the stringent moral scruples that people observed in him a little later.

He was also free, perhaps a bit unbusinesslike, and seemingly unwilling to be tied this early in life to any sort of conventional community pattern.

3

John Chapman was also showing one other very characteristic trait—he already had the knack of sowing folk talk wherever he went. Only bits of it were ever recorded, and these do not help much with clearing away the shadows, but their very existence in a region that left little in writing for this period is significant.

"He was a singular character," said R. I. Curtis of West Virginia in 1859.[7] *"I knew him in Venango county, Pennsylvania, nearly sixty years ago, when a child of eight or nine years."* That would have been around 1800. . . . *"He was very fond of children and would talk to me a great deal, telling me of the hardships he had endured, of his adventures, and hairbreadth escapes by flood and field—some of them I remember."*

And what nine-year-old wouldn't have cherished some of those stories! One yarn, Curtis recalled, was a first-rate hairraiser about an escape from the Indians. John had been scouting around up on the peninsula in the neighborhood of Erie. Then he discovered that he was being hotly pursued by a party of red men, who, he had good reason to think, were hostile.

But all escape had by this time been cut off, and the Indians were obviously closing in upon him. There was only one thing left that he could do to elude them. He crept out into the shallows of the lake and lay down in the water among the thick growth of reeds and cattails.

His pursuers searched long and angrily for him—so long, in fact, that he actually took a nap in his weary hide-cut before he finally got a chance to slip away.

In French Creek Township, historian Newton heard the hint of another story, that on one occasion young Chapman "walked several miles on the ice *barefooted* [the italics were Newton's] merely to show off his powers of endurance. He seemed to be as much at home with the red men of the forest as with his own race." [8] All his life bare feet and ice were to vie with apples as appropriate symbols of John's career.

In another story mentioned by Curtis, John was a mighty woodchopper. He worked occasionally for the settlers who were making clearings in the French Creek district and he must have acquired some local fame for muscularity for Curtis remarked that "he could chop as much wood or girdle as many trees in one day as most men could in two." Years later in one of the best of the Johnny Appleseed stories from central Ohio, John would even be credited with having the devil chopping for him, and in the late extensions of the myth he has taken on for his chief adversary the forest-destroying Paul Bunyan himself.

The striking difference between these tiny scraps from the earliest of the John Chapman tales and the well-known ones of the later tradition is that the earlier ones center chiefly in physical prowess, not in apples or in any kind of sentimentalism. Life in the French Creek and Allegheny valleys was both rough and crude, and John seems to have fitted easily into some of its more extravagantly strenuous activities. True, none of the traditions admit that he was an actual hell-raiser or rip-tailed roarer, but if he did not indulge now and then in some high and mighty talk and do a little showing off in the best style of the boom-town boaster, then there is little to explain these hints of colorful yarns that have been preserved in enough independent ways to show that they once had considerable circulation. They suggest hearty and brawny tales— not the prettied-up sort that would be told in Ohio and Indiana of the aged Johnny Appleseed. They are rather grotesque and earthy. They belong to a young man. Judge Wetmore's narratives of the tussle with the snowstorm was obviously of the same cycle.

One of these stories was concerned with privation. "On an

island in French Creek," wrote Curtis, "he subsisted one whole winter on butternuts." Curtis did not elaborate, but this winter of remarkable endurance and vitamin deficiency may have been the same one that is preserved in a colorful Chapman family story set down about 1875 in Washington County, Ohio.[9] The author, William M. Glines, wrote out for a country literary society the stories that he had heard when a boy from John Chapman's brothers and sisters who had been his neighbors in southern Ohio. On at least one occasion, Glines said, he even heard some of the tales directly from the aged John Chapman himself. Glines's details are sometimes improbable or even impossible, but the fact that most of his yarns have parallels preserved from wholly independent sources not only shows that they were once current but increases the likelihood that they stem from actual experiences. Two of them parallel Curtis's stories from Venango County.

About John's hard winter in the Allegheny Valley, Glines wrote as follows:

At about the age of 28 years he succeeded in inducing his half-brother, Nathaniel, to run away with him. Nathaniel was a boy about 14 or 15 years old at the time. They made their way through the wilderness on foot to "Fort Duquesne," now Pittsburgh, Pennsylvania.

From there they went up the Allegheny to Olean in the State of New York where they remained about one year. The country being new and unsettled, they often suffered for want of the necessaries of life. Johnny finally concluded that he must go to Pittsburgh for provisions, and leave his brother to do the best he could; he said one would live there better than two, unless they had more provision. At length he left his young brother to look out for himself.

Some way or another, not exactly known, Johnny succeeded in procuring a muley steer which he led by a halter all the way to Pittsburgh and back again to his brother, using him as a pack horse for whatever he could procure. He was gone on this trip about four weeks.

During Johnny's absence Nathaniel became very much reduced and must have starved to death, but for a tribe of Indians who were wandering through the country who found and relieved him of his suffering; they taught him the use of the bow and arrow to success in killing small game.

In spite of the apocryphal details in the yarn, there may be some truth in it, too. John would have been twenty-eight in 1802, while his half-brother Nathaniel, oldest of Captain Chapman's second family in Longmeadow, would have been fifteen in 1796. But both Power's and Hale's trading-post accounts in Franklin carried the names of John and Nathaniel Chapman at now unidentifiable dates between 1797 and 1800 —the latter apparently about 1798. There was no "Fort Duquesne" in these late years, of course, and Olean on the upper bend of the Allegheny in New York was not founded till 1805. Whether John and Nathaniel were indeed near the present location of Olean or whether they were down in Venango County, they would have stocked supplies from posts much nearer than Pittsburgh. The likelihood is that this was the winter, probably between 1797 and 1800, spent on John's claim somewhere up French Creek, and any Indians who assisted them were very likely the friendly Senecas and Munsees that followed the trails regularly to and from Franklin.

The most delightful story in the entire group of fragments from these Allegheny Valley years concerns John's remarkable feats on floating ice. Again the episode has been saved in both the Curtis and the Glines accounts.

French Creek is "a turbulent stream when high," wrote

Curtis. "He once floated down it many miles on a cake of ice."

Glines transferred the incident to the Allegheny, made it an episode in the brothers' adventure-packed year together, and gave some additional details.

During the winter [he wrote] Johnny wanted to go down the river a short distance, and as the ice was running, he concluded to take a small canoe they had procured and started on his journey, but finding it rather troublesome to keep his canoe right side up, he concluded to drag the canoe to the center of a large strong cake of ice.

Having succeeded, he laid down in the canoe, made himself as comfortable as he could, went to sleep and when he awoke found himself about 100 miles below where he intended to stop.

He, however, managed to return to his brother who had suffered much during Johnny's long delay.

The future Johnny Appleseed slumbering peacefully in a canoe, atop a cake of ice as it bumped and dived its way for a hundred miles down the turbulent and rock-strewn Allegheny River marks the climactic point in these early hints of high adventure in western Pennsylvania.

3

APPLES ON THE BORDER

ALTHOUGH, as we have seen, appletree growing appears in John Chapman's story from the very first traditional account of his trek into the West, it does not emerge in official records until 1804, when he was thirty years old.

In February of that year, for reasons not now clear, John still in Franklin, Pennsylvania, signed two promissory notes.[1] In the first of these, dated February 1, 1804, he agreed to pay the sum of one hundred dollars to the children of Elizabeth and Nathaniel Rudd of Charlemont in the Commonwealth of Massachusetts. Interest was to be paid till the children were of age. Elizabeth Chapman, John's older sister, had married Nathaniel Rudd of Charlemont in December, 1799. John must not have known in February, 1804, that both of their children—John and Elizabeth, three and one years old respectively—had died only eight days apart during the previous September. The Rudds' third child would not be born until September 24th next, when possibly because of the nearness to the adventuring uncle's birthday it would be named John Chapman Rudd.[2]

Three days after signing this first note, John wrote another for the same amount to be paid to Nathaniel Chapman. Since it is the earliest documentary evidence of John's apple nursery interest, the exact text is sufficiently significant to quote entire:

"Franklin, February 4, 1804, for value received I promise to pay Nathaniel Chapman or order the sum of one hundred dollars in land or apple trees with interest till paid as witness my hand.

John Chapman"

Both notes were witnessed by Adam and John Harper.

Which of the Nathaniels this second note was intended for—the father who was still in Longmeadow, Massachusetts, or for John's younger half brother, who had been adventuring with him along the Allegheny—cannot be determined now. The half brother had now gone on west into Ohio and was settling in the vicinity of the new town of Marietta. The father was just about to move his Longmeadow family out to the same locality. Perhaps the notes were concerned with an adjustment of funds due the children of Captain Chapman's first wife. Anyhow, John appears to have been borrowing the money, and his prospects for realizing a return from it involved both land and appletrees.

As for the appletrees, John's neighbors around Franklin were beginning to see something of a pattern taking loose shape in their unpredictable associate's free life. Curtis remembered from French Creek that he would clear little patches in different places suitable for his purpose *"and where he thought at a future day appletrees would be wanted; then, in the fall, repair to Allegheny county, Pennsylvania, and wash out of the pomace at cider mills a bushel or two of seeds, and return with them on his shoulder, plant them at the proper time, enclose the spot with a brush fence, and pay*

*some attention to the cultivation. He never secured title to
the land for his nurseries. He never grafted any."* [3]

Except for the comment about land titles, Curtis's account
might be used to summarize John Chapman's horticultural
routine through all the rest of his life.

Today, Chapman's method seems quaintly primitive, especially to anybody who knows modern horticultural pro-
cedures, and this quaintness has been played up for far more
than it is worth in story and verse, song and drama. John
Chapman's plan for wholesale production of appletrees was
really no more picturesque than many other operations of
squatters and first settlers in the breaking of the wilderness
and—as soon becomes apparent—had some unusually practical
aspects. To his fellows on the border, it was neither quaint
nor impressive. To them, gathering seeds at the cider presses
in the older settlements and sowing them for future orchards
in the new clearings was nothing unusual. Other settlers did
it commonly.

What people did not see in Chapman's work—in fact, it
can be seen only from the backward glance long afterward—
was the drama of the larger plan that was slowly taking shape.
Perhaps it was a clearly conceived plan, perhaps only an accident; whatever it was, John himself seems not to have talked
much about it. Concerning his adventures, he chatted freely
enough wherever he went, but concerning his business, Yankee that he was, he was tight-lipped. Few people even when
he died in 1845 would fully realize the extent of the business
operations he had carried on, not even his family or the executors of his estate.

It is silly, of course, to say as uncritical sentimentalists have
sometimes done, that John Chapman brought the first fruit

trees into the Middle West. Orcharding was a venerable business in America long before his day. Even when John's remote ancestor Edward was nurturing his precious trees in Ipswich a hundred years before John was born, the French were already carrying the fruit along the Great Lakes and into the Mississippi Valley. When John first left New England, orchards of aged growth could be found around old Indian towns across New York, northern Ohio, and Indiana. In some of the valleys where he himself would be sowing nurseries in the 1820's and 30's, he would find awaiting him appletrees so old that their size rivaled that of the native hardwood patriarchs. Here in Pennsylvania, the southwestern counties around Pittsburgh—Allegheny, Westmoreland, and Washington counties in particular—had been settled with well-established orchards for at least two generations before John Chapman began visiting their cider presses for seed.

Nor is it correct to say that he was the first man to set up a seedling appletree business in the West. Many another enterprising frontiersman, realizing the value of the fruit tree market, had set out to profit from it, and the seedling business dominated the trade.

By 1790, for example, Ebenezer Zane had planted a nursery on Wheeling Island seventy-five miles down the Ohio from Pittsburgh, and on the Virginia side of the river opposite Yellow Creek, Jacob Nessley was developing another. On down, at Marietta, Rufus Putnam by 1796 had set out an apple nursery not with the usual seedlings but with grafted stock that carried all the well-known varieties of the Eastern states.[4]

The one unique thing about John's seedling tree business, as it eventually emerged, was his scheme for moving it with the frontier. Few other nurserymen could adjust their lives and business to such a plan. So far as records now make known, no one else ever did.

The urgent need of the frontiersman for apples is something that the twentieth century can easily overlook. Apples have been relegated in normal modern diets chiefly to side dishes and casual eating. Even the family orchard, only a generation ago a requirement on every well-balanced general farm, is rapidly disappearing. It is hard to realize that in the pioneer history of most American communities the first apple crop once marked a first stage of permanency. No other fruit could be started so easily, and none could be put to so many essential uses.

To the first settlers on the Allegheny, Beaver Creek, and the Muskingum, apples meant not just fruit in season; they were one of the few crops that remained basic through the year. Choicer varieties provided a family with hand-eating and cooking from the first mellowing in the summer until the last cold apple buried late in the autumn had been dug up out of the frosty earth in early spring. Bushels of them were cut and dried in the fall to be strung and hung from the kitchen ceiling or the attic rafters until needed for sauces in the winter. On pleasant Indian summer days, in big brass kettles over outdoor fires many bushels more were cooked down into gallons of apple butter, one of the few preserves that the pioneer housewife with her limited equipment could keep for many months.

Late every autumn all the remnants of the crop that were useless for storage or butters were hauled by the wagon load to the cider presses for the precious juice. It was the cider age in American history. No well-established home could exist long without it, and usually many barrels were essential. The sweet drink was luscious and healthful in early autumn, growing increasingly enticing as it began to take on the sparkle of effervescence. In the man's world, at least, hard cider was a normal social drink, as well as its even more efficacious distillations into apple brandy or applejack. In the woman's domain, cider was a concern of fundamental practical importance, for boiled cider and vinegar were the two basic flavorings and preservatives without which her normal winter store of pickles, preserves, butters, and mincemeats would have merely dropped out of existence.

It was the age of barter, too. When hard cash was scarce, apples or vinegar toted to the nearest trading establishment could be exchanged for perhaps a dozen eggs, a fat hen, a deerskin, or a beaver pelt. In time, apples would even pioneer in a broader commerce, for apple brandy from the trees that spread over the Ohio Valley's hillsides in the first wave of settlement would be one of the first important inland products to be shipped on down the Mississippi to the markets of New Orleans.

Every settler, therefore, hoped to have a goodly plot of appletrees set out and bearing in the shortest stretch of time. Often, the trees were even a legal prerequisite to a claim, as in Kentucky's "Sapphire Country" where the planting of appleseeds or peachstones was a common guarantee to warrant the establishment of a title. At Marietta, when the Ohio Company in 1792 set up the "Donation Tract" to encourage migrations to the backlands up the Muskingum and Duck Creek, they stipulated specifically that to acquire a hundred acres a settler put out not less than fifty appletrees and twenty peachtrees within three years. When orchards had been established, the land had been mastered.

The problem was to get the trees. Land was cheap, and the orchards when once started took little care. After five years at the most, they would produce steadily increasing crops for a long time to come. But somewhere there had to be a beginning.

No one today ever plants seedling orchards or would suppose their fruit worth marketing. Appleseeds still sprout vigorously enough, as every farm boy knows who has explored the pleasures of fence rows, but it is one of the commonplaces of horticulture that appleseeds rarely grow up to produce fruit that is true to the parent type. Large apples may give small ones, yellow ones green, and sweet ones sour. One can never be sure that he is getting a Baldwin or a McIntosh or a Grimes Golden unless the kind has been transmitted from a known tree of that variety by a graft or a bud carefully set by skilled surgery into a vigorous seedling stalk. The "wild" or "native" or "common" or "Johnny Appleseed" apples, as seedlings are called today in various parts of the country, are never cultivated now except for a rare individual tree that chances to give desirable fruit and that may be worth perpetuating as a valuable new variety.

But it was seedling stock that started the pioneer apple orchards across America. Not that grafting and budding were unknown. These arts were already highly developed in the 1790's. But the transporting of such stock into new country was a difficult and expensive venture. When trips from Connecticut to Ohio often took many weeks, a considerable number of young grafted appletrees would have pre-empted precious baggage space needed for family essentials, and would have demanded a constant vigil to keep the tender roots moist and alive. Even if such trees could have been imported, few of the first settlers could have afforded to buy them.

That is why not just John Chapman but many another traveler headed west in the 1790's, even though he had no concern whatever with the nursery trade, was packing bags of appleseeds and peachstones over the mountains. And it is why nurserymen here and there were hurrying like John to have patches of seedling trees ready to sell. For seedlings could be produced cheaply in large numbers and could be sold profitably at a low rate so long as the market in any neighborhood continued.

Whatever the quality of the seedling fruit, it would be useful for something. Almost any apple would make butter or cider. A few seedlings in every lot were bound by the law of chance to be fairly good, and some would be superior. Sooner or later a Northern Spy would appear in New York, a Grimes Golden in West Virginia, and a Stark in Ohio.

Furthermore, once the seedling trees had been set to growing in an orchard plot, the pioneer could "top-work" them to his heart's content with grafts and buds from better fruit wherever he could find it.

The first orchards in almost every state began in this way. In New York, S. A. Beach, in his monumental study of the state's apple history, reported as late as 1905 the remains of seedling plantings that were from fifty to a hundred years old. In Ohio and Indiana the traces of such orchards that were started from John Chapman's stock alone extend over hundreds of square miles.

Such was the moving market of the advancing frontier that John had begun to anticipate in a chain of little wilderness plantings lengthening westward.

2

Although late legendry has now planted many other nurseries and orchards for John Chapman during these Pennsylvania years over much of New York, New England, Virginia, and West Virginia, all evidence suggests that his actual trail was leading from the Allegheny River communities directly west into eastern and central Ohio. Whatever other preoccupations John may have had, a major one from his very first authenticable appearance in the West to the last of his travels was cheap land, and the next immediately handy land-opening after northwest Pennsylvania was in Ohio.

Before following the growing links of his nursery chain, however, it is only fair to say a word more concerning the important legend of his early residence in Pittsburgh. Now that John has become beatified in popular feeling, it would be sacrilegious to ignore this favorite episode, even though imaginary, for it has fitted perfectly into the idealistic trend the Appleseed myth has taken in late years and it will doubtless continue long.[5]

John came riding into Pittsburgh one summer's day in 1794 (sometimes it is 1789 or 1790), the story usually runs, sharing the driver's seat of a canvas-topped freight wagon from Philadelphia. He had chosen Pittsburgh because this frontier trading post was the gateway to the West. Here where the Allegheny and Monongahela join, the dreamy-eyed young man from Connecticut (sometimes from Massachusetts) had the initial labors of a mission to perform. In the leather bag beside him, as he rode into town, were the treasured seeds with which he was to begin his work of preparing a way in the wilderness for the men and women who would develop America.

His first step was to buy a few acres in Pittsburgh, plant his seeds for a nursery, then settle down for a dozen years while his plans and project grew. For a while he worked about the river rafts and scows that were carrying the steadily-growing stream of westward travelers down the Ohio to the new lands. Then he built a log house on Grant's Hill, later Pittsburgh's celebrating "Hump," and provided there a haven for the weary and the shelterless.

"His cow, his garden, his orchard, his trees, and his bee-hives," says the American Guide pamphlet on Pittsburgh, "satisfied his wants, with plenty to spare for all who stopped at his door."

"The bees," John would say, "work without wages. Why should I not do the same?"

From his nursery he gave trees to the families going on into the new land. Or, sometimes he gave them little leather packets of appleseeds to plant for themselves. Finally, however, the pattern became apparent for the fulfillment of his larger mission. The time was at hand to go ahead into the wilderness himself. His trees must be ready waiting when the moving column of settlers arrived. So, on a June day in 1806, he left Pittsburgh and faced down the broad Ohio into the Old Northwest where in time his kindly deeds and appletrees were to prosper very richly in American idealism and ima-ginations.

The real John Chapman seems never to have resided in Pittsburgh or anywhere in the neighborhood, though he must have visited the locality. To have chosen that particular door-way into the West would have been entirely alien to his char-acter. To the end of his years, John Chapman shied away from larger towns. He never took the broad highway into a new region if there was a chance to slip in by a less conspic-uous route. Nothing hurt his bare feet quite so much as beaten paths. This charming Pittsburgh episode in his saga, though it has been retold in prolific detail and with many variations in schoolbooks, local histories, biographical volumes, horticultural and historical society reports, and motion pictures, was given its basic form as honest fiction by Mrs. Eleanor Atkinson in her charming little historical novel, *Johnny Appleseed: The Romance of the Sower* in 1915.[6]

Most of the northwestern counties of Pennsylvania, too, now claim Johnny Appleseed as a pioneer orchardist. Very possibly he visited them all, but the traditional nurseries in Warren and Venango are the only support to the many late-day rumors.

Out of dream plantings also seem to have sprouted the trees and orchards attributed to him in such widely separated spots as LeRaysville, the Allegheny state forest, the Cornplanter Indian reservation, and Washington County in Pennsylvania; Olean, Salamanca, the south shore of Lake Ontario and the Hudson Valley in New York. No less a chronicler than Van Wyck Brooks has told of Johnny Appleseed's visiting James Fenimore Cooper in Cooperstown—but it must have been the Johnny who came of the same substance as Leatherstocking.[7] John Chapman's myth has gathered many a famous name and place into its folk fancies.

There is possible fact back of a family tradition that Chapman used to visit the cider press of Frederick Medsger near Smithton in Westmoreland County, Pennsylvania,[8] and that he may have helped a bit with the orcharding that flourished early in West Virginia's "panhandle" country. He certainly traveled these regions. But he just as certainly did not establish the first orchards there, as late fancies like to say, and there is no whit of proof that West Virginia's most famous fruit product now, the Grimes Golden apple, should be attributed to one of his seeds.

3

John's main road for carrying apple stock to the border led west, and the earliest report that has been preserved of his first appearances across the line in the Northwest Territory comes from sometime about 1800.

From French Creek and Franklin on the Allegheny hundred-mile trails ran west to Beaver Creek, down that toward the Ohio, then on west around the north bend of that stream, over the territory line directly into the first land surveyed by the federal government north of the Ohio. This was to be Ohio's famous "Seven Ranges." Though the tract had been surveyed as early as 1786, settlement had continued sparse, for Indian troubles had made this first chunk of the territory just over the river one of the hottest on the frontier. Even after the treaty of Greenville in 1795, white and red killings and other troubles continued intermittently, and border scouts had to be maintained.

Besides, the government had established a policy of selling no tracts here of less than 640 acres and had pegged the price at two dollars an acre. Land down the river in the Symmes' tract around Cincinnati was going for sixty-seven cents, and up in the Connecticut Reserve on Lake Erie for fifty. Economics and fear left the Indians to roam undisturbed unusually long in the rolling wilderness just west of the river and closest to Pennsylvania.

Nevertheless, the "Seven Ranges" held immediate promise, and it is not at all surprising that border scouts James Downing, Isaac Miller, John Cuppy, and James Foulks said many years afterward that they saw John Chapman there, on one of their patrol trips just before the end of the century when he visited their camp one evening and warned them of some hostile Delawares in the neighborhood.[9] Their beat circled the area from the mouth of Captina Creek up through the area now included in Ohio's counties of Belmont, Harrison, Carroll, and Columbiana, then back into Pennsylvania and down to the mouth of Beaver Creek. It crossed all the main Indian thoroughfares that converged on the Ohio here from the west and north.

Here, in fact, was the beginning of a great triangle of early Ohio trails and watercourses that lay with its apex on the Pennsylvania edge of the Northwest Territory near the big north bend of the Ohio River. One leg of the triangle followed the course of the Ohio a hundred miles down to Marietta at the mouth of the Muskingum, and the other extended seventy-five or eighty directly west along the land trails into the heart of the new Ohio territory. The third side of the triangle was the long course of the Muskingum River from the center of this Indian country back south to Marietta. John Chapman was on the three sides of this area many times in the early years, and afterward when his main trail had swung farther west he was back again and again, even into old age.

This is favorite country now for the romancers of the frontier, and Johnny Appleseed is a favorite and handy device. Whenever an author finds his characters caught in a difficult moment, he merely has a kindly, lanky figure step suddenly out of the thick bushes, with long hair streaming, a Swedenborgian tract resting in his bosom and a buckskin bag of appleseeds in his hand. Then, providentially, he directs the travelers to the right path, or warns them of Indian prowlers, or restores a lost child, or brings a crucial message, then disappears again into the shadowy depths of the great forest.

The delightfully appropriate thing about this use of John

Chapman as a literary *deus ex machina* (or *apparitio ex silva*) is that John was indeed roaming the Ohio territory with the first blazing of the trails and to the people who saw him actually gave an impression of mysterious unexpectedness. Any author is safe to use him if he times his story from the unquiet lull on the Indian border just before 1800 down to about 1806 and stages his action anywhere along the great triangle of trails that opened the territory.

Settlement in the "Seven Ranges" was not slowed long. By 1800, Jesse Palmer, famous hunter, was living on a branch of Still Fork (present-day Carroll County). John Jackman built a cabin on the Elkhorn about the same time. Then almost at a stride the neighborhood and the whole east edge of what was soon to be the new state of Ohio had been filled up.

Chapman's chain of appleseed plantings had already arrived before the big push, however. The first traditional planting inside the Ohio territory was near the present town of Carrollton. Nothing else is known about it.

Other nurseries soon appeared a bit to the south. In 1801, he arrived at Wellsburg on the left bank of the Ohio in what is now West Virginia, having come, the early story preserved in Jefferson County, Ohio, specifically states, from Venango County, Pennsylvania.[10] He was packing along a quantity of seed in leather bags and must have been riding a horse, for the old account says that he rode up to Cox's Ripple, crossed the river there, and touched Ohio soil near the mouth of George's Run, some four miles below the town of Steubenville. This would have been in the neighborhood of the Mingo flats—famous early Indian camping ground and village site and the beginning of the old Mingo Trail into the central part of the territory. The town of Mingo Junction now spreads

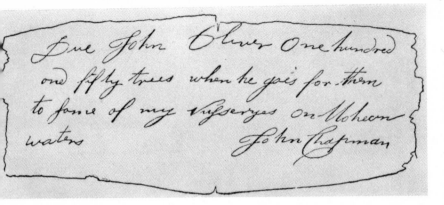

APPLETREE ORDER ABOUT 1820
From *Ohio Archaeological and Historical Quarterly*, IX, 315.

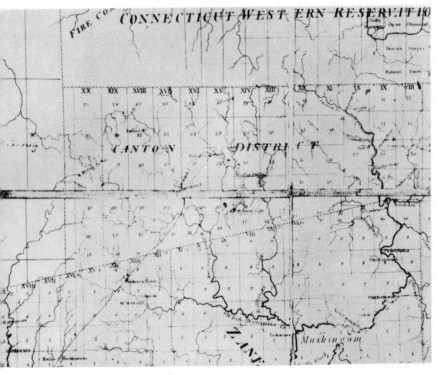

THE JOHNNY APPLESEED COUNTRY, 1806
Detail from John F. Mansfield's "Map of the State of Ohio, Taken from the returns in the office of the Surveyor General," 1806. "Green T." on the upper extension of "Mohecan John's Creek" was burned in September, 1812, and the other Indian towns in the area abandoned. The region marked the most easterly remaining extension of the Indian border. Note the locations on the east branch of the Muskingum of the Moravian Christian Indian settlements, Schoenbrun and Gnadenhutten, famous for the notorious massacres of 1782. (From original in Ohio State Archaeological and Historical Society Library.)

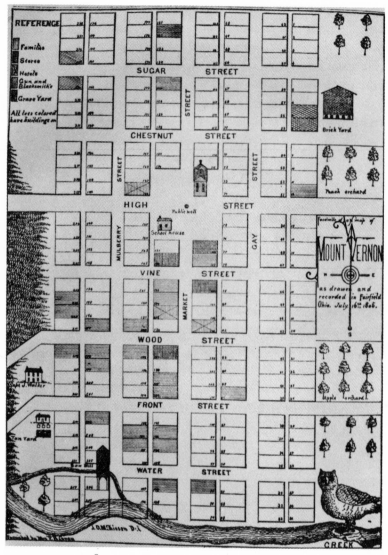

MOUNT VERNON, 1805

Facsimile of a map "as drawen and recorded in Fairfield, Ohio, July 16th, 1805," reproduced from N. N. Hill's History of Knox County, *1881. The hand-colored original hangs in the Mount Vernon Public Library. John Chapman owned lots 145 and 147 (the last and second from the last on the left at the foot of Market Street). The shading on 145 indicates presence of a building but not of a resident family. The "apple orchard" was in the general direction of Chapman's nurseries, one on the "Indian Fields" along Owl Creek and the other on Center Run.*

along the level that was once covered with tepees and corn-
fields.

He spent the night and planted a batch of seeds somewhere
in the neighborhood. Some say it was at the flats, some at the
site of today's Brilliant, down the river opposite Wellsburg,
West Virginia.

When someone urged him to remain in the locality and
develop a nursery business there, he declined, saying that he
was going farther west. There the livestock would not destroy
his trees before they were ready to sell, and there also he
would be ready for the settlers when they arrived.

"They are starting one up the river on the Virginia side
and talking of grafting," he is reported saying, referring to
Jacob Nessley's extensive plantings up the river opposite
Yellow Creek. "They can improve the apple in that way but
that is only a device of man, and it is wicked to cut up trees
that way. The correct method is to select good seeds and plant
them in good ground and God only can improve the apples."

Such advice, if Chapman uttered it, represented either a
blind fanaticism or simple ignorance of horticultural laws.
Most orchardists found that the Almighty liked to use their
skills and blessed their grafted orchards abundantly.

John was on his way at this time to the Muskingum Valley
in the interior, it was believed. In that event, he would have
swung southward to Zane's Trace that cut almost due west
from the mouth of Wheeling Creek across the northern half
of present-day Belmont County. There, a long-persistent tradition insists that he stopped to plant more seeds above where
Morristown was laid out the next year along the trace. The
nursery was on Big Stillwater Creek in the direction of Freeport.[11]

These river counties of the Seven Ranges, being close to

the main thoroughfares developing from Pittsburgh and Wheeling to the center of Ohio, were to fill up very quickly. Stories say that Chapman was back there often during the next ten years, going to and from Pennsylvania, attending to his plantings en route, and getting seeds for his newer nurseries farther west. The traditions are plausible, for many people who saw Chapman later in central Ohio had known him first in these river counties.

In the same year—possibly on the same trip—he showed up at the extreme west corner of the triangle in the Licking bottoms, seventy-five miles into the interior.[12]

This was at the wilderness end of the road that Ebenezer Zane and his men had been cutting since the summer of 1796, the first of the white men's major roads, piercing like an arrow directly to the Muskingum Valley and into the midst of the Indian country. Though its purpose had been primarily military—to cut through the mid-portions of the wilderness and connect the old Cumberland road from Pittsburgh to Wheeling with Boone's trail at Limestone (now Maysville), Kentucky—the effect upon the immediate economic development of the Northwest Territory proved to be gigantic. By 1800, towns were already being laid out along its course, and the rich lands of the interior were being readied for sale.

On the Muskingum, Zane had selected a hundred-acre tract, one of the three he was entitled to along his new trace. There in 1799 with his son-in-law McIntire, he had laid out the town of Zanesville. By 1801, a tavern, several cabins, and some trading establishments had accumulated. The new road was as yet only a cleared path wide enough for horses and foot, but the stream of newcomers over it was steady and was growing every month. The 2,500,000 acres of the United States Military Lands established here in 1796 had been surveyed in

1797–98 and had now been parceled out to meet bounty claims of officers and soldiers in the Revolution. The remainder was just about to go on the market. Zane's town in the center of the virgin country would be the chief migration objective and regional supply depot for several years.

Although at Zanesville the trace itself turned south through southern Ohio toward Kentucky, the waters of the Muskingum River came down out of a network of picturesque and tillable valleys to west, north, and east, and up these the newcomers were scurrying.

The Licking River, being the closest tributary on the west, had already drawn more than a dozen families. Squatters Elias Hughes and John Ratliff had brought their large families upstream twenty miles as early as 1798. John VanBuskirk, long a spy on the Indian frontier, had settled on a 3,100-acre tract in 1800. In 1801, John Larabee, Revolutionary veteran and Indian fighter, was living in a huge hollow sycamore tree while he cleared a few acres and planted corn. Among others, Isaac Stadden had just moved in with his wife from Northumberland County, Pennsylvania.

As William Stanbery, who came to the Licking Valley in 1809, heard the story, Chapman appeared in the Licking bottoms sometime in 1801 with a horse loaded with appleseeds packed in leather bags. These he had gathered from cider presses in western Pennsylvania. Stanbery, later one of Ohio's prominent jurists, a state senator, and a congressman, knew Chapman well for many years and presumably got his data both from him and from pioneer residents in the valley. It was his understanding that John in 1801 made a planting "near Newark on the farm of Isaac Stadden" and that "from this were planted all the early orchards of Licking County."

Long afterward, Mrs. Stadden, jealous in her belief that

she herself had set out the first fruit trees in this rich agricultural valley—having brought them from her former home in Pennsylvania—used to deny that Chapman had grown trees on her husband's land. But she had known John well and, whatever the specific circumstances, there is no doubt that he was in the neighborhood very early and afterward returned there often.

This corner of his travel-triangle had brought John Chapman, at last, to the edge of the north-central Ohio country that was to become peculiarly and richly his personal domain.

4

THE JOHNNY APPLESEED
COUNTRY

John Chapman was to take over all of inner Ohio from Zanesville and Newark and the Licking River north and west up the valleys of the Muskingum watershed and over the state divide across the narrow lake plains to Erie.

Today the area is marked by the busy little cities of Coshocton and Mount Vernon, Mansfield, Bucyrus, Ashland, and Wooster. A network of good highways now crisscrosses the wooded ridges and narrow rivers that interweave with broad meadow bottoms and rolling uplands. In 1803 the natural gateway for the main push of migration into the heart of this beautiful country was at the forks of the Walhonding, the main upper west branch of the Muskingum River. Approximately twenty miles above Coshocton, the Mohican comes down through a high-walled exit to join Owl Creek or, as it is now called after its old Indian name, the Kokosing. Both streams come from many long, tenuous branches that wander down through the counties of Knox and Holmes, Morrow, Crawford and Richland, Ashland and Wayne with their beginnings far up on the broad east-west land divide only a few miles below the shore of Erie. Like most of the Muskingum's upper valleys, these of the Mohican and Owl

Creek grow less precipitate as one follows them north and west beyond the gnarled ridges that frame their lower unions, then smooth out into softly rolling countryside as the miles move up onto the broad flats of the divide and then tip over into the shore plains.

These valleys hold some of America's finest farming country now. But in the years just before the War of 1812 their development, especially in the upper reaches, was coming very slowly. They were too far removed to keep in easy touch with the main lines of commerce below. Roads came grudgingly. The Indian border remained here long enough to bring one last terrible reign of burnings and scalpings when the second war with Britain broke out in 1812.

The upper Muskingum watershed is the kind of country that holds history and traditions well. Rugged sections always cling to the past better than flatlands, and stories haunt this varied countryside now like the clouds of serviceberry and dogwood that scatter along its ridges in spring, or like the white-bleached sycamores whose skeletons in winter stand tangled in gigantic *danses macabres* along the edges of the corn bottoms. The red men and the first white invaders left many marks here. Some of the Indians' favorite towns dotted the region. Their major trails through Ohio crossed it. In the seams of certain ridges here, they had found the greatest flint deposits in eastern America. To these valleys came the earliest of the white men's military expeditions into the West—Boquet's, Brodhead's, Williamson's and others. Moravian Indians were massacred here and Colonel Crawford was burned. There is scarcely a township in all these counties today that does not boast some important relic of the aboriginal era or the frontier that swept it away.

In recent years, however, the past is likely to be represented often enough by Johnny Appleseed. His presence is everywhere. A monument in Ashland greets visitors at the entrance to the main thoroughfare (it served appropriately during the second world war as a travelers' aid center for hitch-hiking G.I.'s).[1] A memorial seat in the public library tells his story in beautiful carved wood.[2] In Mansfield his monument in the pleasant city park stands not far away from an original blockhouse preserved from the last of the Indian raids—John Chapman must have climbed in and out of its doorways.[3] A junior high school has been dedicated to him, and a Boy Scouts area operates under his name. Motorists down the long, picturesque Black Fork road past the new Charles Mill conservancy reservoir find his name carved on an old monument in the open country below Mifflin, set up there many years ago to commemorate the families and soldiers who were slain by the Delawares in 1812.[4] Stop in any village along the way and ask about Johnny Appleseed, and people start telling family traditions or lead the way out to some quiet fence corner to point out his trees, for every seedling appletree springing up by a brookside has come to be known in the vernacular as a "Johnny Appleseed tree."

There are even broader and more pervasive indications of his continuing presence. Here in his own country, as elsewhere across the land, John Chapman has become the patron saint of the earth and the streams and the forest, and lingers near to bless everything good that comes of them. Open any of Louis Bromfield's recent books about the American soil, for instance, and Johnny will be striding across the page, for the author's experimental Malabar Farm is in the very heart of the Johnny Appleseed domain.[5] A fork of the storied Mohican runs through an actual "Pleasant Valley." And an integral part of the whole is the ghost of Johnny always lurking near to watch the efforts of modern scientific farming to restore fertility when soil has been depleted, or coax back undergrowth to denuded hillsides, or turn furrows with the contours of the slopes to hold back disastrous wash. It was he who guided the C.C.C. boys in setting out the many acres of pine and spruce whose green now mingles with the russet of native bur oaks along the steeper slopes in winter. He watches over the beautiful Mohican state forest here that encloses many hundreds of the non-tillable acres to preserve their treasures of natural beauty and wild life for the people's pleasure and good.

At least fourteen huge conservancy dams hold back the headwaters of these upper forks now, in long reservoirs that break the disastrous floods with which the Muskingum Valley has been devastated in later years. They make beautiful inland lakes, some of them covering the very spots where John once tucked his appleseeds into wilderness mold.

He no longer spends his time peddling seedling trees for a fippenny bit, or looking after stray horses, or lending a helping hand to some newly-arrived settler, or warning settlements of Indian scalpings. He has much more in his keeping. He walks the fields to look for the returning mantle of humus. He beckons the herons and wild ducks back in larger numbers each year to the reservoirs and streams. And from town to town he preaches the gospel of beauty and of neighborly co-operation to accomplish community good.

But this apotheosis has come long afterward. John Chapman had happened into a region just at the right moment for that rare, perfect combination of place and man that occurs from time to time to work inevitable magic—Daniel Boone in Kentucky, Crockett in Tennessee, Abe Lincoln on the Sangamon. But it would take time for the folk alchemy to work, and neither John Chapman nor any one else in 1803 or 1804 dreamed of the gray-headed saint of a half-century hence.

2

Shortly after John's first appearance in the Licking Valley about 1801, he turned up in the beautiful Indian fields along Owl Creek twenty-five miles farther north. Today if a pinpoint be set down somewhere near the approximate center of an Ohio map, it will likely fall within at least twenty-five miles of the city of Mount Vernon. In 1803, it would have found the same general relation to the hut of Andy Craig, buried in the deep wilderness, at a spot where what is now called Center Run flowed down from the north into Owl Creek.

"From all we can learn," historian A. Banning Norton wrote in 1862 after painstakingly interviewing numbers of old residents, *"we are of the opinion that contemporaneous with* [Craig] *was the oddest character in all our history, Johnny Chapman, alias Appleseed, who was dicovered in this country when the Walkers, and Butlers, and Douglasses and others landed here, and whose name is found recorded among those voting at the first election ever held in this district."* [6] John Butler had settled near the mouth of Owl Creek in 1803. William Douglass and Captain James Walker came in 1804. Ben Butler arrived in 1805.

John had apparently pushed in ahead when the only residents were the half-wild, daredevil squatter Craig and the hulking, raw-boned trollop from Wheeling with whom he was hanging out here in a hut near the mouth of the run. On up the stream were John Stilley, his wife, and twelve children living much like the neighboring Indians. Stilley had been captured by the Wyandots twenty-five years before when a child in Washington County, Pennsylvania, and had been brought like many other border captives up through the Indian towns in these valleys. Released at Detroit after the Revolution, he had gone to Kentucky for a while, had served Anthony Wayne as a scout, but unable to forget the tangle of picturesque valleys and streams, high rock walls and rich meadows of this north-central Ohio wilderness had eventually sought it out.

The Indian fields directly west of Andy Craig's shack on Center Run were a series of low, deep-soiled grassy flats that separated the river from the forest to the north. The Delawares had camped and planted there for generations and still came and went freely though their main villages had been moved above the treaty line fifteen miles north.

John must have made his first plantings here in the flats, along the west bank of the run near Craig's place, sometime between 1801 and 1804, for he had trees ready to sell to settlers in 1806.[7]

Perhaps the best clue to the probable time of John's transition to the north-central Ohio frontier is the opening in 1803 of the United States Military Lands for sale to the general public. John was now hunting land more vigorously than ever, and in 1803 all portions of the military tract in central Ohio not taken up by Revolutionary bounty claimants had been offered for sale at the land offices. Under an ordinance of the new-founded state of Ohio, all government land sold after 1802 would be free from taxation for five years from the date of purchase. Furthermore, in 1804, the size of tracts purchasable was cut down to as small as quarter sections. The land laws were being adjusted at last to the reach of the common man for whom, so it was commonly stated, the whole vast experiment of the Northwest Territory had been intended.

John apparently had little ready cash available. He would not be able, in fact, until 1809, to make the small beginning of his long series of extensive land purchases and leases in this area. But it is very likely that his financial adjustments with members of the Chapman family back in Franklin, Pennsylvania, in February, 1804, were concerned with prospective land investments here.

The Franklin documents also give the last evidence of John as a resident of the Allegheny region. He was back in Pennsylvania often in later times to get his seed supplies, tradition says, but the year 1804, in which he appears to have been both on the Allegheny and in these upper branches of the Muskingum, seems to mark his shift to the Ohio country.

By the next year, Ben Butler, Thomas Patterson, and Joseph Walker had staked out the bounds for a town here on Owl Creek, that was to extend from the stream in the neighborhood of John's nursery up through the woods on the north slope. In keeping with the grand scale that marked many Western enterprises, they named the potential town after Washington's estate on the Potomac, Mount Vernon. The enticingly decorated, hand-colored map that they drafted, to file for incorporation at the county seat of Lancaster fifty-three miles south, shows that they laid out a total of 240 lots.[8] Thirty-five of these, the drawing indicates, had buildings erected on them, though the plat did not understate and there are no records today to account for half that many residents. All buildings but one were probably of logs. Around the north and east sides of the plat, the draftsman either proudly or hopefully sketched in a large setting of apple and peach orchards. John's trees here on Owl Creek may have already been salable in 1805 though no mention of a planting from his nursery has been found previous to those that James Love-ridge set out the next year. Loveridge was making a clearing on Owl Creek just above Walker's and Douglass'. In 1806, he set out an orchard of Chapman's trees, some of which were to live until the 1870's and '80's.[9]

In the spring of 1806, Owl Creek held its first election. Fifteen eligible males gathered into Mount Vernon from the surrounding woods, said Norton (who had examined the records), including John Chapman.[10] It was an off-year local election: the year before, both President Thomas Jefferson and Ohio's first governor, Edward Tiffin, had been rein-stalled for second terms, so that there was little of outside political excitement to stir the far-out fringes of the settle-ments.

3

Sometime in 1806, too, John was back in Pennsylvania after seeds, it was reported. An old pioneer of Jefferson County, Ohio, recalled that he had seen Chapman for the first time that year. John was going down the river with two canoes lashed together, well laden with appleseeds secured in western Pennsylvania.[11] Another informant for the same year says that John stopped at George's run in Jefferson County to visit an acquaintance made on the trip of 1801.[12]

Some people have surmised that John was boating seeds from Western Pennsylvania down the Ohio to Marietta. It is true that by 1806, the rest of the Chapmans had established themselves near Marietta, and that fact has stirred a lively Johnny Appleseed tradition around the mouth of the Mus-kingum.

"In the year 1805," says the carefully compiled genealogical record kept by Jabez Colton during these years in Longmeadow, Massachusetts, "Nathaniel Chapman with his family removed from Longmeadow to the western country in winter." [13] Colton must have meant the winter of 1804–05. Both birth records in Longmeadow and census reports in Marietta bear out the date. Badly confused family recollections caught by several early Ohio chroniclers say that John and his half-brother, who had been roughing it together in the Allegheny wilds, had visited Marietta about the beginning of the century and were responsible for the father's moving the rest of the family to the neighborhood.[14]

The Captain was moving his family into the Duck Creek settlement fifteen miles up the narrow valleys above Marietta. No record can be found that he ever owned any of the new land available there, though his sons and daughters would do much better.

Nor is there any evidence to support the late-sprung story that John engaged in nurserying there. The Marietta neighborhood by 1806 neither needed his nursery stock nor would have approved his primitive methods of culture. They had been growing orchards for eighteen years. Settlers, even on Duck Creek, had been putting out apple and peach orchards since 1792. General Rufus Putnam's orchard at Marietta was set with scions from the finest appletrees of Israel Putnam's estate in Pomfret, Connecticut. His Roxbury Russets, Seek-No-Furthers, Early Chandlers, and many other varieties had already started a great orchard industry all around the mouth of the Muskingum. By 1808, a census shows that Washington County had at least 774 acres of flourishing fruit trees.

More likely, any seeds that people in the east Ohio counties saw John boating down the Ohio in 1806 had not only come 50 miles from Pennsylvania but would follow the current of the Ohio a hundred more to Marietta, then be carried north up the Muskingum Valley ninety miles, past Zanesville and the mouth of the Licking, to the branching of the Muskingum and thence along the Walhonding (then often called White Woman's Creek) to the forks, where they would be planted either on Owl Creek or on Mohecan John's Creek (now the Mohican River).

Of the Chapman family that had moved to Duck Creek above Marietta only a little more need be said here, for John's life would take him in other directions. Captain Nathaniel Chapman died in 1807 and was buried in the Duck Creek neighborhood. Lucy Cooley Chapman, his forty-five year old widow and John's stepmother, lingers in thought for a moment. She had borne ten children in twenty-two years and had brought at least half of them into the Ohio wilderness, one an infant in arms. Now left with a good-sized household to look after, little is known of her or of her circumstances except that she seems to have lived on in the Duck Creek locality. When the 1810 census was taken, she was there with her two youngest children. An older boy was living nearby with his wife and small child. Another son, said to have been a mute, was also in the neighborhood, living alone. At least three of the others married and settled in the region. There she fades from view. She must have had a hard life. Her grave like those of John's father and mother is lost today.[15]

The neighborhood has a monument to Johnny Appleseed now, a stone memorial set up in 1942 along the roadside just south of Dexter City.[16] Above, at the top of a steep slope are the remains of a pioneer cemetery containing the graves of a half brother, Parley, and members of his family. A few old appletrees among the stones have, naturally, been attributed to John's planting.

The memorial is pleasantly appropriate, for although Marietta and Duck Creek probably saw much more of the other Chapmans than they ever did of John, his mythical orchards have sprouted all over the country. Remnants of his supposed trees may be seen in Marietta's Campus Martius Museum, and, it is sometimes even said that he started the fine commercial orchards that now grow all along the slopes overlooking the Muskingum and the Ohio. Of course, in historical fiction he has come to know all the famous figures of Marietta's heroic beginnings—General Putnam, Commandant Whipple, Dr. True, and the rest. He once even visited the Blennerhassets on Blennerhasset Island, a story goes, and was first drawn to Swedenborgian mysticism there.[17]

4

John Chapman's operations at the moment were actually developing at the Walhonding Forks. It was strategic geography over again. John, now in his early thirties, had acquired not only an amazing ability to get about over the trans-Appalachian landscape but a clear sense of future migration routes for the first-comers; the place where the Owl Creek and Mohican branches joined would be the natural doorway for many years into a vast area of new country to the west and north. Here the appletree plots that he had started at least by 1806 would still be flourishing ten years afterward, and were to be among his most widely famed nurseries in the region.

One of these was growing on the upland south of Owl Creek in present-day New Castle Township of Coshocton

County. It was located on the 4,000-acre tract of Robert Giffin, with whom Chapman may have planted by arrangement, for Giffin had spent several years near St. Clairsville in Belmont County, John's earlier territory in eastern Ohio.[18] "Many earliest settlers recognized in him an old acquaintance," said historian Norton, "who had wandered for years along the streams of western Pennsylvania, engaged in the same pursuit and preparing the way for those who might follow upon his trail to have their own orchards." [19] Giffin, who in 1808 rowed his household goods in a pirogue all the way down the Ohio and up the Muskingum and the Walhonding to his tract, set up a cabin close by Chapman's nursery, then went back to bring his wife and four children overland by way of Zane's trace. Having but three horses, the six of them had to take turns walking and riding. With them, or soon after came Martin Cox, John Ely, David and Thomas John, Timothy Hawkins, Matthew Duncan, John Wolfe, and James Pigman, all of whom bought portions of Giffin's land and started their earliest orchards from the Chapman trees. David John set out his first orchard about 1808.[20]

Though this New Castle plot was small—only about seventy-five feet square—its trees ultimately supplied a great many of the pioneer orchards in southwestern Coshocton, northeastern Licking, and eastern Knox counties. Newcomers to Jackson Township, in the extreme southeast corner of Knox, trudged some ten miles to get a start of them in 1810; John had been down in their hills advertising his wares, old residents remembered.[21]

Five miles north, John had a larger planting started along the Mohican fork.[22] It too was in Coshocton County, near the county line on the big bend of the river in present-day Tiverton Township. The wild, ridge-hemmed terrain remains even today very thinly settled. But it was an excellent location so far as the river was concerned, for the trails followed the river course and the Mohican itself was navigable to small boats and rafts and for a decade would be a major route for new families going as far as thirty miles upstream. John Chapman's nursery on the lower Mohican was long a familiar sight. He had it going before 1807, say the first chroniclers. Apparently he had merely taken over a wilderness location to his liking, undisturbed by any thought of formal lease, for the 4,000-acre tract on which the nursery stood was held by an Eastern landlord who never moved in.

The most reliable tradition says that this Tiverton plantation was about one acre in extent and that John at one time planted three bushels of appleseeds there. While in the vicinity tending it, he would stop at the cabin of John Butler about a mile away over the line in Knox County. From this plot a great number of trees eventually found their way to orchards in Coshocton, Knox, Holmes, Richland, and Ashland counties. Isaac Draper, who came from Virginia in 1806, the first settler in the township and the only resident land owner until 1817, started an orchard from it on his quarter section a few miles north.[23]

To glance ahead a moment, this large Tiverton nursery was still operating in 1812, and in 1816, even though Chapman's principal activities by that time had shifted twenty to fifty miles upstream. One of the most precious of Johnny Appleseed's autographs is an original draft for trees from this site, now in the possession of the Mansfield, Ohio, Boy Scouts, reading:

"October 1812, for value received I promise to pay or cause to be paid to Benjamin Burrell one hundred and

fifty trees at my nursery near John Butlers in the month of March such as they are when called for. John Chapman." [24]

Chapman's business along the trails seems to have been conducted very largely by means of such written orders to be presented by the holders to local agents in whose care he left his trees.

Another planting site in the same neighborhood is sometimes referred to by local historians as "Nursery Island" in the Mohican, a short distance from the Knox-Coshocton line. The location is uncertain now. From it came many a fine tree, said the residents of Butler Township in the Owl Creek Valley. Here John, they said, during these first years of opening up the forest spent considerable time among the Rileys, Shrimplins, Staats, Carpenters, and Benjamin Butlers, sharing their hospitality for days and nights at a stretch. All their first appletrees came from him. One tree was pointed out for many years on the Joseph Staat farm. Staat had come to Owl Creek in 1816.[25]

These people along Owl Creek and the Mohican were the kind of people that John Chapman liked, and theirs was the stage of frontier life in which he had come to feel his most comfortable adjustment. They were a rough border breed for the most part, and beginnings of communal living in the edge of the wilderness often made them even rougher than they were by nature. Many sentimental contrasts have been drawn in late-day stories of John's refined gentility among these hardened liquor-swillers and Indian killers. But his early conditioning certainly never interfered with his easy mingling among all kinds of people who lived in the semi-wild-ness of the first-line settlements.

The Owl Creekers could do with any refining influences that might happen along. By the spring of 1807, the makings of a real settlement within the newly platted bounds of Mount Vernon were most evident in the fact that Ben Butler had opened up his cabin as a tavern to accommodate the stream of new arrivals, and James Craig had begun dispensing whis-key. Gilman Bryant started a store in a small sycamore cabin. Sometime that year a Baptist preacher reached the neighbor-hood, and a Methodist circuit rider soon after him. Both were badly needed. The Owl Creek folks were no worse than the average, but James Craig, for example, was one of the hardest drinkers in the central Ohio settlements and probably the most notorious fighters in the county. Hardly a day passed without a brawl about the town center. Craig had as many as four fights in a day with Joseph Walker. Once he and Ben Butler had a terrific set-to in which Craig was badly mauled—but the next day they took a drink over it and called the quarrel ended.

Prodigious quantities of corn whiskey had begun to flow along Owl Creek, as in most up-valley inland regions. Corn was the first big crop that could be raised with little trouble on the alluvial meadows that bordered the streams. There was always a sale and at prices no raw crop would bring for a good many years. Besides, it was the standard social drink, and the only alcoholic one that could be produced locally on a sizable scale in the first years. Though habitual drunkenness was something to be regretted, total abstention was looked upon as singular, and even the mild-mannered John Chap-man, was not a teetotaler. It was corn whiskey and not cider in the very first years that warmed circuit riders and lawyers to their oratory, provided cheer at weddings, and drowned sorrow at wakes. It sealed all business deals. Few towns in their founding escaped the raucous, liquor-drenched boom years. It is not surprising in looking over the earliest records of Mount Vernon to find that the township officers devoted much of their labor to the licensing of public houses and the handling of assault and battery cases. Mount Vernon of John Chapman's years has left a rather fuller record of this over-sized roughness than some of its neighbors, but the fullness is due not so much to unusual excesses as to the heart-warming fact that some of the town's first chroniclers preferred the vigor of ugly truth to any amount of anemic sentimentalizing.

Even huge chicanery could be a good joke if the right man came out on top, as witness the fixing of the county seat in 1808. When the state commissioners were considering the proper center for the new county of Knox, they set a day to view the possibilities in both Mount Vernon and the town of Clinton a mile and a half away. Knowing that the commissioners were coming, the Mount Vernonites knocked off drinking, trimmed their language and deportment to a semblance of refinement, were hard at work in all kinds of orderly pursuits when the officials arrived, and managed to put on altogether a splendid show of gracious, respectable hospitality and business decorum. In Clinton, however, Ben Butler, Joseph Walker, and other Mount Vernon leaders had provided a well-primed band of rowdies from the country around, who greeted the commissioners with such a disgustingly boisterous and disreputable exhibition of human depravity that the dignitaries were glad to hasten back and designate Mount Vernon the new seat of government. That night, of course, the lid went off again in Mount Vernon. Great bonfires were lit in the public square, live trees were blown open with charges of gunpowder, and corn whiskey flowed uninhibited once more for the rejoicing mob.

Ben Butler used to like telling about his rough handling of the town's first doctor. It was a good example of the frontiersman's brawny way of dealing with uncertainties. The doctor was "too damned lazy" to practice, Ben said. One day the doctor happened by the field where Ben, who was trying to plow, had just worked himself into a lathery rage at the beech roots that kept catching the share. The doctor said he had been inoculating a child against smallpox and wanted to inoculate Butler's child.

"God damn you!" Ben exploded. "Haven't I moved away up here to get rid of the damned smallpox, and damned if you shall inoculate my child!"

Then he drew his knife and started for the medico, who fled in terror and soon afterward moved away from town. No other doctor dared show up during Butler's residence.

No incident stands out in more grotesque contrast with the humanitarian John Chapman of later reputation than the public whipping recorded for this same noisy year of 1808. William Hedrick had stolen a watch, a bay mare, a pair of overalls, and a bell and collar. He had been fined a total of $119.50, three months' imprisonment, and forty strokes from a rawhide. One May day in 1808, accordingly, he was tied hands over head to a small leaning hickory on the square and given the full course of the law even though left hideously mangled. A few onlookers protested, but most of them were unsympathetic.

It was not that human nature was extraordinarily callous on the frontier, but that life on the edge of the wilderness permitted few of the nicer gradations of feeling. The need to chop away forests, push back Indians, fight off wolves, and clear out rattlesnake dens; to endure severe winters in the inadequate shelter of the early cabins, and malarial seasons inevitable with the land undrained; to make long journeys through dangerous, unsettled territory—merely keeping alive —demanded massive strokes in action and thought. Feelings corresponded. There were extremes of violence in a community's punishments, quarrels, treatment of wild beast and of Indians, but the same people could be passionately tender in personal relationships, hospitable without limit, warmly co-operative in all neighborhood functions, and intensely emotional in their religion.

A dominant current in the founding blood came from the earlier border of Pennsylvania, Maryland, Virginia, and the river counties of eastern Ohio, and they gave their peculiar coloring to much of the frontier life. They had been suckled in the last years of the Revolution. In their culture, they came chiefly from a generation that had kept just a little ahead of the refining graces moving from the coast. They lived close to nature, and like nature they accepted life as a harsh struggle in which violent extremes were considered a matter of course. They had seen the cutthroat land wars in western Pennsylvania, and they knew that the law was usually on the side of the strongest. In their conquest of the wilderness they could not be squeamish about the little humanities. Without a qualm of mercy they could skin a wild wolf alive and turn it back into the woods to warn off the rest of the pack. They believed that the only good Indian was a dead one and boasted of how many times they had provided that guarantee. On the average they were brave, sturdy, solid, enterprising men and have to be judged now by the rules of conduct that the majority accepted, no matter how disgustingly coarse or sickeningly barbarous some of their actions appear to later observers.

There were exceptions here and there—whole communities of them—as in nearby Granville with its transplanted New England colony, or the Quakers who were settling above Mount Vernon. But it was not these outsiders who really opened the new country—it was the borderers.

John Chapman was not of border blood, of course. He had been reared in finer-grained New England communities, and he was touched by definite scruples of humanitarian conduct, as time would show. A half century after the primitive, Rabelaisian extremes of the central Ohio wilderness years, settlers looked back and remembered John as standing out sharply against the harshness and brutality that they had accepted as necessary. But he was no weakling. Few men could match his endurance. His life was strenuous, his accomplishment huge. He had been conditioned to a half-wild manner of living and liked it. The semi-tamed edge of civilization was exactly the stage of society in which he had come to be at home and he was to cling to it all his days. He seems not to have liked the exaggerated grossness. But his own tendency toward humility and kindliness was only a natural complement to it. Extremes were as normal on the border as winter and summer.

5

In September, 1809, when he was thirty-five years old John Chapman bought a couple of Joseph Walker's town lots in Mount Vernon, paying out fifty dollars for them in good United States money.[26] It was the first real estate he had ever owned. Samuel Kratzer, local merchant, tavern keeper, justice of the peace, and commander of the militia, witnessed the deal.

Both lots were on the south side of the new town out toward his nursery. One of them, at the corner of Market and

Water streets with "Plumb Alley" in the rear, is a valuable city business block today.[27]

The other lot bordered on Owl Creek, and John's deed specifically gave him all water rights pertaining thereto. According to the plat, a sawmill was already in operation just west of him. This lot now lies mainly in the bed of the Kokosing River.[28]

What use he made of his land is not clear, whether for a cabin or for appletrees or for both.

Considering the time he was spending on long trips, however, and the fact that he was keeping a chain of nurseries growing even back into western Pennsylvania, he could not have called any spot more than temporary headquarters.

To the south, he was often in the Licking Valley, filling it in time with lively family traditions that have flourished very luxuriantly around Newark, Granville, and Alexandria—of his overnight visits, his gifts of trees and seeds, the orchards set out from his stock or by his hand—though very little of specific fact ever happened to get set down in writing.[29]

The raw town of Newark had sprung up at the forks of the Licking. John knew it well enough to have a bad impression. It was worse than Mount Vernon. Years afterward, when expounding his Swedenborgian concept of hell, he said that it must probably be much like early Newark.[30]

William Stanbery knew him there from 1809 on. John once spent a night with the Stanberys in Newark, sleeping by preference in a grove nearby.

Mrs. Isaac Stadden downstream formed a definitely unfavorable impression of his vagrant ways, considering him a rather trifling sort.[31]

His one recorded nursery in the Licking Valley was on the

north side, about three miles northeast of Newark. For some reason, he soon abandoned it, old-timers said, leaving it unenclosed so that farmers' stock browsed over it and left few trees that were worth transplanting.[32]

Civilization's main attack upon the wilderness was now in the other direction, north from Mount Vernon up the upper branches of the Mohican.

The progress was slow because of the isolation. There were few highways in central Ohio yet, and none at all into the wilder country to the north. A petition from the inhabitants of Licking and Knox counties in January, 1808, for instance, states that the region had no road whereby people could "receive letters or any kind of intelligence or any private conveyance nearer than Newark or Zanesville." They wanted a road from Newark to Mount Vernon, thence about thirty miles farther north to the settlement of Mansfield just getting under way, and from there to the mouth of the River Huron on Lake Erie.

The main advance had to be chiefly up the streams. There were a good many long upper branches of Owl Creek and the Mohican. John was having a look-around on most of them. In the summer of 1809, for example, he was seen on the site of newly-platted Mansfield, and later clues suggest that he probably had plantings on the most northerly extensions of the Muskingum system: the Rocky Fork, the Black Fork, and the Lake Fork of the Mohican River.

Meantime, the seeds that he had been planting for the past six or eight years, whatever their breed, must have had the sap of patriarchs in them.

Trees from his Owl Creek nursery near Andy Craig's shack

at Mount Vernon would still be growing fifty years later. Some that James Loveridge set out up Owl Creek in 1806 or soon thereafter were standing in 1881, and one of them had a circumference of nearly eight feet. Another cut down in the 1870's had at least seventy annular rings.[33]

A tree that K. B. Cummings planted from the Tiverton nursery on the Mohican was still standing in 1881, a venerable pioneer twelve feet in circumference broken down but still able to send out blossoms every May.[34]

One that David John transplanted from the New Castle plot in 1808 was also standing in 1880, although only one branch remained. It too had been a mighty tree. The trunk measured ten feet, two inches, a foot above the ground. People had long taken grafts from it, for its fruit, though "natural," was good. One year a late owner had picked eighty-four bushels of fruit and estimated that the whole crop would have made 140 bushels if harvested. The foliage in its prime had shaded a circle forty-four feet in diameter.[35]

There were giants in the earth in those days.

These recorded trees have never matched in longevity and size, however, those that have sprouted later in popular fancies around the branches of the Walhonding.[36]

Five great Johnny Appleseed orchards, says one story, once spread along the Walhonding, producing various grades of fruit. Chapman's big Mohican nursery was five acres in size, says another. On it, says still another, he planted in 1806 as much as sixteen bushels of appleseeds brought from western Pennsylvania and eastern Ohio. That would have been a lot of seeds. There are about 336,000 appleseeds in a single bushel, it has been estimated; sixteen bushels would have had some 5,376,000. After deducting one-fifth for the field mice, the chipmunks, and other deterrents to germination, Johnny Appleseed would have had at least four million trees growing on his Walhonding Valley acreage!

This goodly supply is apparently not yet completely exhausted after 145 years, for an increasing number of trees and old orchards all over central Ohio now claim John Chapman's sowing. Obviously, the ghost of Johnny Appleseed is still very actively peddling his wares, and the mythical nurseries at the forks of the Walhonding must still be his major source of supply.

PART TWO

DURING THE WAR OF 1812, when the frontier settlers were tortured and slaughtered by the savage allies of Great Britain, Johnny Appleseed continued his wanderings, and was never harmed by the roving bands of hostile Indians. On many occasions the impunity with which he ranged the country enabled him to give the settlers warning of approaching danger in time to allow them to take refuge in their block-houses before the savages could attack them. . . . Large bands of Indians and British were destroying everything before them and murdering defenseless women and children and even the block-houses were not always sufficient protection. At this time Johnny travelled day and night, warning the people of the approaching danger. He visited every cabin and delivered this message: "The Spirit of the Lord is upon me, and he hath anointed me to blow the trumpet in the wilderness, and

The Voice of One Crying
in the Wilderness

sound an alarm in the forest; for, behold, the tribes of the heathen are round about your doors, and a devouring flame followeth after them."

Harper's New Monthly Magazine, November, 1871

In doctrine he was a follower of Swedenborg, leading a moral, blameless life, likening himself to the primitive Christians, literally taking no thought for the morrow. Wherever he went he circulated Swedenborgian works, and if short of them would tear a book in two and give each part to different persons. He was careful not to injure any animal, and thought hunting morally wrong. He was welcome everywhere among the settlers, and was treated with great kindness even by the Indians.

HENRY HOWE, Historical Collections of Ohio, 1846

The stalking Indian
  The beast in its lair
Did no hurt
  While he was there.

ROSEMARY AND STEPHEN VINCENT BENÉT

A Book of Americans

THE WATCHMAN AT THE GATES

THE time had now come when the queer nursery-man, who operated in the edge of the wilderness just ahead of the main settlements and who had an inordinate knack for leaving talk spinning behind him, was to be elevated into a border hero. As early as 1805, when Chapman's young trees were just getting a first hearty stretch out of Owl Creek loam, the Indian border all the way from Missouri to north-central Ohio had begun to feel an under-pulsing of new and serious agitation. The Shawnee Prophet, brother of the reknowned Tecumseh, had begun to have wondrous dreams. He was receiving revelations from the Great Spirit concerning the future of the Indian tribes, and the significance of these visions he had begun to expound to the Senecas, the Wyandots, the Ottawas, and other tribesmen who gathered at his meetings along the Auglaize and the St. Marys in northwestern Ohio.

Throughout 1806, the Prophet and Tecumseh were living in Greenville, where the latter had refused to sign the peace treaty with the other major chiefs in 1795. Visitors from far tribes were often at their quarters. The Prophet was now prophesying with amazing power. Had he not foreseen the eclipse of the sun that came during the summer? Surely he spoke as the earthly agent of the Great Manitou, and his revelations concerning the red men's future freedom and of a great sovereign confederacy among them came only from divine wisdom.

In 1807, it was beginning to be obvious that Tecumseh was attracting many followers and was accomplishing some sort of intertribal organization. Drums and council fires told of superstitious rites being revived throughout the Indian territory that still covered two-thirds of the Old Northwest from central Ohio to the Mississippi.

In the spring of 1808, Tecumseh and the Prophet moved with their followers to the Tippecanoe branch of the Wabash River in northwestern Indiana, there to strengthen their organization and consolidate the tribes.

Depredations began in 1810, border burnings and killings here and there. Pent-up bitterness could hold back no longer. Various immediate factors were stirring it—Governor William Henry Harrison's maintenance of garrisons at several posts in the territory contrary to the tribesmen's will; his aggressive land-buying policy, against which the Indians realized they were helpless; consistent mistreatment by the whites everywhere along the border; and, especially just now, the encouragement of the British who were not only inciting the Indians to attack but smuggling quantities of firearms and ammunition to them from Canada.

Harrison acted swiftly and decisively in the autumn of 1811 and, as every schoolboy likes to remember, met the combined forces of the Indian tribes on Tippecanoe Creek where he defeated them in a sharp battle on November 7.

A lively tradition has made Johnny Appleseed an heroic participant in the Battle of Tippecanoe, though all the facts indicate that he was devoting his energies at the time entirely to his chain of appletree nurseries in central and eastern Ohio. He was able "to render splendid service to General Harrison and the soldiers," said a publication of the Chicago Historical Society in 1926, "but he steadfastly refused to take up arms himself, calmly informing the officers whom he served that he had no right to take the life of any living thing."

Another account, given by Henry A. Pershing in 1930, has even said that John served Harrison as an intermediary and a scout before the battle, then tended the wounded and dying when the hostilities could no longer be averted. He was struck by two bullets, but the Testament he carried over his heart saved his life. One bullet lodged appropriately, in Romans 14:8.[1]

This Tippecanoe episode is a very recent addition to the saga. It has come entirely from fiction and has been inspired by the fact that Chapman most certainly was a colorful participant in the Indian troubles—not in Indiana in 1811—but a year later in his own north-central Ohio when the smoldering northern border burst into flames with both British and Indian attacks in the War of 1812.

The ominous tremors had been felt across western and northern Ohio all through the months preceding the formal announcement of June 18, 1812, that a second war with Great Britain had begun. The Indians' range, which still covered the whole northwest quarter of the state, reached east in a thinning spear of wilderness that followed the general line of the land divide between the Erie and Ohio River watersheds. Although by the spring of 1812, white pioneers had penetrated most of this Indian country in northern Ohio, there

was still a scattering of native villages between the white settlements pushing down from the lake and the main population
creeping up the streams from the south. Farthest up toward
the tips of the valleys, the white men were far outnumbered
by the reds.

Earlier in 1812, settlers had begun seeing some of the Indians from the villages along the Sandusky and the Maumee
moving to the Canadian side of Lake Erie. Groups of warriors
were heading west and north. Personal clashes were growing
more frequent at the trading posts. Harrison's defeat of the
confederated tribes at Tippecanoe had, it is true, destroyed
any plans for an immediate uprising, but it had not removed
the red man's hope of allying with the British and driving the
Americans back south across the Ohio River.

Up the tributaries of the Mohican where the frontier was
just advancing into what is now Richland and Ashland counties, two Indian towns still remained. Both were small. But
their presence brought fears that were soon to be cruelly
realized.

One small village stood on Jerome's Fork near the present
site of Jeromeville eight miles southeast of Ashland. The nearest white settlements were at Mansfield, eighteen miles to the
southwest, where cabins had been going up since 1808, and
at Mount Vernon twenty-seven miles farther south. Indian
Jerometown's thirty bark huts housed a group of Delaware
families headed by Captain Pipe. A great chieftain in an earlier day, Captain Pipe had been embittered by the ruthless
and unnecessary slaughter of the Moravian Indians at Gnadenhutten in 1782; had helped burn Colonel Crawford shortly
afterward; had taken part in the defeat of St. Clair in 1791;
and had led in the general border fighting that had continued
till the Greenville Treaty of 1795. Now he was old. His band

had lived peacefully with the encroaching whites since 1795 and he had no desire for more hostilities. Some of his younger men were joining the British in Canada, but in 1812 when war was actually declared, he broke up his village and in August, when news came that Hull had surrendered to the British at Detroit and that the hostilities were likely to sweep into Ohio, led his band to the fort at Cleveland and placed them under the protection of the United States government. Though some of his younger men were later caught spying in the region and proselytizing other Indians to the British service, Captain Pipe and his people never returned to their favorite valleys of the Mohican and had no part in the tragic events that followed there.

The other Indian town, a larger one, was ten miles nearer Mansfield on a handsome bluff overlooking the Black Fork. It had been called Greentown after Thomas Green, a Connecticut Tory sympathizer with the Indian massacre in Pennsylvania's Wyoming Valley in 1778, who had fled to the Middle West and joined the Delawares, among whom he came to wield much power. Like the Jerometown Indians, those of Greentown had fought against General Wayne in the Battle of Fallen Timbers and like them for the past seventeen years had maintained friendly terms with the white settlers pushing into their territory.

Of the two races, the Indians had generally shown the nobler grace, history painfully reports. Abuses on the part of the whites had been frequent and flagrant. Every white settler in the region knew, when the border began to take fire in late 1811 and early 1812, that the Indians lacked no provocation and could let loose generations of pent-up animosity.

The Greentown Indians, therefore, became an immediate and serious worry to the dwellers in the Mount Vernon and

Mansfield area, especially after General Hull's disastrous surrender at Detroit.

John Chapman probably knew the seventy-mile hinterland between the lower settlements and Lake Erie as well as any other white man. The statement is no sentimental exaggeration. To become familiar with the land, to judge its course of settlement, to plant in strategic spots, and to know where all the cabins were going up had become his business.

In the summer of 1809 when George Coffinbury drove the first team into the new town of Mansfield, John was one of a group of eight men who shared a dinner cooked on the public square. By 1812, he had at least one nursery growing, a few rods northeast of the Mansfield settlement, on the west bank of the Rocky Fork near its "Big Bend." [2]

Also beginning in 1809 a chain of cabins had been spreading up the wildly beautiful Black Fork Valley six miles east of Mansfield, both above and below the Indians at Greentown. The Reverend James Copus from Pennsylvania, who preached to the Indians, had been one of the first to build there. Martin Ruffner from Shenandoah County, Virginia, and his brother-in-law Richard Hughes came in the spring of 1812. John had a nursery on the Ruffner quarter section very early. [3]

Fifteen miles still farther east on the Lake Fork, he was familiar with the clearing that Alexander Finley from Mount Vernon had begun in 1809 five miles below the Indians in Jerometown. There tradition says he had a nursery growing quite early. [4] All these neighborhoods were upstream from his big Tiverton planting on the lower Mohican. The distance to some of these upper outposts on the branches is suggested by an early historian's statement that Alexander Finley needed three days for a boat trip back down the Mohican to Owl Creek, then up to Mount Vernon. One motors it in less than an hour today.

By 1812, John had pushed on north over the land divide into the Lake Erie watershed. Seventeen miles north of Mansfield, the waterways begin to flow north, gathering quickly into the Huron and the Vermilion rivers to run in short courses across the lake plain. The Huron drains much of the 781 square miles that had been reserved by the state of Connecticut in 1792 as a donation tract for certain of its residents whose homes had been burned by the British in the Revolution, the tract now known as the "Fire Lands." Indian titles had been quieted in 1805, and the first regular settlers had begun arriving along the lake front in 1808. By 1811 cabins were scattering southward up the main branches of the Huron.

Here, Chapman's name is now most closely associated with that of Caleb Palmer, who by 1812 had penetrated farthest up the Huron south from the Erie lake front. Palmer had come through this country early as a surveyor, had bought land in 1810, and the next year had built a cabin and moved his family thirty miles back from the lake on Marsh Run near the west branch of the Huron. The place was so far upstream in the wilderness that the easier access to an organized settlement was not by way of the river north to Erie but on over the wood paths south to the few cabins at Mansfield. Mail had begun to come through from Mansfield to the mouth of the Huron in 1810, and a state road was being cut through in the same direction. Palmer's neighborhood was still so isolated, however, that by the summer of 1812 there were only three families close by in what is now New Haven Township, and only two more downstream in what is now the adjoining township of Greenfield.

Whether or not John Chapman planted a nursery this early in New Haven Township is not clear (he had one flourishing there twenty years afterward), but he had found the neighborhood and by 1812 was living with Palmer. He was there through much of that year and the next—that is, living there and at Mansfield, for Palmer was driven out of his cabin three times during the hottest of the Indian trouble and Mansfield was the refuge. John became a part of the war story in both places.

Things came rapidly to a climax in northern Ohio after Hull's surrender to the British at Detroit on August 16, 1812.

There had been rumors of approaching hostilities before, but little of immediate danger to worry about. True, in April near Sandusky a couple of hunters had been murdered, but the two Indian killers had been quickly apprehended—one was hanged, the other committed suicide. Nearly every paper through the spring and early summer had brought stories of devastations and killing along the settlement front from western Ohio to Missouri. On May 22, the *Western Intelligencer* in Worthington printed reports from Urbana that great numbers of Indians in Western Ohio were moving their families to Malden, Canada, and that whites had begun leaving the Indian territory. There had been scalpings near Greenville, Defiance, and the Chicago River.

War with Britain was declared on June 18. Papers began reporting that the Shawnee Prophet was moving a considerable force toward Greenville, and that all the young Indian warriors at Greentown near Mount Vernon had left to join him.

Then the news began coming in of the Americans' military catastrophes in the north. On July 17, the garrison at Mackinac surrendered to the British and Indians without firing a shot. On August 6, two hundred riflemen of the Ohio Volunteers were caught in an Indian ambuscade at Brownstown near Detroit and, it was rumored, the greater part of them were slain. If the enemy broke through and swept through to Ohio, the Erie front area would be the first to suffer, not only from the invaders but from the resident Indians. The surrender of Detroit proved to be just ahead.

John Chapman, accordingly, was engaged by the few families up the west branch of the Huron to go regularly north down the river to the lake and keep them in touch, at least once a week, with developments there.

He was living with Palmer. Nearby was the cabin of a man named Woodcock, and it was agreed, when the danger of an attack became imminent, that if Indians were discovered a signal gun should be fired, and that on no account whatever should guns be fired on any other occasion.

The first resulting incident had a chuckle in it. One morning, Palmer and John, who were at work in the field, heard a gunshot in the direction of Woodcock's, then a second and a third about as fast as a man could load. They raced to the house, caught their horses and prepared for a hasty retreat.

John decided to reconnoiter. He threw on some Indian garb, took his gun, and started in the direction of the alarm, with the understanding that Palmer should wait until he returned or heard something from him. An hour passed, then two and three, without the return of John. But let the *Fire Lands Pioneer* of March, 1859, recall the events in its own way:

Palmer tortured with all manner of doubts and apprehensions, had taken his gun and gone out to the edge of the clearing on the bank of the Marsh Run, in the direction of Woodcock's, to await his return. After a short time he discovered a dusky form dodging among the bushes, and presently saw something red, and supposed it was the red leggings of an Indian. The conviction instantly flashed upon his mind, that it was an Indian intent upon murder and pillage.

He grasped his rifle, determined to dispute the ground to the last extremity. Being within short rifle range, he raised his piece for the fatal shot, but a movement caused him to raise his head and take another view. Again his weapon was leveled upon the dusky form, but a desire for a more certain aim caused him to raise it a moment, and again it was leveled upon the human form, and just as his finger pressed the trigger . . . Johnny Appleseed stepped out into full view.

The adventures of the morning were soon explained. An unlucky deer had presented himself very near to Woodcock's cabin, and the latter having no meat had determined to have some venison, Indian or no Indian. When John had found out the innocent cause of the alarm, he had turned in and helped skin and dress the deer, and afterwards at his leisure had started for Palmer's with a venison ham. It was this hanging down by his side that Palmer had seen and supposed it to be the red leggings of an Indian.[5]

The big alarm came on Friday, the twenty-first of August.

It was late afternoon. Hanson Reed who lived downstream from Palmer's place in today's Greenfield Township was out in the woods rounding up his cows for the milking. According to the family story told by Mrs. Reed and her sons years later, John Chapman's voice was suddenly heard shouting through the clearing, "Flee for your lives—the Canadians and Indians are landing at Huron!"[6]

The families of the neighborhood—Reed's, Erastus Smith's,

NORTH CENTRAL OHIO

THE JOHNNY APPLESEED COUNTRY

Photograph by Ohio Department of Highways   MOHICAN STATE FOREST

THE MANSFIELD BLOCKHOUSE OF 1812

*The last remaining example of this type of
frontier fort in Ohio*

THE COPUS MASSACRE
MONUMENT

*Erected in 1882 near the
Black Fork of the Mohican,
Mifflin Township, Ashland
County, Ohio, this monu-
ment to the pioneers who
died in the killings of 1812
also bears the oldest of the
many memorials that have
been erected to John Chapman in various parts of the
United States*

and a few others—immediately collected the cattle and some household goods and made their way upstream through falling darkness to Palmer's in New Haven. Rain during the day had made the ground very difficult for travel, and part of the way a road had to be cut through the underbrush. It was a terrifying trip.

The next morning, the New Haven residents were all rounded up—the Palmers, Luther Coe, Alvin Coe and his wife, and the Reverend James McIntyre. A special express en route from Detroit to Washington, they learned, had brought news that Hull had capitulated at Detroit, that the British and Indians were on the march; that the River Raisin, the Maumee, and smaller settlements had already been overrun; and that two thousand Indians commanded by the British were on their way to Sandusky.

What happened next to the isolated families on the upper Huron has been told in various confused and conflicting ways. The safest version seems to be the one given in a letter written three days later from Fredericktown by one of the refugees, Alvin Coe.[7]

It was agreed, he wrote, that they must go immediately to Mansfield. The trip must be made at night, and as quickly as possible. With Caleb Palmer guiding, they started at nine o'clock. The Huron was full to the banks, so that teams and cattle had to swim. At last they reached the east fork and the state road, and, after a strenuous journey, arrived at Mansfield on Sunday morning. Here the few cabins offered little protection; so they proceeded on south toward Fredericktown twenty miles away.

Halfway there, while they were crossing Clear Fork, a horseback rider caught up with them to say that the Indians had now driven all the white people from the mouth of the

Huron, and that men, women, and children were fleeing help-lessly through the woods.

Similar news had reached the militia in Cleveland on Saturday evening. Nine boats laden with three hundred British regulars and six hundred Indians had landed at the River Huron, it was reported, and had driven out the settlers, who were still unorganized for resistance.[8]

When the facts finally caught up with the rumors, it turned out that the nine boats had really contained American prisoners released by the British at Detroit under the terms of Hull's surrender and sent by water to the nearest landing on the south shore of Lake Erie.

Nevertheless, the terrors of the unprotected settlers who fled from the Huron Valley during the week end of August 21-23 had been real enough, and their suffering en route had been severe on the long march through the woods in heavy rains that sent the streams to their brinks and turned the primitive paths to mud.

John Chapman had inadvertantly spread a false alarm, but the reality behind it was still fearful enough and the climax was still ahead.

2

Now that the British were actually on their way to Ohio, every Indian below Lake Erie was a potential menace. Colonel Kratzer of Mount Vernon, who took command of the local militia, was determined to remove all the inhabitants of Indian Greentown to Piqua or Urbana immediately.

Accordingly, the soldiers descended upon the village one day early in September taking with them the Reverend James Copus who lived close by. Copus held the Indians' confidence.

He had lived by them for three years, had preached to them, had gone and come freely among them, and was a particularly warm friend of the old half-breed chief, Captain Thomas Armstrong. For that reason, Kratzer had persuaded Copus much against his will to help convince the Indians that a temporary move was to their best interest. All their property, they were told, would be carefully protected.

The Indians were in great excitement. Greentown being an old and favorite village, they did not want to leave. They loved it for its pleasant and strategic location and for its long traditions that went far back into the days when it had been a stopping place on the captive routes in the Indian wars. Their burial ground was there. They could take few of their accumulated possessions with them.

Persuaded at last by Copus' sincere assurances, however, they agreed and set off with the soldiers for Mansfield.

Scarcely were they out of sight before smoke rising from among the trees behind them told them that their homes had been immediately fired. The entire village was destroyed.

Though the burning had not been authorized (some vengeful soldiers having perpetrated the act without orders), neither that fact nor the Reverend Copus' chagrin could allay the bitter dismay of the tricked refugees.

At Mansfield an even more shameful wrong was committed. The Indians were herded into camp under guard, with orders that any Indian seen loose in the woods should be shot on sight. During the short stop, a Wyandot named Toby, not a resident of Greentown but known to local citizens as a quiet, civil man, came to Mansfield to meet his twelve-year-old daughter who had been visiting friends among the Delawares. Not being allowed to leave the camp openly, Toby and his daughter slipped out at a time when the guard was at the blockhouse with a young couple who wished the chaplain there to marry them.

A mile west of town, they were fired upon by two soldiers, Morrison and McCullough from Coshocton, who then ran to the garrison to tell of their exploit. Colonel Kratzer immediately sent out a party with the two soldiers to find the Indians and bring them in.

The child had escaped unwounded and, according to John Chapman's later information, eventually reached the Wyandots safely.[9]

But old Toby was badly wounded. He had staggered a few paces and fallen into a little creek, later known as Toby's Run, and was lying in the water. Still able to speak, he protested that he was a friend and begged for mercy.

Morrison pulled a tomahawk from the Indian's belt, however, and handed it to McCullough who had recently lost a brother in the ambuscade at Brownstown, with the words, "Take revenge for your brother's blood." (Another version says that McCullough had lost a friend killed by the Indians near Coshocton.)

McCullough walked up and deliberately sank the hatchet up to the handle in the old man's skull. Then the soldiers cut off the head, scalped it, brought it back to town, and stuck it on a pole in the street where it remained till someone took it down in disgust and buried it. The soldiers filled the scalp with whiskey, witnesses have declared, passed it around, and drank from it even though the liquor was turgid with blood.

Old Toby's body was so casually buried that the ribs could be seen projecting above the ground for two or three years thereafter.[10]

Indian revenge for the several outrages was not long in arriving. After the Greentown Indians had left Mansfield under the escort of local troops, there was a few days' lull. No further reports of hostile parties in the neighborhood had come in, and Mansfield, it was supposed, was comparatively safe. Everything was very quiet.

Trade was so dull that Levi Jones, the current merchant, grocer, and whiskey vender, sauntered out one afternoon to where John Wallace and a man named Reed were clearing off a new brickyard northeast of the village center, just west of and adjoining Chapman's nursery on the west bank of Rocky Fork. A little later, returning by a trail around through the woods, Jones was suddenly fired upon by Indians ambushed behind some bushes and logs. One shot passed through his left hand into his right breast. He did not fall, but ran forward until thrown back on the ground by a tree limb. The Indians overtook him, stabbed him several times, scalped him, took his hat and handkerchief, gave the scalp yell, and fled.

A couple of men working some fifty rods away heard the shots and the cries, ran to town, and gave the alarm. Immediately everything was in an uproar. Wallace and Reed were missing and had probably been murdered too. Their wives were frantic.

The ten families in the immediate vicinity were soon gathered into the blockhouse for the night. But the local soldiers were away with the Greentown Indians, and there was no knowing what the attacking savages would do before morning. Not only did the Mansfield dwellers need help, but they must get warnings to the outlying residents.

John Chapman volunteered to make the long hazardous trip to Mount Vernon to get assistance and to warn settlers along the way of their danger.

This expedition that night has been celebrated in many a tale and verse. According to Norton, the earliest historian of the event, he made the journey on horseback. But later chroniclers have insisted that he ran barefoot and bareheaded the whole precarious thirty miles to Mount Vernon, stopping only at the cabins to wake the occupants and tell them of the Indians. Norton was probably right, for the situation called for dispatch, and no messenger in his right mind would have gone afoot in a life-or-death emergency if horses were available. But the foot race has made the more favored story, whether or no.

The settlers never forgot Chapman's dramatic shouts in the still September night. For years his words kept echoing and gathering dignity as the tale was retold. Some said that he merely called out that Jones, Wallace and Reed had been killed and that the Indians were passing south.

"Flee for your lives," Amariah Watson of Washington township remembered the call. "Flee for your lives. The British and Indians are coming upon you, and destruction followeth in their footsteps."

Another recalled the precise wording as:

"The spirit of the Lord is upon me, and he hath anointed me to blow the trumpet in the wilderness, and sound an alarm in the forest; for, behold, the tribes of the heathen are round about your doors, and a devouring flame followeth after them." [11]

There may have been some quaintly religious turn in John's calls, and it may have continued to stir imaginations long after the original words faded.

Johnny Appleseed's race through the Ohio forests in September, 1812, to warn the countryside of impending massacre and to bring help to the beleaguered families in the blockhouse, has remained one of the favorite stories out of the Middle Western frontier. Other details of that terror-haunted night drop away leaving only Johnny running through the moonlight, barefooted, shouting his fearful alarm. A hundred persons can tell about his race with death to one who can remember the name of the murdered trader or who knows whether one or a hundred citizens were killed.

As it turned out, Wallace and Reed had come in unharmed shortly after John had left for Mount Vernon. The residents who had huddled in the blockhouse during the night were unmolested, and there were no further immediate signs of hostility. John had the reinforcements from Mount Vernon there by dawn. They recovered Jones's body and buried it, found the killers' trail, and set off in pursuit.

Later the story was told that Jones had incurred the anger of several Greentown Indians by having refused, when they were moved, to return to them some rifles that they had left as security for trading-post debts. His death was commonly attributed to revenge.

As always happens when danger brushes close but seems to have been narrowly averted, people laughed a little. They had done some silly things in their fright. Maybe, after all, John Chapman's heroic journey in the night was just a bit funny.

At Fredericktown, halfway to Mount Vernon, when John's shouts had roused citizens in the dead of the night, Samuel Wilson, who lived near the Quaker meetinghouse some distance from town had been so badly scared that he had run all the way to the blockhouse with just his overcoat on—his pantaloons under his arm.[12]

A day or two after Jones's murder, a couple of young

blades from Mansfield on their way to the Newman clearing half a mile north of town, were frightened nearly out of their buckskins when a horseman suddenly appeared in the distance and fired. They ran back to the cabins and reported that they had heard five shots in the direction of Newmans and that no doubt Newman, his wife, and three children had already been massacred. A few minutes later the regular mail carrier from the lake front rode into town saying, "Don't be alarmed, I only shot off my pistol!" [13]

The Fredericktowners two weeks later had an even severer scare. Captain Douglass and the fifteen volunteers who had been trailing Jones's murderers unsuccessfully to Upper Sandusky were returning to the settlements by way of the army road to Fredericktown. They wore handkerchiefs on their heads for hats and were a grimy, grizzled lot, for they had been out in the dirt and weather for sixteen days.

Coming out of the bush at Fredericktown, they fired their guns to announce their presence and immediately sent the nervous populace in a wild stampede to the blockhouse. Two women fainted.[14]

The laughs were short-lived, however, for the danger had not been imaginary and tragic bloodshed had not been averted.

3

News of the slaughter that now descended upon the cabins along the Black Fork began reaching the outside world on September 13.

"The day before yesterday," Brigadier General Reasin Beall wrote from his camp near Wooster to Major General Elijah Wadsworth at Cleveland, "the Indians killed and scalped four persons on the Black Fork of Mohican, about twenty-five miles west of this, and eight miles east of Mansfield." [15]

Five days later, the *Western Intelligencer* at Worthington got the story:

A family has been lately murdered by Indians, six miles from Jerometown, (Indian village about 60 miles northeast of this place, on the waters of the Muskingum,) consisting of Mr. Henry Zemore, his wife and daughter, and a man of the name of Martin Roughner.

The murder is supposed to have been committed by a party of Armstrong's Indians, who inhabit the place and Greentown, but are now all at the treaty at Piqua, except a few disaffected who refused to accompany the rest of their tribe. Both Jerometown and Greentown have since been almost entirely burned down by the whites.[16]

Already there had been more killings on the fifteenth, and two days later General Beall, who "for want of the necessary supply of Forage and provisions" was still prevented from proceeding beyond his camp three miles west of Wooster, was writing apologetically to General Wadsworth:

. . . it is with extreme regret that I have to inform you that on Tuesday last the Indians killed three men, wounded two men, and one woman about three miles above Greentown, and eight miles east of Mansfield (at the house of one Cobus) one Indian was killed and others wounded, the indians retreated—the indian killed was one of those who formerly lived at Greentown and was recognized on his way with the others (indians) who were escorted through Mansfield towards the settlements for their protection . . . I strongly recommend to the quarter Master department to proceed to owl creek and the Mohekin settlements which is within eighteen miles of the place of my intended destination to commence the erecting block houses . . .[17]

In the meantime the slaughter had been even more extensive than General Beall reported, and great excitement was spreading through central Ohio and down the branches of the Muskingum.

Out of many confused stories that local chroniclers have left concerning this last tragic Indian episode in the Muskingum watershed, a few facts are certain.

First, on the afternoon of September 10, a party of perhaps ten Indians had killed an elderly German, Frederick Zimmer (Zemore, Ziemer, Seymour, and other variant local spellings), his wife, and daughter Catherine, in their cabin on the east side of the Black Fork above Greentown and a couple of miles north of the home of Reverend Copus. A neighbor, Martin Ruffner, who had seen two Indians near the Zimmer cabin had hurried to warn the family only to be caught in the attack and slain. His body found in the yard and his gun bent nearly double from clubbing showed that he fought off the assailants desperately. All the victims had been scalped.[18]

Zimmer had incurred the hatred of the neighboring Greentown Indians, John Chapman explained later, because he had tied clapboards to their ponies' tails in an effort to frighten them from his cornfield. Any injury to an Indian's horse or dog was an insult to be avenged.

All the families in the region immediately fled to the nearest blockhouses. On September 14, however, the Reverend Copus insisted upon returning with his family from Beam's blockhouse on the Rocky Fork to his cabin on the Black Fork. He had the friendship of the Indians, he was sure, in spite of his recent share in the removal of the Greentown Indians and the shameful burning of their property. Nevertheless, Captain Martin insisted that nine soldiers accompany him, his wife, and nine children to the cabin.

The next morning, a party of about forty-five Indians descended upon the troops and the cabin. The siege lasted for about five hours, during which time, Copus and three of the soldiers were killed, and several other persons, including little Nancy Copus, were badly wounded.

The Delawares believed, of course, that the minister had played them false in the shameful Greentown removal. Indeed, the evidence must have appeared very black against Copus, although there does not seem to be the least doubt, now, that he was entirely free of any treachery and was thus the innocent victim of other men's shameless deeds.

Beside the slayings, the savages burned cabins here and there for many miles up the valleys.

Outlying cabin life was now at an end. The devastation in the Mansfield area, increasing disturbances around Sandusky, and the imminence of a British invasion by way of the Maumee resulted in immediate evacuation by most civilian families from northern Ohio and the setting up there of at least a semblance of military protection.

General Beall's troops got their "Forage and provisions" at last and were able to move from Wooster into the forks of the Mohican.

I have detached from my Command the troops of Horse and part of a Company of rifle men to the Clear fork of Mohekin— [he wrote General Wadsworth on the twentieth], two companies to Jaromestown, they are erecting Block houses, and at the same time scouting parties sent from each—one small company at Kenney's station eleven miles East of Wooster on Sugar Creek and two Companies at Wooster for the like purposes— Colonel Williams with a small force from General Cass's Brigade is stationed at Mansfield,—the remainder of Bay's detachment at Beam's Mill three miles east of Mansfield on the Black Fork of Mohekin—and Col. Kratzer ten or twelve miles north of Mansfield on or near the Huron road . . .[19]

Blockhouses went up quickly all down the streams, even as far south as the forks of the Walhonding, where one was put up on Giffin's land a few rods from John Chapman's New Castle nursery.[20]

Though there were few killings in Ohio after September, 1812, and though the main British invasion never reached the state, there was no general return to abandoned homes till the following summer after the news of Perry's victory over the British fleet on Lake Erie, September 10, 1813.

When the settlers came back, the Indians were gone forever, except for the forlorn visitors who straggled back from the West for many years to view the beautiful country that had been a happy home.

John Chapman's part in the tragedies on the Black Fork is not at all clear now. Wesley Copus, son of the murdered preacher, was the authority for saying that John acquitted himself with distinction at the time.[21] Seemingly, it was in his usual role of messenger to the other endangered settlements.

Seventy years later when a monument was erected in the Black Fork Valley to commemorate the men killed at the Copus cabin, Chapman's name and the dates of his life were included in the inscription. It is the earliest of the many memorials erected to him.[22]

Literary and folk simplification has tended to combine all the various frights and bloodshed of the Ohio border in 1812 into one great attack and John Chapman's several trips of warning to various communities into one magnificent race against death. Probably, over a period of several weeks, he gave a less spectacular and much more practical type of service than the romancers have imagined. Pioneers insisted that he got around to most of the far-removed neighborhoods. He was up Owl Creek many miles above Mount Vernon, they said, telling outdwellers in what is now Morrow County of the Zimmer murders.[23] Others said he went down the Walhonding in the other direction as far as Coshocton, and even passed on up the Tuscarawas to Newcomerstown and the Moravian neighborhoods around Gnadenhutten. Obviously there has been much exaggeration. Late folk tales have even transported this trip of warning to places as far away as Indiana and Missouri. The facts have long since dropped away leaving only the general outline of a fearless messenger racing through the danger-haunted forest, and this pattern has in time turned into a symbol of self-immolating human courage.

6

A PIECE OF GROUND

JOHN Chapman's life story now comes to a chapter that has been completely lost in the popular telling of the Johnny Appleseed myth. Plain facts have always had a hard time sticking fast to Chapman, of course. Odd bits that brought chuckles or seemed to want to burst into poetry fared pretty well, but the day-in-day-out routine of hewing down trees, grubbing in the soil, and carrying on business with his fellows were soon forgotten. The fact that the Yankee tree grower once held rights to hundreds of acres of land in Ohio and later in Indiana was completely forgotten in the generation following his death and never appears now in the legend proper. Instead he is usually called by such kindly but misguided words as those on the otherwise appropriate memorial in the Ashland, Ohio, public library, "an eccentric pauper-philanthropist." John had become eccentric enough by these middle years and there are evidences of his philanthropy, but he was never a pauper. In fact, just after the war, he seems to have set out with a fixed determination to acquire land rights on a rather extensive scale.

I

By the time the battle smoke blew away in 1813 and people were scurrying back into northern Ohio to make short work with the last miles of wilderness, thirty-nine-year old John Chapman had settled in the general area of which Mansfield was the rapidly expanding business center. "Settled" is only an approximate word, of course, since finding Chapman in any fixed spot at any given time is like nothing quite so much as laying finger on the proverbial flea. But he flea-hopped over the townships of Richland and adjoining counties for about twenty years, and that was longer than he was ever "settled" within any other such narrowly defined bounds.

Tradition places him in the Fire Lands with Caleb Palmer at the close of the war. The doughty Palmer was driven out of the Huron Valley twice more after the August flight of 1812 and returned the last time in the fall to find his cabin and crops burned. Of Chapman, Daniel Sherman of Ridgefield in the Fire Lands wrote in 1864, "I saw this noted character at Parker's Block House in 1813"—that would have been twenty-three miles north of Palmer's and seven miles from the lake front.[1] But John was also selling appletrees from his big nursery on the lower Mohican eighty miles south in October, 1812. As usual he was getting around.

If rumors are to be trusted, his nurseries by this time had appeared at the following points on the upper Muskingum watershed: farthest south, at least one in the Licking Valley; to the north, several more on Owl Creek and the Mohican; up the branches, one at Finley's on Lake Fork, another on the Black Fork on Ruffner's quarter section and another over the stream near a fort at the top of the hill across from the present

town of Mifflin; another a mile and a half west, referred to as
being between Mansfield and Charles Mills; one on the big
bend of the Rocky Fork at Mansfield, more to the west and
southwest in what are now the counties of Crawford and
Morrow; in the north, one on the Springer farm southwest of
present-day Ashland, where one story says he lived and
worked for three years; farthest north, one in Huron County
close by the big marsh in New Haven Township.[2] There is
no verifying most of these traditional sites. Some may have
come earlier or later, and some may be just pleasant folk
claims. It is doubtful that he had so many going all at one
time.

Previous to 1814 John Chapman had been exercising in his
business what the average American following the frontier
has always considered his inalienable right, the privilege to
"squat" on unclaimed (or even on merely unoccupied) new
land. Though John owned two town lots in the village of
Mount Vernon on Owl Creek, there is no actual record that
he ever planted or even lived there. He roamed and camped
and nurtured his trees on other people's ground, claimed or
unclaimed. Sometimes he may have had an informal agreement with the owners.

This pattern of his relationship with the soil was now about
to change.

On May 31, 1814, he and a Mrs. Jane Cunningham of
Richland County signed together a 99-year lease with the
state of Ohio for a quarter section—160 acres—in the extreme northeast corner of Washington Township four and a
half miles southeast of Mansfield.[3]

Of Mrs. Cunningham and of Chapman's associations with
her nothing more has been preserved except the fact noted
in an early memoir, that she was one of the first settlers in

THE BLACK FORK MASSACRE

The first news story of the killings on September 10 and 14 appeared in the Worthington (Ohio) Western Intelligencer of September 18, 1812. The page contained various other reports and rumors from the warfront some fifty miles away. (From original in the Ohio State Archaeological and Historical Society Library.)

The Western Intelligencer.

WORTHINGTON:

FRIDAY, SEPTEMBER 18, 1812.

The long desired alteration of the mail, having at length taken place, it is found expedient to alter the day of publication.— Our paper will therefore, in future, be published on WEDNESDAYS, omitting the next.

A family has been lately murdered by Indians, six miles from Jeromestown, (an Indian village about 60 miles north-east of this place, on the waters of the Muskingum,) consisting of a Mr. Henry Zemore, his wife and daughter, and a man of the name of Martin Roughner.

The murder is supposed to have been committed by a party of Armstrong's Indians, who inhabit that place, and Greentown, but are now all at the treaty at Piqua, except a few disaffected, who refused to accompany the rest of their tribe. Both Jeromestown, and Greentown have since been almost entirely burned down by the whites.

The British have removed nearly all the cannon and military stores from Detroit, except sufficient to keep up a small garrison there, and are fortifying Malden, and other places upon the other side of the line.

It is reported by some persons who were sent by Col. Crozet, to Lower Sandusky as spies, that on their approaching the place they saw the buildings all on fire, upon which they thought proper to return.

THE ZIMMER (SEYMOUR) CABIN

Frontispiece in J. F. M'Gaw's Philip Seymour, *1858*

THE OHIO COUNTRY, 1804

Map drawn by Samuel Lewis, engraved by A. Lawson, 1804. Chapman's objective was
Army Lands newly opened beyond the Seven Ranges. Zane's recently cut path can be tra
west from Wheeling to the juncture of the Licking and the Muskingum, and from t
southwest through Chillicothe to the Ohio. In the Army Lands, the stream marked ".
hickon John" became the Mohican River, and the one marked "Owl C." and "W
Woman's R." came to be known as Owl Creek and later as the Kokosing River, wl
joins with the Mohican to form the Walhonding branch of the Muskingum. (From c
in the Ohio State Archaeological and Historical Society Library.)

Washington Township. Since John did not bother to enter the lease at the county recorder's office, the transaction and the subsequent history of it would have been lost had not a few incomplete records of the Mansfield land office happened to be preserved in the Ohio State Auditor's office.

The deal ushered in the series of big-lease ventures that marked the next few years of John Chapman's activities and that do more than any other contemporary records to fill in the substance behind the shadowy seed-plantings and forest-trampings of the Johnny Appleseed tales.

Chapman and Mrs. Cunningham had leased a quarter section of Ohio's Virginia Military District School Lands. One famous innovation in the Continental Congress's Ordinance of 1787 setting up the Northwest Territory had been the stipulation that a thirty-sixth of all the new land, or the revenue therefrom, should be reserved forever for the maintenance of free common education. Ohio, coming to statehood in 1803, had been the first of the American commonwealths to enter the experiment. The inauguration of the plan stands now as a landmark in the history of American education.

These school tracts in Ohio could not under the original regulations be sold, but were managed by district land offices that were permitted after an act of February 17, 1810, to lease them at a low rental for periods of ninety-nine years. The terms seem very reasonable now, if one forgets that a dollar of legal tender in 1814 was often harder to get than a hundred a century later. By paying ten dollars of contingent expenses, Chapman and Mrs. Cunningham had acquired what amounted to permanent use of 160 acres of virgin land. They were to put up within three years a good, comfortable cabin and to clear at least three acres of ground in the quarter section. Furthermore, commencing at the end of five years, they were to pay a yearly rental of six per cent on the appraised value of the land. Since this value was two dollars per acre, they would owe an annual rental of $19.20. There would be no taxes.

The drawback was that even though a man could do the necessary work to establish his leasehold, the saving of even so small a sum as $19.20 in cash from the profits of 160 acres of new land was sometimes a superhuman task in the back country, and if the lessees defaulted in so much as one of the stipulations, the tract was immediately forfeited to the state without refund.

It was the first time, all evidence suggests, that John Chapman after following the opening of new land for nearly twenty years had been able to get a substantial parcel of it in his own right. Earlier, the land laws had played up mainly to the big speculator and to the man with available cash. Most of the government land in central Ohio had been gobbled up in the first decade by such purchasers. Now, through the land office of Winn Winship, newly opened in Mansfield, some twenty-five hundred acres in north-central Ohio had been placed on the market for permanent lease on the level of the little investor.

Only—it soon appeared—John was not setting out to be a small investor. On August 27 following the Washington Township lease, he signed a second indenture for another quarter section of school lands, five miles north of the first, just northeast of Mansfield. It was in Madison Township, on the east side of the Rocky Fork.

Then, the next winter, on February 28, 1815, he purchased from Richard Whaley the rights to still a third quarter thirty-five miles to the east, south of the village of Wooster, in the neighboring county of Wayne. This deal cost him a hundred dollars.

Nor was this all. On the following April 10, he contracted for still a fourth quarter, this one again an original lease from the land office, in what is now Green Township of Ashland County (then part of Richland) on the Black Fork of the Mohican. It was fifteen miles southeast of Mansfield and immediately down the fork from old Indian Greentown.

Even this was not to be all, but there was a pause of three years in his land expansion. In the interim, it is interesting to note, by the spring of 1815, John Chapman, forty years old, in the third year of the presidency of James Madison, had come to hold 640 acres of tiptop land under lifetime leases, and owned outright two town lots in Mount Vernon. No further cash payments would be due until 1820 and there would be no taxes on the leases. In addition he had a chain of appletree nurseries, the number undeterminable now, running through the whole region, from which he could expect at least some occasional income.

No feat of imagination is necessary to see the job that John had laid out for himself during the next few years if he attended to business. By 1817, cabins had to be put up on four rather widely separated quarters, and twelve acres of land had to be made tillable. Besides, the tracts must be set to earning in preparation for the interest payments that would begin at least by 1820. Whether he did his own work or supervised it, he had laid out a fairly rigid pattern of life for himself.

2

Recorded traces of him in 1816 suggest that the pattern was not holding him from his usual travels.

On the Fourth of July, he was up among his old acquaint-ances in Huron County delivering an Independence Day ora-tion at the celebration held in the Miner Cole home south of Norwalk. It is the only time when Chapman, who was said to be remarkably well read and to speak informally with great power on subjects dear to his heart, is reported to have held forth in formal public address. A son of Lexington and Con-cord, Bunker Hill and Valley Forge, he should have come easily by his theme.

Martin Kellogg recalled the event because it occurred dur-ing the famous cold summer of 1816, just after the killing frost in June. In Huron County, it even killed the sturdy leaves of the beechtrees.[4]

The same year, he is said to have shown up in the southern part of the Muskingum Valley, probably on a visit to his family, and had a hand in starting at least one orchard in Mor-gan County.

In 1816 [says a Morgan chronicler], he planted a large orchard on a farm now owned by William Argo [in the western part of Bristol township] for a gentleman named Fuller. In 1818, Fuller sold the farm to a Massachusetts man named Johnson who placed the property in charge of an agent. On visiting it in 1822, he was surprised to find that his young orchard had been transferred to a farm on Bear Run.[5]

In 1818 he was dabbling in real estate again. On June 1, he purchased from Henry H. Wilcoxen town lot No. 265 in Mansfield, paying $120 for it. He sold it the following Octo-ber 30 to Jesse Edgington.

Also on June 1 and again in November, he was selling off leaseholds from his Madison Township hundred and sixty to Alexander Curran, John C. Gilkinson, Henry H. Wilcoxen, and Matthias Day. In the end, he kept seventy acres in this tract, and these turned out to be a life-holding. If someone had started at the southwest corner of this Madison Township quarter in 1818 and walked seventy-six perches north, he would have come to an oak tree that served as a landmark. On it he would have read, say the courthouse records, the initials of Henry H. Wilcoxen and John Chapman—a large "H.H.W." and "J.C." carved deeply into the bark. Among all these rather dry minutiae of the real John Chapman's dealings, the thought of his initials—Johnny Appleseed's monogram—on an oak tree in the Ohio woods is captivating!

In the meantime, on April 27, he had expanded his holdings further by purchasing of a William Huff the rights to still another 160 acres of school lands in the western edge of Richland County. The quarter section lay about eleven miles west of Mansfield in Sandusky Township. The locality was still very wild, swampy, and mainly unsettled. The 99-year lease had been taken out originally by Moses Modie in 1815 and, apparently proving somewhat hopeless in the undeveloped stage of the township, had passed through several hands.

Although the specific story is lost, John evidently managed on at least three of his quarter sections to get the preliminary improvements completed inside the limits of the land laws. Five years after his initial investment he still held in addition to his Madison Township parcel the Washington tract with Mrs. Cunningham and the Green tract along the Black Fork. On the latter quarter he had also planted a nursery. On the Holmes County land no facts concerning his labors have been preserved.

On the new Sandusky Township quarter taken over in the

spring of 1818, he apparently set to work immediately to complete the technical requirements, for the lease had been given originally in 1815, and the cabin and three-acre clearing had to be accomplished at once to come within the three-year limit. To begin with, he had a nursery growing very quickly, from which are reported to have come all the first orchards in the neighboring portions of Richland and Crawford counties. On one occasion, George C. Coffinbury, Mordecai Bartley, Joseph Welch, Richard Condon, Matthew Curran, and Jonathan Beach, all early residents of the Mansfield vicinity, made a trip in a company to get trees here. They found John living in a lean-to shelter made of large pieces of elm bark set up against a log. They spent the night with him, sharing his supper and breakfast, both of which consisted wholly of coarse mush made from Indian corn meal. His camp equipment, they noted, included one kettle, a plate, and spoon. They carried away a load of apple seedlings on horseback.[6]

Though neither lease nor deed can be found now, John was said to have had still another nursery growing on another school quarter section southwest of his Sandusky Township tract in a portion of Delaware now included within the bounds of Morrow. Persistent references to such a planting must have some basis in fact, though the location is now lost. In 1819 Harlan Simmons of Greenfield, Huron County, went to it with his father and brought home all the trees that could be packed on their two horses. John had cleared about a quarter acre in the woods, Simmons remembered, where he had sown the seeds broadcast like grain. The trees that had been felled about the spot served to fence it in. The seedlings were growing quite thickly at the time of their visit. John appeared to be "about fifty years old"—actually he was forty-five. He was sociable, Simmons said, and talked intelligently.[7]

All this meant hard confining work. The folk tales have always tended to make John's life sound like a ballet of the seasons: Johnny Appleseed's rhythmic goings and comings! The springtime ecstasy of planting! The scratching in the wild, fragrant earth! The tamping in of magic seeds! The blossoms of May! Autumn's fruition! The winds and the rains and the woodland creature to fill in the choreography! Actually, his practice here on the school-land tracts seems to have been to establish a rude camp for himself where he could live while he cleared the ground, prepared timbers for and set up a simple cabin, and started any planting. "Near his plantations which were remote from any habitation," said George C. Coffinbury who knew Chapman well during the early Mansfield years, "he provided comfortable shelters from the inclemency of the weather. Hollow trees and hollow logs, provided with a nest of dry leaves served their purposes in some cases." [8]

He hired occasional help. Mansfield people used to tell of one boy who went out to help John make a clearing but who became too disheartened to last it out after he had tried one day of John's simple woods' diet.[9]

3

He was living in the crudest of outdoor camps in the midst of the swamps and forest about 1819, getting timber ready for a cabin, when the two Vandorn boys from Washington Township went out to help him raise the logs and spent a very miserable night sharing his open-air hospitality.

John had introduced himself to the Vandorns soon after

they moved to Richland County in August, 1814. They had settled in the southwestern corner of Washington, nine miles south of Mansfield. John's quarter section, taken up with Mrs. Cunningham in May, was in the northeastern corner of the same township. It was John's practice—a good business practice—to find a path sooner or later to every new cabin door, perform some neighborly courtesy if possible, and make known his appletree supply.

This time he was carrying a bunch of catnip, E. Vandorn recalled years afterward—also some literature setting forth the religious views of the Swedish mystic, Emanuel Swedenborg.[10] Since John arrived at the Vandorn place late in the day, the family persuaded him to remain for the night.

The catnip was to be freely used, John told them, to prevent the ague. Many of the early accounts of John in the Mansfield area mention this interest in medicinal herbs.[11] One of his main ideas, says one memoir, was to equalize the distribution of all efficacious plants—notably dog fennel, pennyroyal, catnip, hoarhound, dandelion, wintergreen, mullein, rattleroot, and any other plant supposed to be helpful. Such practice can in no way be considered eccentric, since medicinal herbs were desired in every well-organized frontier garden. Their use was normal routine, and the exchange of them a neighborhood courtesy. One has only to note the patches of catnip, hoarhound and motherwort that flourish today around most old Middle Western farmsteads to be convinced of the widespread pioneer use of them. In the Johnny Appleseed region, the initial appearance of dog fennel (also called "Mayweed," or even "Johnnyweed") has been attributed to him. It is an ill-smelling plant that was once thought effective in a tea for ague, or malaria, but that now infests every barnyard and stocklot. The attribution is both a dubious and an improbable honor.

As for the Swedenborgian literature, it was of far more curiosity to the settlers than the herbs. The early church life of the Mansfield rural neighborhoods had been dominated by the simple frontier fundamentalism of the Methodists, Baptists, United Brethren, Presbyterians, and Disciples. The revelations of the New Jerusalem that had been set down by the Stockholm philosopher scarcely a half century before, were still young in America and certainly novel in the Ohio midlands. The mystical nature that these new accounts of heaven and hell held for the uninformed must have seemed all the more fantastic because it was John Chapman who was introducing them.

The account given by E. Vandorn in a letter to the *Ohio Liberal* of Mansfield many years afterward gives one of the earliest known reminiscences of John's common way of life in these years: [12]

After talking about his nurseries and relating some of his wild wood scenes, encounters with rattlesnakes, bears and wolves [Vandorn wrote], he changed the conversation and introduced the subject of Swedenborg; at the same time he began to fumble in his bosom and brought forth some three or four old half-worn-out books. As we were fond of reading, we soon grabbed them, which pleased Johnny. I could see his eyes twinkle with delight. He was much rejoiced to see us eager to read them.

Vandorn was outlining here what was later to become the standard picture of Chapman as a colporteur of Christian literature among the frontier cabins—the evening call, the overnight stay, the yarn-spinning, the shift to Swedenborg, the books left for perusal. In fact, the famous account in *Harper's Magazine* of 1871, that gave the picture national popularity, seems to have been drawn entirely from the Mansfield locality.[13] One wonders, though, how the young, book-hungry boys got along in their perusal of such tough-going volumes as *The True Christian Religion, Divine Love and Wisdom, Divine Providence, Arcana Coelestia, Conjugal Love, Heaven and Hell*, or the *Four Doctrines*, any of which from the works of Emanuel Swedenborg were available in American editions in these years and some of which must surely have been among the volumes that John had available for reading and distribution. The Vandorn letter continues:

Johnny partook of a hearty supper, and gave us a full history of the Seymour [Zimmer] family and blockhouse scenes, etc. When bedtime arrived, Johnny was invited to turn in, a bed being prepared for his especial accommodation, but Johnny declined the proffered kindness, saying he chose to lay on the hearth by the fire, as he did not expect to sleep in a bed in the next world, so he would not in this.

Some time later, probably about 1819, John sought the help of the boys in raising a cabin in his Sandusky Township clearing, Vandorn said. The location he remembered as the "Wetstake" woods some distance from the new village of Lexington. The cabin was to be fourteen by sixteen feet, made of small logs.

"I was to go where a man lived by the name of Harding," said Vandorn, "and then follow a line of blazed trees, marked for some four miles in the wilderness, to his camp, and there we found him on a certain day."

John's section lay on the headwaters of the Whetstone River about sixteen miles from the Vandorns and six miles from the settlement of Lexington. The region had been opened relatively late and would be settled even later because of the wetness of the land and the impassable thickets and forest that set up a formidable barrier. Wild game abounded there. It was, in fact, one of the most famous hunting spots in the state. Indian trails like narrow sheep paths threaded it in various directions.

The Hardings were among the more substantial of the early permanent residents. Amos Harding settled here in 1819. His great-grandson Warren Gamaliel was to be the twenty-ninth president of the United States.

When the time came around, after preparing some lunching, guns, ax, butcher knife, etc., we set out on our journey, which was at that time a dense forest, shaded with heavy trees and thick underbrush, and arrived at Harding's about two o'clock in the afternoon.

After partaking of some refreshment and being put on the trail, we struck out, and after encountering swamps, tree tops, and some seeking about after deer, which was very plenty at that time, arrived there safely.

In the dusk of the evening we saw smoke curling up amongst the tree tops, and directly we saw Johnny standing close to a fire kindled by the side of a large log, an old tree which had been torn up by the roots.

I never shall forget how pleased he appeared to be when we came up to him in the wilderness, four miles from a living soul but Indians, among bears, wolves, catamounts, serpents, owls and porcupines, yet apparently contented and happy.

Here Johnny had some poles put on crotches, covered with elm bark. Some five or six rods from this were logs cut for a cabin and some clapboards for a roof.

After sitting down and chatting for a while, Johnny poked in the ashes with a stick and dragged out some potatoes, saying, "This is the way I live in the wilderness."

"Well," one of the boys replied, "you appear to be as happy as a king."

"Yes," said Chapman, "I could not enjoy myself better anywhere—I can lay on my back, look up at the stars and it seems almost as though I can see the angels praising God, for he has made all things for good."

The boys unloaded their trappings. Cornelius untied the provision sack and laid out on a pile of clapboards some bread, butter, and dried venison. He then invited Chapman to partake. John needed no urging. He helped himself to their bread and butter, and they to his potatoes.

Johnny entertained us until late bed time [Vandorn wrote],—gave us a history of the Seymour family and the Dutchman Ruffner. He said the Indians had a spite at the Seymour family. For some time the Indians' horses were unruly and troublesome to the first settlers and various tricks were played on them such as tying sticks in their mouths, etc., and not long before the slaughter of the Seymour family two horses belonging to the Indians came running into the Indian camp with split pieces of clapboard tied to their tails and blazing with fire. This the Indians charged upon the Seymours, which caused them to seek revenge.

Johnny blamed the whites for all the mischief done by the Indians. He said the Indians had done him no harm, but were friendly. Two Indians came to his camp one night and told him the fire was coming, and they helped him keep back the fire round his camp and nursery.

While fighting the fire, they had pulled back an old log and disturbed a rattlesnake, which had protested with a vigorous rattle.

"The Indians don't kill snakes," John told the boys.

"Don't they?"

"Oh, no!" said John. "We walked around it with torches in our hands, talked to it and then left it to take care of itself."

Cornelius remarked that they had done wrong in not killing the ugly thing.

"No," said John, "I killed one once that had bit me, and I am sorry for it."

He talked till the boys got sleepy. They stretched themselves out on the clapboards, with their heads under the bark shed and their feet to the fire.

"I got in a doze," said Vandorn, "but was soon startled by the howling of wolves like so many devils, not far from the camp. I jumped up and snatched my gun, but Johnny requested me to remain quiet."

Cornelius thought that the wolves were really coming and wanted to get up.

"Lay still!" said their host. "They won't hurt you; I am used to them."

"Used to the devil," Cornelius retorted, "who could be used to such howling and screeching?"

"I like to hear it," said John.

"Well, I suppose you are collogued with the devil," replied Cornelius who was a little out of humor and did not exactly trust this strange man of the woods.

The boys got up, took their rifles and fired a couple of shots in the direction of the howling.

"Tut, tut!" said John. "Lay down and go to sleep."

"Well, sleep yourself if you can," said Vandorn, "for I can't."

The older man was already half asleep. "Keep still—keep still, boy!" he directed and began to snore.

The youths loaded their rifles, punched up the fire and lay down again.

"I had got in the land of dreams, and my mind running on ten thousand wolves with all their howlings," Vandorn concluded his reminiscence, "when hoo-hoo-o-hoo-hoo-o goes a great bull owl right over my head, enough to frighten a ghost.

Before I was fairly awake, I was up and had grasped my rifle, and yelled 'Indians! Indians!' "

"Oh, do let me sleep," the boys remembered Johnny pleading disgustedly. "It's nothing but owls—I like to hear them hoot."

So saying, he drew up his feet and turned over as much in comfort as if he had been enjoying a palace.

His young companions would have preferred the luxury of the meagerest cabin. The simple life has often appealed most strongly to those who are farthest from it.

7

A VERY EXTRAORDINARY
MISSIONARY

Just when the smoke of John Chapman's camps was curling up out of his school-land clearings, his story suddenly takes a new and most unusual turn.

Up to John's forty-second year, the records manage to hold most of his personality in a baffling reticence. One is sure of the eccentric adventurer, the tough border scout, the itinerant nurseryman, and the land seeker who seemed bent just now during his middle years on carving out for himself a substantial place in the economy of a particular Ohio community. They assure the actuality back of the folk hero, but they hardly reconstruct a personality. Now, more than halfway through John Chapman's life, the records do begin to relent a little and what comes out concerning the man's inner life is one of the most remarkable of all the revelations in a long life of rather curious happenings.

I

On January 14, 1817, when Chapman was forty-two years old, the story of his unusual career was told in print for the first time, not in New England or in the Middle West, as one would have expected, but thirty-five hundred miles away in Manchester, England.[1] And it was the story, not of a nursery-man or of a frontier hero but of a very devout Christian missionary.

The account appeared in a report of the Manchester Society for Printing, Publishing and Circulating the Writings of Emanuel Swedenborg, and it had been taken from a letter written to the Manchester Society by someone in Philadelphia.

Said the report:

"There is in the western country a very extraordinary missionary of the New Jerusalem. A man has appeared who seems to be almost independent of corporal wants and sufferings. He goes barefooted, can sleep anywhere, in house or out of house, and live upon the coarsest and most scanty fare. He has actually thawed the ice with his bare feet.

"He procures what books he can of the New Church; travels into the remote settlements, and lends them wherever he can find readers, and sometimes divides a book into two or three parts for more extensive distribution and usefulness.

"This man for years past has been in the employment of bringing into cultivation, in numberless places in the wilderness, small patches (two or three acres) of ground, and then sowing apple seeds and rearing nurseries.

"These become valuable as the settlements approximate, and the profits of the whole are intended for the purpose of enabling him to print all the writings of Emanuel Swedenborg, and distribute them through the western settlements of the United States."

Whoever wrote this first contemporary notice of the colorful missionary in the Ohio settlements must not have known John directly, but had picked up a number of the interesting anecdotes that had begun to circulate about him. The striking descriptive bits were exactly the sort that were already going the rounds in the folk tales of Ohio neighborhoods that had seen much of him. The description corresponds, in fact, almost item for item with one that was to be put together in the Mansfield area twenty-eight years later by the historian Henry Howe and that has since stayed firmly in the popular story of Johnny Appleseed.

Whatever their origin, these few contemporary paragraphs preserved in rare copies of an obscure sectarian report from England in 1817 send a shaft of revealing light directly to the heart of John Chapman's vigorous middle years and give much depth of reality to the mere surface picture that later generations have usually seen. No religious group has ever been more warmly appreciative of humane values than the sensitively intellectual followers of Emanuel Swedenborg. Thanks to their rich regard for such personal services as Chapman's and to a scholarly respect for carefully kept records, a most important chapter that had been nearly lost can be partially restored.

The Manchester report suggests that Chapman's fame was well known in Eastern circles of the Church of the New Jerusalem. In fact, a letter written in 1822 by Mr. William Schlatter, most eminent of the Swedenborgians in Philadelphia, indicates that he had been corresponding with Chapman since about 1815. No definite clues are available now to trace the beginnings of John's associations with the New Church faith, but he must have been one of the first Swedenborgian followers in the Middle West and, for that matter, one of the earliest New Church converts in America. For, the Church of the New Jerusalem was still very young in this country in the years of John's first contacts with it, and even as late as

1817 was just organizing its first "General Convention" in Philadelphia and had something less than four hundred "receivers" of the teachings in the whole of the United States.

Within so small a group, when it consists primarily, as has always been the case in the New Church, of keenly literate people, it is fairly easy to identify particular families and leaders responsible for the extension of the organization and its faith. In the New Church circle, the accumulating evidence shows, John Chapman had at various times a fairly wide variety of contacts and acquaintances with such people, some of which must have been established very early in his career.

He knew members of the Bailey family for example, most prominent of all the earliest New Church adherents in Philadelphia. In 1784—when John was a ten-year-old youth in Massachusetts—James Glen, returning from London to British Guiana, had lectured in Philadelphia on Swedenborg's science of correspondences. Among his hearers had been Francis Bailey, an elder in the Presbyterian church, publisher of *The Freeman's Journal* during the Revolution, printer to the state of Pennsylvania, friend of Benjamin Franklin and witness to his will. Bailey had become the first "receiver" of the Heavenly Doctrines in the United States. A reading circle was formed at his home. He projected an American edition of Swedenborg's writings, to which Benjamin Franklin, William Morris, and other distinguished citizens were subscribers. From this circle the New Church—bound by its finely sensitive intellectual nature to be a small and restricted one—had slowly spread into Maryland and Virginia and particularly westward across Pennsylvania into Ohio, the sanctuary and hoped-for-harvest-ground for all sects new or old in the first half century after the establishment of the Northwest Territory. Bailey and his children after him were very prominent throughout this extension of the New Church doctrines, both in Pennsylvania and in Ohio. In 1826, John Chapman revealed to Colonel John H. James of Urbana, Ohio, who had married Bailey's youngest and twelfth child, that he had known the family for years.[2]

He appears also to have known Judge John Young of Greensburgh, Pennsylvania, who had married Maria Barclay, who lived in the Bailey home. Young had been a clerk in the office of Sir Walter Scott's father in Edinburgh, had migrated to America when he was seventeen, and at twenty-two had heard Glen's lecture at Bell's Book Shop in Philadelphia. He became a follower and an intimate member of Francis Bailey's reading circle. In 1790, seven years before John Chapman is known to have reached the West, Young had moved his law practice over the mountains to Greensburgh in Westmoreland County, where he continued to introduce the doctrines throughout a long career as lawyer and judge of the western Pennsylvania bar. Through Young, an unproved New Church tradition has long claimed, Chapman first had contact with the faith and received books that he distributed in Ohio, but there were other active New Churchmen close enough to the line of John's travels for him to have touched one or another very easily.[3] In 1789, a group had been formed in Bedford, Pennsylvania, the first of the church west of the mountains. In 1794 another had been founded in Steubenville on the Ohio River by a Bailey convert. And there were others.

He also knew the Eckstein family and visited in their home. John Eckstein, late sculptor to Frederick the Great of Prussia, had migrated to Philadelphia and in 1808 was a member of Bailey's group. His son Frederick, a fine artist in his own right, married Bailey's daughter and went West to Cincinnati, where he not only continued a distinguished family line but became the "father of Cincinnati Art," if not of art in the Middle West. Their daughter, in turn, married Alexander Kinmont, a brilliant young Edinburgh scholar who had come to America in 1823, was converted to Swedenborgianism while teaching in Bedford, then moved on to Cincinnati, the cultural capital of the new West, to found his own school. When Chapman called on Colonel James in Urbana in 1826, he bore a letter of introduction from Kinmont. Furthermore, Alexander's brother William, who followed from Scotland in 1824, settled for a time in John Chapman's neighborhood near Mansfield where a Swedenborgian society had begun to flourish.[4]

These and other tenuous personal leads weave a network of tradition that has long been preciously cherished in New Church families.

It has been a much more fine-grained and dignified tradition, of course, than that which has flourished popularly, for Johnny Appleseed to the New Churchmen has always appeared primarily a servant of the Church, a colorful but reverently useful frontier missionary whose oddities minimize when viewed in the light of his Christian service.

Most of John Chapman's acquaintances in the Middle Western settlements neither knew about his personal relations with people such as these nor even suspected that such existed. He was not a man whom one associated with people that frequented formal reading circles and academic halls. His strange looks and ways made an initial impression of uncouthness and ignorance. He was often good for a laugh. Not many listened to his particular interpretations of the Christian faith, and of those who did very few comprehended.

2

The most extended of these New Church contacts, of which records remain, was with William Schlatter of Philadelphia.

Schlatter, a wealthy importer and wholesaler of dry goods, had inherited Francis Bailey's earlier position as sponsor of the Swedenborgian society in Philadelphia. Since his conversion in 1814, he had not only given of his extensive means to build a temple for the group in his city and published at his own expense for free distribution various of Emanuel Swedenborg's writings, but he had built up contacts with practically every other prominent New Churchman in America and England and maintained a voluminous correspondence. Fortunately, some of his letter books have been preserved.

It was he, we learn, who by 1817 was supplying at least part of the church literature John was distributing in the settlements, for he wrote on May 4 to the Reverend Richard Goe, pastor of the New Church society in Wheeling:

"I am not without hopes of seeing you . . . I have sent some books to Mr. Chapman, do you know him and has he received the Books, he travels about in Ohio and has much to do with appletrees; I am told he is a singular man but greatly in love with the New Church doctrines and takes great pains in deseminating them." [5]

In July and August of the same year, the Reverend Jonathan W. Condy and the Reverend M. M. Carll, both of Philadelphia, on a joint evangelistical swing through Maryland, Pennsylvania, western Virginia, and Ohio, had a chance somewhere to talk with this "singular" New Churchman.

Condy, who was a man of discriminating mind, having been not only a distinguished lawyer and promoter of his church but once the Clerk of the House of Representatives in Congress, reported to Schlatter that he found Chapman to be intelligent with an absorbing desire to promote the doctrines of his church.[6]

Sometime the next year, a young minister of the Methodist persuasion named Silas Ensign found his way to Richland County, Ohio, and began putting up a cabin six miles northeast of Mansfield in the vicinity of Chapman's Madison Township lease. Whether Ensign had already imbibed of the Swedenborgian mysticism before meeting John is not now clear, but very shortly after coming to central Ohio, he became an ardent exponent of the New Church doctrines and was soon gathering about him a group of followers. Among these, John Chapman was not only an enthusiastic worker but the chief contact man with the central church organization in Philadelphia.[7]

According to Ensign's own testimony, Chapman was the only "receiver" in the Mansfield area when he arrived there, but by late 1819 or early 1820, sufficient numbers had been attracted to their teachings that Chapman was writing Schlatter asking that Ensign be properly licensed as a lay reader for their group.

Schlatter's reply to Chapman is reconstructed below from his letter book: [8]

Philadelphia, March 20, 1820

My dear friend,—

I had the satisfaction of receiving your much esteemed favour of the 20th ult. in due time, and laid it before our brethren. It gives us great satisfaction to find you were so desirous to promote the cause of truth not only by your desire

*for the book, but also to have brother Silas Ensign as a lay
reader.*

*I refer you to my last letter, dated 20th Feb. in reply to
your inquiry about the Book in which I informed you the
society had it not in their power to [enter] into the arrangement you desired, say to barter books for land at fair price,
and also that I wanted [you] to answer me. I referred you to
our friends Wright and Marcus Smith of Cincinnati who have
lately published some of Emanuel Swedenborg's works and
might find it [possible] to exchange some for land. I informed
you our Book society were indebted to the English society
for the books imported, and that we could not on that account
barter them but only sell for cash. I hope you will receive
that letter. I directed it [to] Richland county, Ohio, it was
the only direction I had.*

*In reply to your request to have our friend Silas Ensign
licensed, we beg leave to point out the regular mode of application which no doubt your society of readers will cheerfully
comply with us. It is all important, to have some regular order
in those matters. You will therefore have a meeting of some
of those brethren who wish Mr. Silas Ensign to be your
reader and draw up a recommendation which can be signed
by yourself and friends, and forwarded to me and your request shall be granted, this has been the uniform mode pursued with other societies and I make no doubt you will see
the propriety of continuing the rule.*

*I am truly glad to hear the doctrines are spreading in your
section of the country, and I make no doubt if you had more
books they would increase faster. I informed you in my last
I would furnish you with a few of my small works if you
would write me by some of your merchants, when they came
on this spring, our worthy friend, Mr. Daniel Thuun has seen*

*your letters, and will be glad to hear from you, he is one of
the most zealous members.*

I must now conclude

Your friend,

Yours in affection

Wm. Schlatter

"Our friends Wright and Marcus Smith of Cincinnati"
were two of ten brothers whose energetic, progressive lives
were widely felt not only in the Church but in artistic, the-
atrical, publishing, and early cultural movements generally in
the Middle West. "Our worthy friend, Mr. Daniel Thuun,"
was one of the oldest and most faithful of the Philadelphia
New Churchmen. The business of Mr. Ensign's appointment
as lay reader was taken care of duly and properly, and two
years later forty "receivers" in his flock were petitioning to
have him ordained as a full-fledged minister.

One item in this letter that starts imagination soaring is
Schlatter's implication that John had recently offered to ex-
change some of his Ohio land for New Church literature.
Schlatter discussed the proposal further in a letter to the
Reverend John Clowes of Manchester, England, on April 16,
1821: [9]

"*I have received a letter from a zealous member of the New
Church, and one who appears most anxious to spread the doctrines of truth,*" he wrote. "*He offers land for books but as
our societies have no books on hand it is out of their power
to supply him. It is my intention to send him a few books I
had published.*

"*I enclose a copy of his letters that you may know something of his character. He is a singular man and our friend Mr.*

Condy who has conversed with him in Ohio states him to be intelligent and says the great object of his life appears to be to promote the doctrines. If some of the printing Societies or any of our friends have books to spare I think they will be faithfully distributed by Mr. Chapman.

"*The land that he offers is valuable and if your society had the books we would send them and receive the land and appropriate it for the use of a new Church and School and the support of a new Church minister. You will have the goodness to make known his wishes to our friends and I make no doubt they will send him some books and sermons which they can spare.*"

The following May 15, Daniel Thuun was also writing about Chapman's offer of land, in a letter to Margaret Bailey in Cincinnati: [10]

"*. . . To add something more to the New Church news, there is Mr. John Chapman near Wooster, Ohio, who wrote lately to Mr. Schlatter that he found an increase of Receivers all around his neighborhood and that they are spreading as far as Detroit, he proposed to make a Deed over to the New Church for a Quarter Section of Land and take payment in Books of the New Church. We contemplate how best to fulfill his wishes. This is the Appleseed man you certainly must have heard of, who goes around in the Country to plant Apple trees.*"

Which of his land holdings Chapman was thinking of devoting to his church is an interesting speculation. The four quarter sections that were still in his name in 1820 were held not in full possession but under 99-year leases, any of which could have been assigned but which would have also entailed an immediate interest payment obligation upon the new lessee. In fact, as the records soon reveal, John himself was beginning to feel a severe money pinch.

The proposal for transferring the quarter section to the Church of the New Jerusalem was never carried out, but one's fancy is stirred, surely, to think that John Chapman had almost been the founder of another denominational school in the Old Northwest. Popular romancing, which has credited its apple-hero with almost every other possible philanthropy, has never happened to hit upon a Johnny Appleseed college! But then, popular belief has never been able quite to catch up with the strange happenings of John Chapman's real life.

William Schlatter had for years been printing and distributing at his own expense the teachings of Swedenborg. No other person in America had yet done so great or so generous a material service to the church. Being a merchant with very extensive connections, it had been his custom to send out packages of the books with his merchandise, often inserted in bales of cloth, to customers over the country. He had sent them even to India and to the Emperor of Haiti, but especially to the inland merchants of Middle Western America. In 1819, he could state that in the past few years he had purchased and published about "7,000 Books and sermons on the sublime doctrines of the New Jerusalem of which about 6,000 have been distributed gratis and the remainder are yet on hand for that purpose." [11]

But beginning in 1818, the nation's financial debacle that had been intensifying since the last war with Britain had begun to make great inroads upon Schlatter's business. "I have had great tribulation in my worldly matters," he wrote in December, "my business . . . is extensive and my connections in the Western country extended. The deranged state of the currency and the pressure of our Banks has caused great distress among merchants generally and particularly those who are engaged in the Western trade." By 1820 and 1821, it was indeed out of Mr. Schlatter's power to respond to John's request as he would have liked.

Nevertheless, he continued to help all he could and in November, 1822, he was writing to Silas Ensign at Mansfield:

"... I am truly delighted to find there is so many members of the Lord's new church in and near Mansfield and also that they have appointed you their leader and request a license of ordination for you ... we shall act on your request in the course of this week ...

"I make this communication ... to say to Mr. Chapman that I have written him three if not four letters since I have had a line from him. I wish to know if he received my letters and the last books I sent ...

"I shall be glad to hear from you often, and hope you will communicate fully any interesting church news. Mr. Chapman has no doubt been very instrumental in spreading the truth." [12]

And another letter on November 18 to the Reverend N. Holley who was teaching and preaching in Abingdon, Virginia:

"Mr. Ensign says when he first went there, there was but one receiver and that was Mr. John Chapman, whom you must have heard me speak of, they call him John Appleseed out there. If you do not know his history I will give it to you in my next if you desire it, as it is interesting ... I corresponded with Chapman for seven years." [13]

"John Appleseed"—this allusion in 1822 is the earliest known mention of John Chapman's sobriquet. Its form is that which was probably most commonly used during his lifetime. The childish diminutive "Johnny" came with old age and the myth.

None of Schlatter's other communications concerning his missionary correspondent in Ohio are now available. But one suspects it was he who was responsible for the bright tribute printed in the journal of the Fifth General Convention of the New Churchmen held on June 3-5 of that year in Philadelphia:[14]

"In the state of Ohio throughout," the Committee appointed to select from communications of church extension reported, *"the great work is going on still more extensively.*

"Besides the society established at Steubenville . . . and Lebanon and the very numerous church of Cincinnati . . . one very extraordinary missionary continued to exert, for the spread of divine truth his modest and humble efforts, which would put the most zealous members to the blush. We now allude to Mr. John Chapman, from whom we are in the habit of hearing frequently. His temporal employment consists in preceding the settlements, and sowing nurseries of fruit trees, which he avows to be pursued for the chief purpose of giving him an opportunity of spreading the doctrines throughout the western country.

"In his progress, which neither heat nor cold, swamps nor mountains, are permitted to arrest, he carries on his back all the New Church publications he can procure, and distributes them wherever opportunity is afforded. So great is his zeal, that he does not hesitate to divide his volumes into parts, by

repeated calls, enable the readers to peruse the whole in suc-cession.

"Having no family, and inured to hardships of every kind, his operations are unceasing. He is now employed in travers-ing the district between Detroit and the closer settlements of Ohio.

"What shall be the reward of such an individual, where, as we are told in holy writ, 'THEY THAT TURN MANY TO RIGHT-EOUSNESS SHALL SHINE AS THE STARS FOREVER.' "

3

The rest of the testimony to John Chapman's religious labors comes from the stories that followed him along the trails.

He was no blindly fanatical colporteur. He both read his tracts and discussed them freely and intelligently, even though many did not know what he was talking about. The scriptural interpretations of Emanuel Swedenborg were too toughly intellectual to appeal widely in a frontier culture where illiteracy ran high and religion was popularly a com-bination of naive literalism and emotional demonstrativeness.

Judge Stanbery of Newark, who knew John well in Lick-ing, Knox, and Wayne counties from 1809 to 1830 and saw him again in Bucyrus in 1831-32, used to say that his own knowledge of Swedenborg came entirely from talking with Chapman. "His main bump seemed to be to leave the books of Swedenborg whenever he could get anybody to read them," he said, "and leave them until he called again . . . His books were very old. He got them somehow from Philadel-phia. He had great thirst for making converts." [15]

The Emry family settled in Richland County in June, 1816. Emry, who was a Baptist preacher and a widely read man, soon heard of Chapman's unorthodox religious views from the neighbors, some of whom thought he was crazy, while others thought he was possessed of the devil. At the first opportunity Emry invited Chapman into his home and engaged him in religious discussion. To the preacher's delight, says the family tradition, he found that the strange man of the trails had one of the best informed and brilliant minds he had ever known. Thereafter Chapman was always a welcome visitor in the Emry home. Sometimes he stopped for three or four days at a time.[16]

John spent a night in 1819 with Henry Roberts, a Quaker whom he had known for years near Mount Vernon. A short time before, returning up the Muskingum Valley from a visit with the Chapman family, John had met Henry's son, Isaiah, en route by foot to Missouri, and he had promised the boy to stop at his father's and tell of their meeting.

During the evening, John spied a copy of Hosea Ballou's *Treatise on the Atonement* which, since 1805, had been setting forth the beliefs of the Universalist sect to American readers. At first, John was caught by the reading, for a disciple of Swedenborg could go along at least a little way with the Universalists. He could accept, for instance, their hostility to the Calvinistic notion of election. Christ had died not for the selected few, but for men universally.

But Chapman soon threw down Ballou in disappointment and disgust. No New Churchman could follow the Universalists in their basic assertion that in Christ's atonement all mankind is saved and that every individual in spite of his earthly sins will be brought to a state of perfect holiness and happiness in the world to come. Ballou was especially ardent in his doctrine that all retribution is confined to this world. Sin originates in the flesh, not in the spirit. Therefore, death frees the souls from all impurity and all are brought to a state of perfect holiness and happiness in the world to come. In Swedenborg's system there was not only a heaven but a very definite and purposeful hell.[17]

David Ayres remembered Chapman from about 1822. The Ayres family had settled on the banks of the Black Fork twelve miles north of Mansfield in 1815 and along with the Trucks family had procured from Chapman the trees for the first orchards in Blooming Grove Township. Young David remembered the New Church volumes left from cabin to cabin and exchanged on return trips—the first traveling library in the Middle West. But he felt that the immediate results were often negligible:

"The people . . . paid little attention to the New Church . . . doctrine," he said, "it was not orthodox, neither popular, and old Johnny was ragged." [18]

The prime reason for the neglect was not John Chapman's rags but the fact that the doctrine he bore to the settlers was largely unintelligible to them. The generation following the middle border was the most religion-eager any frontier had ever known. Any supernatural teaching that provided ready access to emotions and to simple understanding got a hearing, especially if it offered an escape from the harshness and misery that had to be borne in the breaking of a new land. The flames of emotional revivalism that had begun in New England in the eighteenth century had been kept brightest year after year just in the wake of the new settlements, down the back country of the Piedmont and over the mountains into the bluegrass and saltlick country, then up through all the valleys of the Old Northwest—always just behind the earliest comers.

Never anywhere in all the complicated history of American churches has there been such a heterogeneous mingling of sects and systems as that which surged through western Pennsylvania, Ohio and Indiana from 1790 to 1850. Sabbatarians, Free-Will Baptists, Congregationalists, Bible Christians, Wesleyans, Old School and New School Presbyterians, Covenanters, Mennonites, Unitarians, Universalists, Adventists, Jerkers, Millerites, Friends, Restorationists, United Brethren, and Mormons! James B. Finley, William Otterbein, Joseph Smith, Alexander Campbell, Peter Cartwright, Lorenzo Dow, Joseph Bimeler, and Father Fenwick! Inner light, sanctification, predestinarianism, immersion, justification by faith, authoritarianism, the seventh millenary, universal salvation, communism, atonement, special revelation! Synods, dioceses, districts, phalanxes, conferences, congregations, societies, conventions, communities! Priests, circuit riders, ministers, lay preachers, class leaders, wardens, deacons, lay readers, stewards, elders, overseers, rabbis! Never has such a variety of spiritual interpretations and leadership woven such a complicated interlacing of creeds and disciplines in so short a time in a similar area. New soil brings lush crops—even with shallow cultivation.

The New Church doctrines were too intellectual, however, to thrive with merely surface tilling. They moved deeply, and therefore slowly, in the convictions of earnestly thoughtful people. True, they too were finding their richest harvest west of the Alleghenies, but compared with the ingatherings of the Methodists and Campbellites their totals were negligible. Sixty-three years after James Glen's first visit to Philadelphia, the New Church could list only seventeen societies with about 360 members in nine states. It shunned emotional revivalism as mere sensationalism and depended chiefly upon the understanding of educated minds that follow the slow, solid processes of extended syllogistic reasoning.

Swedenborg's doctrine of "correspondences," the basis of New Church theology, was derivatively Neo-Platonic, and Platonism in any form has always been a method of thought for nurtured and discriminating minds. Whether as a philosophy or translated into a system of Christian thought, Platonism has ever demanded time for leisurely perusal of the printed page and for penetrating discussion. Newly settled country had little of that leisure.

One of John Chapman's warmest disputants for many years was the Reverend James McIntyre of New Haven in the Fire Lands that Chapman had visited frequently ever since the days of Palmer's blockhouse and the Indian massacres. McIntyre, a New Yorker, was theologically untrained except through the few books that came his way, but he had become an ardent local preacher in the Methodist Church and was much renowned for his long-continued war on Calvinism and Universalism. Like Johnny Appleseed, he was famous for his eccentricities of dress. Tall, gaunt, ungainly, with pinched face and small deep-set eyes he would appear to preach in a tow-cloth shirt worn in the manner of a frock, tow-cloth pantaloons held up by one tow-cloth suspender, a freakish hat pulled over his face, and barefooted.[19]

John Chapman's talk about corresponding and coexisting spiritual and natural worlds was wholly incomprehensible to the naive McIntyre. "Man is so created," Swedenborg has said, "as to be in the spiritual world and in the natural world at the same time." [20] The spiritual world is, of course, where the angels are, and the natural is where men are. Man is created with both an internal and an external—an internal by which he is in the spiritual world, and an external by which he is in the natural world. The internal is the spirit and the external the body. The latter derives its being from the former. In fact, the whole natural world "corresponds" to the spiritual world, not only in general but also in particular. "All things which exist in nature, from the least to the greatest, are correspondences. The reason they are correspondences is that the natural world with all it contains exists and subsists from the spiritual world and both worlds from the Divine Being." After death, a man merely abandons the natural form and continues in the spiritual one alone.

To Brother McIntyre this philosophical dualism, in which the material fact and the spiritual equivalent exist as one, was an incomprehensible subtlety.

"I would like to know what your faith is, any way," he would reiterate doggedly after a long discussion. "I would like to know about the life here and hereafter; I have told you what my Bible tells me, now how does it come that you have got something different?"

Chapman would say, "It is no more mysterious to me or even to you that you should live in different zones after death than that you live in this one now."

"Do you call that an argument?" McIntyre would say helplessly.

"That is all I have to say."

After all, how could one explain to a nonbeliever that the Resurrection is not a long-delayed event that comes with the last trump but the simple continuation of the spiritual being without the natural? Or that Divine truth and wisdom come not through special revelations and spectacular conversions but flow directly "into man's thought and by an internal way into his organ of hearing, thus acting upon it from within"? Or that the scriptures are not to be taken literally but are the mere letter record of spiritual meanings, the true significance of which can be known only when the original "correspondence," long lost, is once more revealed—a duty to which the New Church was especially devoted?

People caught the seemingly quaint and spectacular in John's words more often than the deeply spiritual.

His religiously inspired mercies to wild creatures, for instance, brought a multitude of laughs and an endless succession of yarns. Once when mowing he had been bitten by a rattlesnake, which he promptly killed with his scythe. Then, smitten with remorse, he had said, tears gathering in his eyes, "Poor fellow! He only just touched me, when in an ungodly passion I put the heel of my scythe on him and killed him!"

This tenderness, said the storytellers extended to bears, wolves, horses turned loose to die, wasps, mosquitoes, and flies.

But why not? Had not Swedenborg said that "all things in the world exist from a Divine Origin . . . clothed with such forms in nature as enable them to exist there and perform their use and thus to correspond to higher things"?

People were amused by his reports on the nature of heaven and hell. How could literal minds understand that Swedenborg in setting down his revelations had been forced to use merely earthly terms for what were really spiritual values, that communications with angels is not a matter of physical seeing and hearing, but instead "as the spiritual man thinks about Divine things in whatever he does, he is in communion with the angels of heaven, and is therefore united with them so far as he acts in this way." This talk of communication with angels people called mere spiritualism, though nothing could have been farther from the New Church method. The outsider was always confusing the physical image with the spiritual value.

Sometimes John parried queries with a wry joke. When he compared Swedenborg's idea of hell with the notoriously wide-open town of Newark; possibly he had in mind Swedenborg's vivid cataloguing of hellish things: "cadaverous, putrid, excrementitious, filthy, rancid, and urinous matters" with varieties of hell to correspond to each.[21]

They asked him about life in heaven, and he told them it would be a continuation of the earthly except that it would be spiritual in nature. But what of golden streets, sapphire gates, and harps to play? Alas, the blind could not perceive that the meanings of the scriptures are not apparent in mere printed words open to the eye but are heavenly arcana hitherto concealed in the wisdom of the angels.

They asked him why he did not marry, and he replied that he had received a vision of spiritual satisfactions in the world to come. Something he said started the story that he had foreseen two wives in the hereafter, and frontier ribaldry had a good time with that one. But since polygamy was definitely not in the Swedenborgian system, his hearers must have garbled whatever he said.

4

John Chapman's ultimate personal influence in extending the Church of the New Jerusalem is difficult to evaluate.

He certainly took an active part in the formation and the

growth of the Reverend Ensign's society in Richland County, a fact illustrated particularly well by the conversion of John Tucker. Tucker, a native of New Hampshire, had come to Richland County in 1818 and taken up a half section on Sweitzer's Run in Monroe Township southeast of Mansfield. A man of parts to be reckoned with in any community, he left his mark on the early county in many ways. He taught at least sixty school terms, was a surveyor and laid out the town of Lucas for his brother. He was a good doctor. In addition to these pursuits and farming, he took long walking tours to Indiana, northwest Ohio, and Missouri that almost rivaled the jaunts of Johnny Appleseed. He also organized the first church group in his township, a Swedenborgian one, after his interest had been stirred by a tract given to him by John Chapman.[22] A number of families soon joined him, including those of Joseph Applegate, Henry Wyrick, John Eyler, George Shambaugh, and David Crawford. The little flock was allied, apparently, with the congregation of Reverend Ensign, whose members were widely scattered over the region that lies between Mansfield and Wooster.[23]

Between 1820 and 1840, all through the central and northern Ohio counties where Chapman spent his best middle years, a considerable number of small Swedenborgian societies sprang up and flourished vigorously for a time—in Licking, Wayne, Muskingum, Richland, Cuyahoga, Medina, Huron, Portage, Erie, Sandusky, Shelby, and Lucas counties.[24] Chapman is commonly credited with the sowing that sprouted into this sporadic crop.[25]

In the memoirs and traditions of numerous New Church families, stories of his services have continued to appear for a hundred years.

John Smith of Mellagen's Grove, Illinois, who died in 1872,

had been introduced to the faith first in central Ohio by Chapman sometime before 1824.[26]

The Reverend John Randolph Hibbard, who himself had been converted to the doctrines when he found a copy of the *True Christian Religion* in an Ohio log cabin, knew various of Chapman's converts.[27]

One aged New Churchman testified in 1890 that he had first become a disciple of Swedenborg by reading books left by Chapman in his father's house when he was a small boy. "He told them they lived in another world at the same time they lived in this," the informant recorded; "that they had a spiritual existence as well as a natural one." [28]

Chapman visited the Wagars of Rockport near Cleveland, and he left his "leaves" on the well curb of the Nicholases near Vermilion.[29]

In both the Kinmont and Eckstein families in Cincinnati, where he had been a guest, said Miss Edna Silver, careful historian of the New Church in the Middle West, "dwellers in both homes testified to his acceptance of his untoward physical conditions, to his triumph of spirit over matter, to his unwordly faith that heaven would take care of him, to the Master's burning message on his lips. In recalling the radiance of his spirit these ladies had lost all remembrance of his uncouth appearance." [30]

In recent years the returning awareness of these associations with his church has worked to soften much of the grotesquerie that characterized the earlier growth of John Chapman's story in popular fancy. His idealism has become more rational, much of the early cause for ignorant laughter has disappeared, and Chapman himself has become a much simpler and more normally human person. At the same time, he has emerged as increasingly deserving of the legend that has crowned his long and colorful labors.

As the common run of saints goes, the real John Chapman must have been anything but flawless. He was eccentric, often lacking in consideration for the commonest social conventions. But he had qualities that kept the respect of a group of thoughtful men and women who were following some of the most subtly intellectual ethics, esthetics, and theology that America has ever known. The popular mind felt the presence of these qualities too, but it did not always know why.

The spark of Swedenborgianism that stirred the creative fancies in the legend of John Chapman has touched the American mind in many other immeasurably rich ways, in poetry and art, philosophy and religion. The gracious lives of the first New Churchmen left a trail of schools, art academies, musical societies, books and publishing concerns from the East coast deep into the heart of the Middle West. From Plato to Johnny Appleseed is a long tortuous road indeed, and it has developed many by-paths through the twenty-two hundred years other than those that branch from medieval Christian theology, the special revelations of Emanuel Swedenborg, and the need for appletrees on the American middle border.

PART  THREE

His PERSONAL APPEARANCE was as singular as his character.
. . . He lived the roughest life, and often slept in the woods.
His clothing was mostly old, being generally given to him
in exchange for apple trees. He went bare-footed, and often
travelled miles through the snow in that way.

HENRY HOWE, *Historical Collections of Ohio*, 1846

Thus strangely clad, he was perpetually wandering through
forests and morasses, and suddenly appearing in white settlements and Indian villages; but there must have been some
rare force of gentle goodness dwelling in his looks and
breathing in his words, for it is the testimony of all who
knew him that, notwithstanding his ridiculous attire, he was
always treated with the greatest respect by the rudest frontiersman, and what is a better test, the boys of the settlements

The Legend Takes Root

forbore to jeer at him. With grown-up people and boys he was usually reticent, but manifested great affection for little girls, always having pieces of ribbon and gay calico to give to his little favorites. Many a grandmother in Ohio and Indiana can remember the presents she received when a child from poor homeless Johnny Appleseed. When he consented to eat with any family he would never sit down to the table until he was assured that here was an ample supply for the children; and his sympathy for their youthful troubles and his kindness toward them made him friends among all the juveniles of the border.

Harper's New Monthly Magazine, November, 1871

Now we had always heard that Johnny had loved once upon a time, and that his lady love had proven false to him.

ROSELLA RICE IN JAMES F. M'GAW's *Philip Seymour*, 1883

His mush-pan slapped on his windy head,
his torn shirt flapping, his eyes alight,
an American ghost . . .

FRANCES FROST, "American Ghost"

8

PORTRAIT AT FIFTY

B Y 1824, John Chapman's big land operations in north-central Ohio had faded almost as abruptly as they had begun ten years before, and the nursery chain that first had led him into the West was emerging again as his central occupation. It was also adding some new and longer links. The twenty years of his life were still ahead out of which would come the picture that would immortalize him in popular fancy.

From about 1817 most of Chapman's paths—whether from a distant school-land clearing, a round of nearby nurseries, a group reading of *The True Christian Religion*, or a trip to family and cider presses in southeastern Ohio—wound sooner or later down to the village of Perrysville in the valley of the Black Fork of the Mohican sixteen miles southeast of Mansfield.

His half-sister Persis, nineteen years younger, who had been twelve when their father brought the family from Massachusetts to the Duck Creek settlement in 1805, had married a man named Broom, who sometime after 1816 moved his wife and children to Perrysville. There they lived for a number of years, northeast of the village in a cabin on the Mohicanville road.[1] William Broom, who seems never to have

provided much earthly substance for his family, was employed by Chapman on his various properties.

John, in turn, lived with the Brooms—that is, when he was
in the vicinity. He is said to have been passionately fond of
his sister's children, and he clung to the family more or less all
the rest of his life. Dates of residence are indefinite, but the
Perrysville cabin belongs at least to the 1820's and perhaps
earlier. Later the Brooms lived in Mansfield, where John continued to frequent their household from time to time. Still
later, about 1834, when his interest turned to Indiana, they
followed him there, and Broom was in his employ at the
time of John's death in 1845.[2]

This association with his sister's family was the only
approach to normal home life that John Chapman is known
ever to have shared at any time during his mature years. It
must have been a very thin and piecemeal enjoyment. But
the straggling evidence of its continuance over many years
suggests a side of John that has been very easy to overlook.
In the legends he has always appeared happily individual, like
a planet serenely on his own, so that a longing for the sym-
pathetic presence of others, which often grows more intense
as the later years of a man's life bring greater individualiza-
tion and loneliness, has never seemed to be a part of his
character. That such loneliness was often his is clear enough
in the record of his attraction to his sister's family, in his
numerous gifts to children, in his seeking out of cabin fire-
sides for lodging along his routes, and in his eagerness to find
audiences for his tales.

Nor can one overlook the hints in local Ohio traditions
that John had attempted during these years in the West not
only to win a home for himself but to find a wife. John

certainly did not shy completely away from women, though there is no basis for the elaborate tales of him as a romancer that have appeared in late fiction.

The Brooms doubtless came to Perrysville on John's advice. It had long been a familiar locality to him and was to continue a favorite as long as he lived. He had explored and planted up the Black Fork before the war. He had known all the Coulters, Hills, Olivers, Rices, Tannyhills, Haleys, and Cunninghams who first took over the land here in Green Township. Some of them he had known in their earlier homes in Pennsylvania and eastern Ohio. One of his quarters of school land, taken up in 1815, was here on the Black Fork below the site of old Greentown just above Perrysville. His nurseries here, and the orchards from them, began early and grew for a long stretch of years. He left the whole neighborhood saturated with his tradition. The fact that he enjoyed in even a loose and fragile way something of a home here may have deepened his feelings for the place.

Perrysville had been laid out in 1815. Traveler William Cheesebrough from Connecticut, who happened down into the place from the Mohicanville road in October, 1817, noted that there were nine or ten houses, that the Black Fork was boatable to this far inland point from the Ohio River via Zanesville, that the land about was full of "Prairies which are rich but very muddy," that the country abounded with honey (John Chapman is reputed to have been very fond of honey, and Honey Creek joins the Fork from the north just below Perrysville), and that the cattle and hogs roamed and fattened in the open woods. The hogs ran in great droves and fed on mast of the oak, hickory, and beech. "The inhabitants have enough to eat and drink," said Mr. Cheesebrough, "except cider." [3]

No cider yet in 1815, of course, for the first young ochards were not old enough to bear a goodly supply of apples, but John Chapman had been doing his bit to remove the lack. When John Coulter and Edward Haley had come in the fall of 1810 to make a clearing, they had found fruit trees to set out—probably his, for he had been visiting the Black Fork since the first cabins in 1809.[4]

One of John's few autographs is a due bill for trees given at some early date in the Perrysville community:

"Due John Oliver one hundred and fifty trees," it reads, *"when he goes for them to some of my Nurseryes on Mohecan waters."* [5]

John Oliver had come to the Black Fork as a boy with his parents in February, 1811 (when the family had spent the first night in a half-faced cabin without a roof, during a twelve-inch snowfall), had grown up in the neighborhood, and is first listed as a property owner in 1817. As planting an orchard was a normal early step in the development of a farm, the due bill probably dates from about that time.

"Some of my Nurseryes on Mohecan waters"—there must have been several, but where? The big one twenty miles downstream at the forks was probably still operating. Several Perrysville residents had brought stock from it as late as 1815 or 1816.[6]

Another grew for a time on John's quarter section just above Perrysville on the Black Fork. Since he had taken that lease in 1815, the nursery could have been growing there at any time up until the first interest payments came due and he was forced to give up the tract in 1820.[7]

In 1818, however, it appears that he had no trees ready for sale so close as this to Perrysville, for another scrap of old paper shows that he was sending Ebenezer Rice, who lived just above the village, twenty miles north to get a supply from Jerome's Fork of the Mohican in Orange Township near where the present village of Nankin, or Orange, stands.[8]

"Mr. Martin Mason Sir," he wrote, *"please to let Eben Rice or bearer have thirty eight apple trees and you will oblidge your friend*

John Chapman

Richland Co. Ohio
August the 21st 1818."

Martin Mason had come to Jerome's Fork in the northern part of the county in 1814. The next year he had started a mill there, and the spot was fast developing into another enterprising community center. Rice's order is the earliest clue to the existence of Chapman's nursery. Later informants have said that it was a large one along the creek on Mason's land. Many orchards in the northern part of Richland and Ashland counties were set out from it. Fruit growers in Orange, Montgomery, and Clear Creek townships found it their principal source of supply. It was still growing in 1821, for John Aton who came from Allegheny County, Pennsylvania, set out trees from it that year, as did also the Ekey family and Elias Slocum who lived a mile and a half east of present-day Ashland.[9]

Another fragment of paper signifies that John and Ebenezer Rice of Perrysville were still having business dealings in 1820:

"Mr. Odle please to let Ebenezer Rice have the hoops. John Chapman. August 25, 1820" [10]

The nature of the hoops and the identity of Mr. Odle are trivia that time has buried. John was in and out of the Rice home on the edge of Perrysville for many years.

These odds and ends indicate that in addition to his improvements going forward about this time on his Sandusky Township quarter, twenty-five miles west, and his enthusiastic labors for the Church of the New Jerusalem, John was still keeping up his string of nurseries and frequently got back to the village of Perrysville.

2

The return to large-scale wanderings was not sudden. For practical purposes, however, it can be centered in 1823, because that is the year when records make certain that Chapman's large land projects had pretty well played out, and when he purchased the earliest of the small tracts specifically intended for tree-growing that were to form part of a new, long, farther-strung system of nurseries.

The same business recession that had made William Schlatter in 1819 write off as dead losses most of his accounts with Western merchants had laid paralyzing hands also upon the settlers in the back country, especially those who were trying to hold land through loans and leases. If Chapman had possessed a backlog of capital to tide him over the period of scarce money and undeveloped commercial routes that hit central Ohio just after 1816, he might have made a small-sized fortune out of his land ventures. Without it, even if he had possessed unusual business wit and like most settlers had been blessed with a wife and children to assist him in the physical burden of developing the land, he could scarcely have survived the decade that followed.

PUBLIC SQUARE, MANSFIELD, 1830

Original drawing in Mansfield Historical Society Collection

An artist's interpretation (Harper's New Monthly Magazine, *November, 1871*) *that helped shape the national concept of Johnny*

APPLICATION FOR LAND, 1836
Records of General Land Office, National Archives

For a time after the first clearings and corn plantings of 1809 and 1810, the wants of the inrushing immigrants each year had created a demand and good prices for all the surplus corn, wheat, and pork, that the earlier farmers could produce, says H. S. Knapp, the early historian of Ashland County. But about 1816, surpluses began to pile up, outlets to outside communities did not yet exist, and prices tumbled.

It was true, as William Cheesebrough noted (probably from a current gazetteer) that Perrysville was at the head of navigation on the Black Fork, but the navigation was negligible, being confined to small, local boats. There was no general traffic to speak of and never would be. It was eight miles down the narrow fork to the Mohican, twenty-five more to the Walhonding, seventeen more to the Muskingum, and a hundred more to the Ohio. Though individual boats occasionally made the entire trip, they were exceptional. In the spring of 1823, Lewis Oliver and John Davis fitted up a flat-bottomed boat, loaded it with wheat, flour, lumber, pork, chickens, and whiskey, and safely navigated it, not merely to the mouth of the Muskingum, but even down the Ohio and the Mississippi to New Orleans. However, not finding a market there for their pork and wheat, says the Perrysville tradition, the men actually reshipped with their cargo to Richmond, Virginia, and then walked home from there. Until good roads and canals finally penetrated to this north-central area of Ohio, it was practically sealed off from outside markets and was forced to maintain for nearly two decades scarcely more than a local-barter economy.

The nation-wide bank muddle had added severely to the financial hardships on the border. By 1816, the hundreds of unchartered banks that had been permitted to mushroom everywhere had flooded the settlements with paper currency.

The federal act of 1816 ordering redemption in specie had closed great numbers of these banks and embarrassed others, leaving sheaves of devalued or worthless paper in people's pockets.

Up the forks it was the loose operations of the Owl Creek Bank in Mount Vernon that had caused the most trouble. Organized in 1816, the institution had been no more irresponsible than most, and eventually was to make some returns on its paper, but its suddenly deflated notes were held widely in the locality, where they caused much hardship and many bitter feelings. One disgruntled citizen, a story goes, killed a tremendous owl, took it in to Mount Vernon, and threw it down on the counter of the bank exclaiming, "There, damn you! I've killed your president!" To call someone an "*unchartered* son-of-a-bitch" was the depth of contempt. Though counterfeiting too was common and thoroughly condemned in public opinion, the practical difference between counterfeit and bank paper was often only a nice distinction. Good metal coin was very hard to come by.

"This made it especially hard upon the first settlers who had leased Virginia Military Schoollands," says Knapp, "as the interest on their purchases fell due about this time"—i.e., about 1819 and 1820. "Corn, which had in the previous years since the first settlements, found ready sale at seventy-five cents per bushel, could not be sold at any price; and wheat, which had formerly sold for $1.25 per bushel, and even higher, was now reduced to 37½ and even 25 cents per bushel." There were conspicuous reasons why Easterner Cheesebrough, even though his favorite cider was lacking, had found corn whiskey flowing in disturbing quantities. Dry goods and groceries were very costly. Five bushels of wheat were exchanged by Mr. Tannyhill for one bushel of salt, said Knapp.

John managed to pull a little out of these difficult years, but not much. As for his relations with the local banks, it was never his custom to intrust his precious cash to their keeping. Once, fearing that Indians would attempt rob him, a family story goes, he crawled into the hallow where the soil had caved in under a large tree and hid the money under the roots. It remained there safe for three years. Another time, he climbed up to the comb of the roof on his cabin and stuck his money under the clapboards, where it lay for over a year.[11] Such safety hide-outs were common with wilderness dwellers.

But meeting interest obligations was not so easy. The first of his school-land payments was due in 1819 on the quarter he had leased in 1814 with Mrs. Cunningham. Land office records show that they paid the full sum of $19.20, after a year's extension, in 1820. Thereafter, they paid no more interest and the lease was forfeited.

On the Green Township quarter above Perrysville, the first interest would have been due in 1820. Records show no payments ever made, and this lease too was forfeited. Records for both the quarters in Wayne County and in Sandusky Township of Richland are now lost, but the absence of any assignment entries in the county recorder's books suggests that these too lapsed in Chapman's name. Chapman's known proceeds in 1823 from his venture into school-land leases were sixteen acres (later increased to seventy) still held in the quarter section of Madison Township near Mansfield, and whatever funds he had realized from assignments. It is difficult to believe that he profited much from the investment as a whole. At the age of forty-nine, his chief assets still consisted of his nurseries, his freedom of action, and his seemingly limitless endurance.

His next few recorded business dealings are all concerned with acquiring small patches of ground, presumably for nursery purposes.

On June 25, 1823, he purchased of Alexander Finley for forty dollars about three acres along Jerome's Fork of the Mohican, ten miles northeast of Perrysville. Tradition says that John and his trees had been on the stream along with Finley ever since 1809.[12] He held this little tract the rest of his life, though how long he used it is not known. Finley in later years maintained the taxes for him. When Chapman died, it was not sold, inasmuch as his administrators did not know of its existence. After standing for years, it was preempted as abandoned land.[13] The Mohicanville conservancy reservoir now sends its waters in wet seasons up to the site, which lies just south of the village of Lake Fork. As usual, many early orchards in the neighborhood are attributed to John's nursery there. Two gnarled trees said to have come from it as early as 1817 were still standing recently northeast of Jeromeville.[14]

Two years after buying the Finley lot, when Chapman carried the deed to Wooster for record, he took along another that he had acquired the winter before. A few miles above Finley's place Jerome's Fork was joined by the Muddy Fork that swung from the north around in a giant bend through the edge of present-day Wayne County. Not far from the bend, on December 21, 1825, Chapman purchased fourteen acres from Isaac and Minerva Hatch, paying sixty dollars. Presumably this plot too had been or was to be used for a nursery. John was much in Wayne County sooner or later and left a scattering of local traditions, especially along the west edge of Clinton, Plain, Chester, and Congress townships, also farther east around Wooster, and in the Sugar Creek district of East Union Township. Judge Stanbery used to see Chapman in this county. There were New Church families there, seven of Mr. Ensign's flock of forty in 1822 residing near Wooster. John was doubtless a familiar figure throughout the area, though only the real estate records and unspecific traditions now bear out the rumors that his activities extended not only throughout Wayne but on eastward into the Western Reserve.[15]

This Hatch lot Chapman owned until September, 1832, when he sold it to John H. Pile for a loss of ten dollars.

Back at Perrysville on the twenty-second of April, 1826, Chapman signed a lease agreement with John Oliver for a half acre along the Black Fork—and this time the wording of the record leaves no question of the use—*"where the said John Chapman plants fruit."* Oliver was established on Section 27 just east of Perrysville on the Loudonville road. John's half acre was in the southeast quarter of the section.

How long Chapman had been rearing appletrees on the Oliver lot is not recorded. Trees from it had been available soon after 1819, for Isaac Wolf who came from Pennsylvania that year started an orchard from it.[16]

The lease was drawn to run for forty years. *"And,"* says the agreement on file in the Richland County recorder's office, *"the said John Chapman . . . obligates himself . . . that he will pay or cause to be paid to the said John Oliver . . . twenty apple trees as agreed in the consideration."*

The lease was drawn by Able Strong, local justice of the peace, and witnessed by Amsy Marvin and Richard Oliver (his mark). It was not filed with the county recorder till 1829 —but the fact that John bothered to record it then suggests that he still had trees growing there.

From the various nurseries near Perrysville came many orchards in southern Ashland and Richland counties.

Even now, after all these years, and though this region of country is densely populated [Rosella Rice of Perrysville, daughter of Ebenezer, wrote in the eighteen-fifties], I can count from my window no less than five orchards, or remains of orchards, that were once trees taken from his nurseries. . . . One of his nurseries is near us, and I often go to the secluded spot, on the quiet banks of the creek, never broken since the poor old man did it, and say, in a reverent whisper, "Oh, the angels did commune with the good old man, whose loving heart prompted him to go about doing good!" [17]

Sentimental Rosella was probably alluding to the nursery that stood at some time on the school-land quarter up the Black Fork. She was, of course, confusing the "old man" of her late personal recollections with the middle-aged planter of the nurseries. This confusion becomes the common thing in most reminiscences from these years. The truth is that there is no evidence available today to suggest that people as early as the 1820's had yet begun to breathe John Chapman's name in reverent whispers.

The two available personal descriptions of John during this period suggest, in fact, that he definitely was not drawing veneration:

"I was acquainted with Jonathan Chapman, alias Johnny Appleseed, in Richland County, Ohio, in 1822," said David Ayres in 1881, *"when I was yet in my teens. I lost track of him in 1837 or 1838.*

"He was a spare, light man of medium height, and would

weigh about 125 pounds. He had fine, dark hair, which he allowed to grow down to his shoulders and brushed back of his ears. His beard was grayish and clipped with shears, never close. He was always clad very poorly, old slipshod shoes without stockings, the cast-off clothes of some charitable miser. He would not ask for any, and I suppose he never purchased any. He would eat at the table with any family and liked good victuals, but he would also eat scraps which were designed for the slop barrel.

"He slept on the floor on an old blanket. His old slipshod shoes were untidy looking and he seemed to care very little about his person. I never heard of his being sick." [18]

These realistic recollections are borne out by those of S. C. Coffinbury who had known Chapman in Mansfield and vicinity "from my earliest recollections about 1812 until I attained the age of manhood." Coffinbury had read the glowing and overdone account of Johnny Appleseed in *Harper's* for November, 1871, and sat down to write a letter to the Mansfield *Shield and Banner* correcting some of the exaggeration. As to personal description, he wrote:

"John Chapman was a small man, wiry and thin in habit. His cheeks were hollow; his face and neck dark and skinny from exposure to the weather. His mouth was small; his nose small and turned up quite so much as apparently to raise his upper lip. His eye was dark and deeply set in his head, but searching and penetrating. His hair was black and straight which he parted in the middle, and permitted to fall about his neck. His hair, withal, was rather thin, fine and glossy. He never wore a full beard, but shaved all clean except a thin roach at the bottom of his throat. His beard was lightly set, sparse, and very black.

"In 1840, when the writer last saw him in Mansfield this was his appearance, and at the time he had changed but little, if any, in his general appearance, since he first remembered seeing him when the writer was a small boy. The dress of this strange man was unique. The writer here assumes to say that he never wore a coffee sack as a part of his apparel. He may have worn the off cast clothing of others; he probably did so. Although often in rags and tatters, and at best in the most plain and simple wardrobe he was always clean, and in his most desolate rags comfortable, and never repulsive. He generally, when the weather would permit, wore no clothing on his feet, consequently his feet were dark, hard, and horny. He was frequently seen with shirts, pants, and a kind of a long tailed coat of tow-linen then much worn by the farmers. This coat was a device of his own ingenuity and in itself was a curiosity. It consisted of one width of the coarse fabric, which descended from his neck to his heels. It was without collar. In this robe were cut two arm holes into which were placed two straight sleeves. The mother of the writer made it up for him under his immediate direction and supervision." [19]

John's mode of hairdress, it should be noted, though it seems strange enough in the twentieth century, had been a normal one among woodsmen when he had first come into the West twenty-five or thirty years before. The style would follow the American frontier across the West, and a half century after John Chapman's day would have one last flare of popular attention in the publicity attending the picturesque personality of Buffalo Bill. As for John Chapman's shirts, they were merely adaptations of the hunter's pull-over that had been worn by the scouts and trailsmen of John's youthful years. There were, of course, some variations all his own.

9

THE FOLK TALES GROW

ECCENTRICITIES breed folk talk. John had never been reluctant about leaving behind him a good supply of vivid details concerning his own strange doings. Now in his middle years, in the Ohio neighborhoods where he had become as familiar to the countryside as foxgrape and cockleburs his personal oddities and adventures had begun to produce a very heavy crop of popular yarns. Sometimes these were humorous, sometimes reverent, sometimes disgusting, often conflicting and confusing. A hundred years later, admirers of the Johnny Appleseed legend, who do not like to have its fragile idealism jarred, have often shied away from this first wild growth of tales and when forced to face one of them have sometimes called them apochryphal. Doubtless occasional stories were fictitious, but they come from John Chapman's own time and are nearer to the reality than some of the tinseling that has been strung onto the later well-pruned legend.

I

Along the Black Fork, people did a lot of conjecturing about an early love affair. A man of John Chapman's capabilities did not stay single and turn into a lonely wanderer of his own free will.

A girl back in Massachusetts—or in Connecticut—or some-where—had turned him down, or had been forced to marry some one else, or had died, or something. Unrequited love was the popular formula for explaining all lone bachelors and maidens, especially if they were a bit eccentric—much as Freudian frustrations serve with equal glibness a century later.

"We had always heard that Johnny had loved once upon a time, and that his lady love had proven false to him," said Rosella Rice, who gathered up much of the talk about John that had floated for a couple of generations in her neighborhood.

One day in the Rice home, she said, when Johnny was hold-ing a baby on his lap chirruping gaily to him and apparently deeply contented, Mrs. Rice could not resist the urge to ask him if he would not have been much happier if he had settled in a home of his own and reared a family to love him. He opened his eyes wide—they were "remarkably keen, penetrat-ing grey eyes, almost black"—and replied that not all women are what they profess to be. Some of them were deceivers, and a man might not marry the amiable woman after all, that he thought he was getting.[1]

This reputed cynicism was all twisted up with another tale that went the rounds of many settlements in numerous varia-tions. John could not help being attracted to charming little girls. He was very fond of his sister's handsome daughters. Everywhere he went he was drawn to youngsters. He liked to dandle them on his knee, and he occasionally brought them gifts of beads and gay ribbons. There is not a single stroke of evidence that he ever did or said anything unseemly, but his special attentions and remarks here and there, like nearly everything else he did, were shaped into anecdotes that ranged all the way from the casual to the caustic.

"In 1833," said E. Bonar McLaughlin of Mansfield, "he took quite an interest in a little girl of ten or eleven years, the daughter of a friend of mine where I then lived, and he often called there. He wanted the parents to allow him to have her educated, but the parents thought our schools here quite good enough as they seemed to believe that a girl did not require much book learning." [2]

Various people remembered a story that during the war of 1812 he had rescued a beautiful little girl from the Indians near Mount Vernon and had carried her a long way to restore her to friends. Afterward when asked his views on marriage, he had said that if he ever married he would like to take a girl eight or ten—a pure, beautiful virgin such as the one he had rescued—and train her under his care until a fitting age. Then he would be sure as to her purity; he would never marry any other.[3]

As the Rices told it, Chapman had once taken a poor, friendless little girl who had no one to care for her, sent her to school, clothed her, and watched over her. But when she was fifteen, he had called to see her once unexpectedly and found her sitting beside a young man, with her hand in his listening to his silly twaddle. "I peeped over at Johnny while he was telling this," Rosella Rice wrote, "and young as I was, I saw his eyes grow dark as violets, and the pupils enlarge, and his voice rise up in denunciation, while his nostrils dilated and his thin lips worked with emotion. How angry he grew! He thought the girl was basely ungrateful. After that time she was no protégée of his." [4]

In his lonely bachelorhood, his hope of compensations in a Swedenborgian heaven was a great consolation to him, people said.

David Ayres had a little six-year-old sister whom John used to hold on his lap and entertain for long periods of time. "I asked him why he had no wife," Ayres said. "He said he would not marry in this world, but would have a pure wife in heaven." [5]

A favorite popular version of this story had it that he was in frequent conversation with the inhabitants of the spirit land, two of whom, of the feminine gender, had revealed to him the good news that they were to be his wives in a future state, provided he kept himself from a matrimonial alliance while on earth. He thereafter vowed celibacy and never could be prevailed upon to indulge in amorous attentions.

The Vandorn boys of Washington Township ribbed Johnny once about this expectation of two wives in the hereafter. "What good will they do you? You don't expect to sleep with them, do you?" they asked.

"O yes!" Chapman said. "My two wives will sleep in a bed, and I intend to have a wide board planed smooth and nice attached to the side of the bed for me to sleep on!" [6]

Of course, the choicer Rabelaisian allusions to John's sex life never got written down.

On the literary level a half century after his death, John Chapman emerged out of these humble tales as the great romantically tragic lover of the Middle Western frontier, and as such he has been portrayed in some very delightful novels, plays, and poetry.

On the folk-talk level likewise, the tradition of his interest in actual marriage has continued very strong in several of the

Johnny Appleseed counties. A modern investigator can gather
in northern Ohio communities a collection of family stories
that begin: "Johnny Appleseed once proposed to my grandmother." Or, "While he was here, Johnny actually married
Miss ———." Or, "Mrs. ——— who lives over on the corner is
the granddaughter of John Chapman, you know." [7]

There was probably a grain of truth somewhere behind all
the talk. The best clue seems to be that which came in a communication to Henry Howe, the historian, from a correspondent in Perrysville:

"Johnny Appleseed was a frequent visitor here. He was a
constant snuff consumer and had beautiful teeth. He was
smitten here with Miss Nancy Tannehill and proposed, but
was just one too late: she was already engaged." [8]

2

Chapman could bear pain and any other sort of hardship
like an Indian, it was said. Sometimes he showed off a trifle
by thrusting pins or needles into his flesh without a flinch or
tremor. Possibly he used the horny layers of his callous feet
for the demonstrations! If he had a bad cut or a sore, he immediately seared the spot with a red hot iron, then treated it
as a burn. The Indians were said to respect him as a holy man
who could work powerful medicine. [9]

His bare feet caused endless comment. Abner Davis of
Washington Township remembered Johnny's calling at his
cabin one very cold winter morning when there were several
inches of snow. Davis invited him in to warm himself. John
refused a place by the fire but took a seat in the back of the
room and threw his feet up against the logs of the wall as if

enjoying the greatest comfort. "The skin of his feet in time came to look much like an elephant's hide," said Davis.[10]

Shortly after the War of 1812, he stopped at the Amariah Watson house in Washington Township, walked in without knocking, and accosted Mrs. Watson who, not recognizing him and being nervous from the recent Indian scares, was quite frightened.

"Madam," the barefooted caller said, straightening up and assuming considerable dignity, "God bless you—fear no evil— I am Johnny Appleseed!"

Mr. Watson came in presently and asked why he went barefooted.

"Sir," he said holding out a foot, "this one had been guilty of offense in treading unmercifully upon one of God's dear creatures"—a snake—"and as a corresponding punishment I am now exposing it to the inclemency of the weather." [11]

Late in the fall of 1829 or 1830, William McDaniel of Monroe Township met John walking through the snow with an old shoe on one foot, the other bare.

"Johnny, what's the matter with your foot that you have it bare?" he inquired.

"It offended me," said John. "It tread on a worm and crushed it, and I am going to punish it." [12]

Once with another man he had started across Lake Erie barefooted on the ice, it was said. Night caught them. The temperature suddenly began to drop very low, and in the bitter cold, John's companion was frozen to death.

John, however, kept warm by rolling about vigorously on the ice and eventually crossed without feeling any the worse for the ordeal.[13]

One recalls the rides and races on ice and snow that had graced the early Allegheny episodes in John's saga, and the ice thawed by his bare feet, that had even reached print in Manchester, England, in 1817. As in the earlier day, many tales of his ability to bear hardship were probably the progeny of his own narrations.

3

People never forgot his unconventional clothes. Next to his shoes, or lack of them, his headgear was the most famous item. He never seemed to care what he wore for a hat, said Norton, the historian of Mount Vernon. Sometimes it was an animal's skin, sometimes it was something of cloth, or even a tin case—he had been seen with hats of each kind.

For a time just after the war he wore an old military chapeau which some officer had given him. Thus accoutered one day, he came suddenly upon a Dutchman who had just moved into the country. The apparition of a barefooted stranger, with black eyes peering out of a vast undergrowth of black hair and beard, his body enveloped in a coffee sack with a hole through which he had run his head, "one tam mussel shell cocked on his head," well-nigh frightened the honest Dutchman out of his wits.[14]

"His head-covering was often a pasteboard hat of his making," said Rosella Rice. "with one broad side to it, that he wore next the sunshine too protect his face. It was a very unsightly object." [15]

"His first experiment was with a tin vessel that served to cook his mush," wrote W. D. Haley in 1871, "but this was open to the objection that it did not protect his eyes from the beams of the sun."

Just who first told the story of the mushpot hat is not now clear. Not a single authentic instance of its having been actually seen has been preserved. Yet it has stuck most firmly of all the headgears in the Johnny Appleseed tradition and is now inextricably attached to the myth.[16]

4

Nothing was harder for people to understand, or made more laughable anecdotes, than his curious notions about, and his adventures with, the wild creatures of field and wood.

The oft-told rattlesnake tale had probably originated at his brother-in-law's near Perrysville. John had actually been bitten by a rattler, it was said, while mowing grass with a scythe. Dr. Ayres was called to look at him, but John was more concerned about the snake than about himself. They must go look to see if, accidentally, his scythe had injured it. The creature would not, of course, have hurt him except in self-defense.

But it turned out he had killed the snake. Afterward when he told of the incident, tears would well up in his eyes and he would say, "Poor fellow, he only just touched me, when I in the heat of my ungodly passion put the heel of my scythe upon him, and went away. Some time afterward I went back and there lay the poor fellow dead!" [17]

Once when he was out along the trail, another tale declared, a rattler fastened his fangs in Johnny's right hand. An Indian with him struck it a deadly blow. But Johnny reproved him sharply.

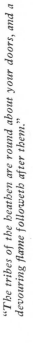

"Here's your primitive Christian."

(Harper's New Monthly Magazine, *November, 1871*)

"The tribes of the heathen are round about your doors, and a devouring flame followeth after them."

DRAWINGS THAT SHAPED A LEGEND

THE STANDARD JOHNNY APPLESEED

Printed in A. A. Graham's History of Richland County, Ohio, *1880, and derived from an earlier engraving in Knapp's* History . . . *of Ashland County, 1863, said to have been drawn in the 1850's (see Frontispiece). The major alteration is in the headgear.*

"News right fresh from Heaven." (Harper's New Monthly Magazine, *November, 1871*)

"The snake didn't go to hurt me," he said, "he didn't know any better." [18]

In most of these stories, people never seemed to wonder at all that John always survived. They thought of his calloused and weather-toughened skin and wondered at the temerity of the wild creatures!

"An attempt to bite through such a hide as his," Charles Parker of Huron County used to say, "would kill a rattle-snake." [19]

Josiah Thomas of Mansfield asked John once if he were not afraid that venomous snakes would bite his bare feet. Rattlers and copperheads abounded in the region.

"No," he said smiling and drawing a scriptural volume from his bosom. "This book is an infallible protection against all danger here and hereafter." [20]

In Green Township he used to take his turn working on the public roads. One day near Jones's prairie, someone stirred up a nest of yellow jackets and one found its way into John's pants. Though it stung him again and again, John very gently and quietly forced it downward by pressing the pants above it until it escaped. Why didn't he kill it?

It would not be right to take the life of the poor thing, he said, as it was only obeying the instinct of its nature, and did not intend to hurt him.[21]

Once in his camp near Owl Creek, the mosquitoes came in great numbers, flew into his fire and were consumed. Taking off the tin headgear he wore at the time, he filled it with water and carefully put out the fire.

"God forbid," he said, "that I should build a fire for my

own comfort that should be the cause of destroying any of
His other created works." [22]

He would never touch tea, coffee, or tobacco, because when
he got to the next world, he said, he could not have them and
so would not cultivate a taste for them here. But milk and
honey were different. "We read that this is heavenly food,"
he pointed out. He drank milk whenever he could get it.

Wild honey almost literally flowed at times in the Ohio
woods, and the settlers helped themselves freely. But if Chapman found a bee tree, he always looked carefully to see
whether the insects had sufficient store for the winter before
he touched the comb. [23]

He was a one-man humane society. Old and broken-down
horses were usually turned loose in the woods to subsist for
themselves and die when they were no longer able to do so.
In the autumn, it was said, Johnny made a diligent search for
such animals, gathered them up, made bargains with settlers
for their keep till spring when he would return and take them
to good pasture. If they were restored to working value, he
would never sell them but would lend them or give them
away. [24]

During his early days around Mansfield, he had once accumulated ten ponies. Then the Indians descended upon him,
he said, and carried off both the ponies and himself. They released him in due time but kept the animals. The affair was a
trifle mystifying to him, because undoubtedly it was the will
of God. The trouble, he decided, was probably that he had
misunderstood the language of God. His release he could read
all right, but how about the ponies? He finally concluded that

the Indians needed them more than he—hence the distribution.[25]

One time, finding a wolf caught in a trap and badly hurt, he released it, doctored it, and nursed it. It became a pet and followed him about like a dog until some one shot it.[26]

Some people said he never killed wild animals for food. All that was necessary to sustain the human body, he said, could be produced from the soil.[27]

However, he once told young David Ayres of feasting on bear meat. He had been lost in the wilderness. The bear he happened to meet had advanced and reared to attack him. John grabbed a long dry pole that was within reach and began pounding the beast, but the pole was so brittle that it broke at every stroke until it was only three or four feet long. Nevertheless by the help of the Lord he slew the bear, had a good supper, and carried both a quarter and the hide into the settlement.[28]

An old hunter used to tell that he had chanced upon Johnny in the deep wood playing with three cubs while the mother bear calmly looked on.[29]

Perhaps she was the same creature that he had befriended in the most famous of all the Johnny Appleseed bear stories.

John had built his campfire at the end of a hollow log intending to crawl into it for the night. He discovered, however, that a bear and her cubs were already in possession of the lodgings.

"Poor innocent things," John is said to have remarked, "I am glad I did not turn you out of your house."

Then he carefully removed his fire and slept on the snow in the open air.

His common sense in leaving Mistress Bear and her children undisturbed is to be commended.[30]

Housewives never knew exactly what to expect of him. In the cabin of Solomon Gladden where he often stayed in Monroe Township, he would never accept a bed though repeatedly urged to do so. He said floors were good enough for him.

On one occasion, he found Mrs. Gladden picking beebread out of the honey. Did she have any buttermilk too? She did and gave him a cupful to drink. Then to her amazement, he asked for some of the bitter beebread to eat with the buttermilk.

"Oh, no!" she demurred. "Not that—I will get you some wheat bread."

"No, thank you," said Johnny. "I would rather have this." Whereupon he ate a hearty meal, Mrs. Gladden declared, of beebread and buttermilk.[31]

Some folks said that he preferred always to take his lunch by himself outdoors, seldom eating inside a house.

Some said he would customarily make his entire meal of one article. Whatever he began with he ended with.

Some said he would never eat meat—that he was a complete vegetarian; others, that he would eat any meat except veal. This was a land flowing with milk and honey, he said, and calves should always be spared.

He liked fruit and vegetables of all kinds—especially potatoes. It was reported that he took snuff, and that he was known to drink a dram of spirits now and then to warm himself up a bit.

Wild fruits and nuts in season often sustained him.[32]

Other people said that he never evinced any abnormalities either in choice of food or mode of eating it.

Willard Hickox of Mansfield, who spent his boyhood in Green and Hanover townships, remembered Johnny's rebuking Mrs. Elias Slocum for waste. Some pieces of bread were floating on the surface of the slop bucket outside the door. John gathered them up in his hand, called Mrs. Slocum's attention to them, and pointed out that the gifts of a merciful God should never be thriftlessly misused.[33]

One morning after he had spent the night on the Slocum's cabin floor, Mr. Slocum found a five-dollar note near where he had slept. He immediately sought out Chapman in town to return it. John examined his pockets carefully, decided the money was really his own, but remonstrated because Slocum had taken the trouble to look him up.[34]

David Ayres remembered that he had never heard John complain bitterly against anyone except landlords, and that was because they would charge twelve and a half cents for a meal of victuals. This was extortion, he thought. In those days, supper and lodging could be obtained for eighteen and a half cents.[35]

Through much of the year, however, at least in his vigorous younger period, John did not bother many housewives or landlords with requests for lodging. Who would want a cabin floor if he could have, for instance, the luxury of a tree-swung hammock. He had learned the knack from the Indians, he said. Near a nursery where he was working he would suspend his hammock from the pliable tops of two trees in such a way that he got a buoyant, springy bed in mid-air. There as happy as a king he would sleep or read and sing when resting from his labors.[36]

Folks who occasionally caught sight of him at such moments sometimes concluded that he was lazy. Young S. C. Coffinbury discovered him once at his nursery near the Big Bend of the Rocky Fork just out of Mansfield. John was lying on his side under a spreading thorntree in the center of his patch. Without so much as arising, he was reaching out with his hoe and extirpating any weeds that happened to be within reach. Coffinbury carried away the impression that he was physically indolent and fond of ease.[37]

6

His benevolences and the stories about them endeared him to the whole countryside.

One old resident of Mansfield declared he had known John to give away as much as fifty dollars at a time to some family in distress.[38]

One November when the weather was unusually rigorous, Elias Slocum found him in Ashland wearing a very dilapidated pair of old shoes. Slocum promptly saw that he was supplied with one of his own pairs, but a few days later was annoyed to find him in Mansfield tramping the snowy streets barefooted. Johnny had given the shoes to a needy family moving West.[39]

Once in Mansfield he bought six breakfast plates at E. P. Sturgis's store. When acquaintances asked him why he needed so many, he told them waggishly that it was to save dishwashing—he would not need to wash them for a week.

The truth was, he carried the chinaware to a poor settler and his family near Spring Mill, who had lost most of their table furnishings in an accident a few days before. He would take nothing in return for his gift.[40]

He often gave his trees to moneyless families. In fact, tradition says the men whom he left in charge of his nurseries in various neighborhoods were given standing orders to give away his trees when those who really needed them were without the customary fippenny bits.

The Hunter children in Green Township were left in a bad way indeed when their father died in 1819 and the mother two years later. There were nine children, the youngest only fourteen months, but David, the oldest, who was but sixteen or seventeen at the time, stepped bravely to the head of the family and did his man-sized job nobly.

One day, coming back from paying his taxes in Mansfield, he met Chapman. They sat down on a log. Hunter shared some cakes and they talked. John wanted to know how the Hunter children were getting along in managing their home.

David should waste no time, John told him, in getting some appletrees started. Young Hunter said he was too poor to buy them. Never mind, the older man said, he would supply fifty or sixty trees if David would call for them of John's brother-in-law, Broom. As for pay, it would be of no moment if they were never paid for. The first consideration was to plant the trees as soon as possible.

From this kindly start, Hunter was able in time to develop a fine orchard of over six hundred trees.[41]

7

As John's religious views often struck the uninformed as fantastic, most of the folks who knew him enjoyed a few jokes about them sooner or later.

He believed this world to be a type of the next, they said. The future world would have the same physical geography, the same phenomena of cold and heat, rains and snows, the same occupations of life, and the same emotions of love and hate, joy and sadness, and so on.

One favorite story turned the trick of the argument against John. A wag was interrogating him on the point of employments in the spiritual world:

"So you think man will follow the same occupations in Heaven?"

"I really do."

"Do people die in Heaven?"

"I think not."

"Then my occupation is gone," said the wag sadly, "for I am a grave-digger." [42]

Usually, he was equal to the banter. Some Mansfield lawyers were rallying him on the same point:

"Mr. Chapman, what business will lawyers follow in Heaven?"

"The woe pronounced against them prevents their getting to that place." ·

"Then where will they go?"

"To Hell."

"And what will engage their attention there?"

"Just what engages their attention here"—great suavity—

"they will be placed in filth up to their knees, and will be striving forever to pitch it into each other's faces."

The lawyers proceeded to question the next witness.[43]

The first Baptists around Perrysville sometimes held services in the White cabin near old Greentown. John was present one day and after the Reverend Otis had finished preaching, asked permission to make a few remarks:

"Are you a preacher?" Otis asked.

"I am a messenger sent before you into the wilderness."

"To what denomination do you belong?"

"I am a believer in the doctrines of Emanuel Swedenborg."

"Ah, indeed! But sir, I stand opposed to those doctrines."

"That's nothing strange, Mr. Otis," was Chapman's firm reply, "when we consider that your father, the devil, is opposed to them too. Children generally follow the teachings of their parents." [44]

Of all Johnny Appleseed's actual or mythical sectarian brushes, the "primitive Christian" incident has become by all odds the most famous. It has been carried on into the legend itself and is always told whenever the nature of John Chapman's mission is being discussed. It has been related so many times, in fact, that it has numerous variations, is set in many different parts of Ohio and Indiana, and several different frontier revivalists are named as the victim of the incident, including the great Peter Cartwright.

It was a Mansfield episode originally, however, and two separate testimonies identify the itinerant preacher who was responsible for it as Adam Payne, an illiterate fanatic, who went about the settlements, with long hair and long beard flying, calling himself "the Pilgrim" and exhorting the citizens to repent of their many sins and be saved.

Samuel Coffinbury remembered that Payne reached Mansfield the year the old courthouse was erected (1829 or 1830), blew a tin horn to announce his presence and preached to an audience sitting on the stones and timbers lying around the public square.[45] John W. Dawson of Fort Wayne recalled Payne's appearing in that town a short time afterward in 1830, where he mounted a box on the northeast corner of Clinton and Columbia streets with the announcement, "Hear ye! Hear ye!" At the conclusion of his rant, John Chapman came forward out of the crowd and asked Payne if he remembered the "primitive Christian" of the incident in Mansfield a short time previous. Payne did.[46]

This is what happened. Though early versions vary, Payne during his talk in Mansfield suddenly spied John lying on the ground resting his feet on one of the stones, and nettled him by saying, "See yon ragged old barefooted sinner and be warned of the paths of sin by his example." Or Payne may merely have raised the rhetorical question, "Where is the bare-footed Christian, traveling to heaven?" John immediately rose and remonstrated, or—as some said—he kicked his bare feet high in the air bawling at the top of his voice, "Here he is!" [47]

The standard telling version of the tale is W. D. Haley's in *Harper's*. The exhorter had punctuated his harangue, Haley said, with the reiterated question, "Where now is there a man who, like the primitive Christians, is traveling to heaven barefooted and clad in coarse raiment?"

When the interrogation had been repeated beyond all reasonable endurance, John Chapman rose from a log on which he was reclining and advancing to the speaker, placed one of his bare feet on the stump that served for a pulpit, pointed to his coffee-sack garment, and said quietly, "Here's your primitive Christian." [48]

In late years the story has come to symbolize the religious significance of Johnny Appleseed's mission on the frontier. He was a John the Baptist of the Western border, living on walnuts and wild honey, clad in cast-off raiment, and preparing a way in the American wilderness for God's people.

As for the fanatical Adam Payne, it is said that he went to Illinois where, during the Black Hawk War a year or two afterward, the Indians murdered him, severed his head, and paraded it on a pole as a trophy.

PART  FOUR

Hitherto he had easily kept just in advance of the wave of settlement; but now towns and churches were making their appearance, and even, at long intervals, the stage-driver's horn broke the silence of the grand old forests, and he felt that his work was done in the region in which he had labored so long. He visited every house, and took a solemn farewell of all the families. The little girls who had been delighted with his gifts of fragments of calico and ribbons had become sober matrons, and the boys who had wondered at his ability to bear the pain caused by running needles into his flesh were heads of families. With parting words of admonition he left them, and turned his steps steadily toward the setting sun.

Harper's New Monthly Magazine, November, 1871

Farther West

Praying, and reading the books of Swedenborg,
On the mountain top called "Going-To-The-Sun."

VACHEL LINDSAY
"The Apple-Barrel of Johnny Appleseed"

10

ALONG THE LAND BRIDGE

EVEN as the valleys from central Ohio to Lake Erie were beginning to teem with John Chapman's stories, he was moving into new terrain. He had already found a bigger and broader stage on which to play the next act of his drama. It would be the last act, too, and the one that would leave to posterity the common concept of him.

Just below where the chain of the Great Lakes swings farthest down to rest Lake Erie on the northern edge of Ohio, the glaciers that scooped out the hollows for these inland seas left a long low ridge, or a combination of them, extending across northern Ohio into the corner of Indiana. The ridge is one of those dramatic lines that ancient nature was always drawing, like chalk marks on a stage floor, to guide the course of ages. This broad swell, rising so easily that motorists on gently graded highways are often unaware of it, forms the land divide of Ohio and northeastern Indiana. Since it was really the old shore line of Erie when the glaciers first relaxed, it sweeps across northern Ohio in the same general curve of the lake shore until it reaches a climactic tip at the end of the old lake bed, where the city of Fort Wayne now stands.

In north-central Ohio it runs along through the upper edge of the Appleseed country, marking the line where the Indian border stayed till 1812. Down off this divide run the headwaters of the short Vermilion and Huron rivers flowing north to Erie, and the long upper forks of the Mohican south to the Muskingum and the Ohio. A little farther west, in what was Indian territory till 1817, it curves along between the broad plains of the Sandusky River on the north and the Scioto-Olentangy system flowing south. Still farther it pushes toward Indiana through the part of Ohio that remained the longest untamed and unsettled, much of it till the 1830's, between the long streams that gather northerly on the one hand into the Maumee River and flow into Lake Erie, and on the other into the Wabash to end in the Mississippi. In places around Fort Wayne, these extended headwaters of the Atlantic and Gulf drainages are only four feet apart. Ancient Lake Erie once spilled south, in fact, into the Wabash and the Mississippi, before its Niagara gate to the St. Lawrence was finally opened. Even in days of the first white settlers, a canoe in high water could cross from the Maumee to the Wabash at the Fort Wayne portage. It was one of the most famous land links in the Old Northwest.

Along the general line of this land divide, across Ohio toward the focal point at the Fort Wayne summit. John Chapman had begun moving in the middle 1820's. For the last twenty years of his life he was to swing back and forth along it with the regularity of a shuttle, weaving for the closing chapters of his story a prodigious pattern among the swamps and rivers.

The thousand square miles touched by this last pattern now spreads through richly favored farm country where the finest of corn and wheat mingle with special patches of celery, potatoes, onions, sugar beets, or peonies to indicate the particular richness of the soil. But in 1825, the land-bridge of the divide led from the relatively well-settled and tillable northeastern counties of Ohio west past the vast swamps and cranberry bogs, impenetrable plum thickets, open marshes, or deep woods that marked the broad sweeps of the Sandusky plains on into the almost impassable mazes of the Black Swamp area to the northwest.

The road west out of Mansfield went directly into this swampland. Twelve miles out, it crossed the old north-and-south Indian treaty line of 1805 that set off with ironical sharpness the retreating redman's rightful domain from the rolling, naturally drained, and therefore settleable lands that the white men had first wanted in the upper branches of the Muskingum. West of this line the water table still stood high and would have to wait for the cutting off of woods and the running of long ditches before its miasmal stretches would be habitable. John Chapman's school-land lease in Sandusky Township had been just in the edge of these wet lands.

By the Treaty of Maumee Rapids in 1817, however, the demarcation of 1805 had been erased and the Wyandots, Ottawas, Delawares, Shawnees, and Senecas had been induced to cede all the northwest quarter of Ohio to the United States Government in return for various promises and ten reservations, large and small, scattered over the area.

By 1826, accordingly, the main trail west from Mansfield ran directly to the new town of Bucyrus on the Sandusky River twelve miles inside this "New Purchase" and from there pushed on into the deep-loamed, mostly unsettled prairies that were alternately desolate and luxuriant, to the big Wyandot reservation that centered in the town of Upper Sandusky. From here there were river and land connections with both Erie to the north and Urbana and other old settlements of the Virginia military lands sixty-five miles to the southwest.

But straight on into the raw northwestern part, there were only primitive trails winding around great swamps or magnificent woodland on the broad back of the divide to the headwaters of various streams that made thin waterways down through the Black Swamp to the Maumee. It was the most desolate of all Ohio's primitive regions.

About fifteen miles west of Upper Sandusky, a trailsman working from the east could reach the upper course of Blanchard's Fork. Today the area is marked by the village of Mount Blanchard in a progressive rural neighborhood sixty miles south of Toledo and Lake Erie, but considering its desolate isolation the place where the paths reached the Blanchard in 1826 might just as well have been six hundred miles from civilization. From there, however, either by land path in dry seasons or by boat at any time, the traveler could follow the Blanchard seventy-five miles down through the long swampy flats first to Fort Findlay, then on past the Ottawa Indian reservation to the Auglaize River, and thence down to the town of Defiance on the Maumee, the business and political center of the whole region. As late as 1830, parties with horses commonly preferred to send them through the Black Swamp by guide while they took the safer canoe course down the Blanchard and the Auglaize.

Historically, the region was richly and venerably famous. Empires had moved back and forth up the Maumee from Lake Erie to the junction of the St. Marys and the St. Joseph where Fort Wayne stands. Harmar's, St. Clair's, and Anthony Wayne's expeditions against the Indians had reached their climaxes along these rivers. The battle of Fallen Timbers had been won here. Hull's and Harrison's armies had plodded back and forth through this mud in 1812 and 1813. Remains of old forts were scattered all along the rivers.

But economic strategy waits for geography longer than military does; settlement came very slowly, partly because of the wet, malarial conditions that prevailed, and partly because of the difficult access. The frontier was to last twenty years longer here than anywhere else in Ohio.

It was inevitable that John Chapman should move into this country just as the flow of final settlement was starting its rush. Anyone who had seen him working west towards the Allegheny in 1797, through eastern Ohio in 1801, at the forks of the Walhonding in 1804, and at Mansfield in 1813, would have known that John had judged with uncanny accuracy the strategic moment to arrive just ahead of another big land push. His career in the West had begun on the Allegheny at twenty-three; now at fifty-four, his nurseries had begun to grow on the Blanchard, the Maumee, the Auglaize, and the St. Marys rivers of northwestern Ohio, and when the first spadeful of earth was turned for the Wabash-Erie Canal in 1832 he had extended his enterprises to Fort Wayne and northeastern Indiana.

As usual no one remembered just when he appeared.

"When I first saw him," said Brockman Brower, early comer to Putnam County in the heart of the Black Swamp, "he was floating down the Blanchard River in a canoe loaded with appletrees, distributing them among the early settlers along the Blanchard, Auglaize, and Maumee rivers." [1]

"Certain is it," wrote John W. Dawson of Fort Wayne, "that in 1830, he was seen one autumn day, seated in a section of a hollow tree which he improvised for a boat, laden with apple seed fresh from the cider presses of a more eastern part of the country, paddling up the Maumee river, and landing at Wayne's fort, at the foot of Main Street, Fort Wayne." [2]

Fort Wayne had now become the western end of the long axis about which the remainder of his life was to revolve.

2

The first mention of a visit to west Ohio comes in 1826.

"He came to my office in Urbana," said Colonel John H. James, well-known lawyer of Champaign county, "bearing a letter from the late Alexander Kinmont. The letter spoke of him as a man generally known by the name of Johnny Appleseed, and that he might desire some counsel about a nursery he had in Champaign County." [3]

John may have been returning from a visit with the Kinmonts and other friends in Cincinnati. The Kinmont contact could have begun with Alexander's brother, William, who had come to Richland County and was settling among the Swedenborgian adherents in Monroe Township south of Mansfield. John Chapman undoubtedly knew him. Colonel James, who had recently married Miss Abbe Bailey, youngest daughter of the first proponent of the New Church faith in Philadelphia, had just come to Urbana in 1826.

Chapman's difficulty over his Champaign County nursery (the earliest planting that is mentioned west of central Ohio) was described by James as follows:

Some years before, he had planted a nursery on the land of a person who gave him leave to do so and he was told the land had been sold, and was now in other hands, and the present owner might not recognize his right to the trees. He did not seem very anxious about it, and continued walking to and fro as he talked, and at the same time continued eating nuts.

Having advised him to go and see the person, and that on stating his case he might have no difficulty, the conversation turned. I asked him about his nursery, and whether the trees were grafted. He answered no, rather decidedly, and said that the proper and natural mode was to raise fruit trees from the seed.

He seemed to know much about my wife's family and whence they came, and this was on account of their church. He did not ask to see them, and on being asked whether he would like to do so, he declined, referring to his dress, that he was not fit, and he must yet go some miles on his way.

He was of moderate height, very coarsely clad, and his costume carelessly worn.

James did not learn until afterward that his visitor's true name was Chapman.

Old-timers in Champaign and Logan counties remembered him well, say the none-too-accurate early county histories. Colonel James and William Patrick both met him several times in Urbana, it was claimed. Patrick had been around since the War of 1812, but there is no reason for assuming, as one local historian does, that Chapman had been seen in the county that early.

In Champaign County, pioneers asserted long afterward, he had one nursery in the southwest part.[4] North in Logan County was another on the Mill Branch of Darby Creek in the southeast corner of the county near Middleburg. Alonzo and Allen West later lived on the farm, and trees set out from it by Walter Marshall and Joshua Ballinger were bearing fruit in 1872. Job Inskeep of Logan remembered Chapman's telling him he had still another planting on the Stony Creek branch of the Miami River on the opposite side of the county. As usual, late tradition has attributed various other old trees and orchards to him, all possible but highly hypothetical.

"About 1830—he left this region and went to the newer portion of the West," says one chronicler.[5]

If he ever had later business dealings as far south as Champaign and Logan counties and the valleys of the Darby and the Miami, no trace is now known, though prized family traditions say that he was in Cincinnati and the lower Miami Valley at times to visit in the homes of such eminent Swedenborgians as Milo G. Williams, Adam Hurdus, Nathaniel Ropes, and Giles Richards.[6]

The main pattern of his life was developing along the state divide in the north.

3

In April, 1828, for example, he was making a typical round of the rivers and swamps of the Maumee Country. It is one of those rare times when records step onto the trail along with traditions to help the inquiring historian over a few leagues of specific journeyings. By 1828, say memoirs of first settlers in Hancock and Putnam counties, through whose portion of the Black Swamp the Blanchard River flows down toward the Maumee, John not only had made plantings somewhere on the isolated headwaters of the Blanchard but even had trees ready to sell to the families that were beginning to push up the streams into this dismal corner of the wilderness.[7]

That was the year, said John Wilcox of Putnam, when his parents bought trees of Chapman as he was paddling down the river in a boat loaded with seedlings from a nursery near Fort Findlay. Wilcox recalled the incident very clearly because of a striking association. The family had settled along the stream the year before. One night, soon after they arrived, Mrs. Wilcox, alone in the cabin with two small children, discovered that the hard rain was bringing the easily-spilled river up to their door. Taking the children, an axe, and a pot of fire, she fled toward higher ground and reached it only after wading water for a quarter of a mile. She managed at last to build a fire, Wilcox always remembered, just "where the first orchard was planted in the subsequent year, the trees being purchased of John Chapman . . ." After fleeing to still higher ground later in the night, the family was rescued the next day by Demit Mackerel in a canoe. The harrowing flight and the planting of the orchard fixed the year in Wilcox annals.[8] Upon such associations, marginal history is always depending for authentication.

There are enough other allusions to a Chapman planting somewhere near Fort Findlay on the upper Blanchard, however, to make certain of its existence. The earliest historian of Defiance County said that it was on the spot where the village of Mount Blanchard was later laid out.[9] This was about where John, after the seventy-five mile trek along the divide from central Ohio would have passed the wide stretches of the Sandusky plains and come at last to the place where he could launch a canoe down the river through the swamps to the Maumee Country. Being just about midway between the Ohio and the Indiana ends of his patch, it was a point through which he was to pass back and forth regularly during most of the remaining years of his life, sometimes several times a season. Though for him it was in 1828 the entry place to this new country, for the real settlers in the Black Swamp region, paddling up the streams from Fort Defiance, it was the backdoor. His usual strategy had appletrees there ready to meet them.

In 1834—to look ahead a moment—after the village of Mount Blanchard had been laid out on this lonely spot, John bought three town lots along the river bank. These he held for five years.[10] Since in the earliest atlases no evidence can be found that these lots had ever been built upon, one wonders whether, like other small tracts that Chapman had recently acquired, they had accommodated one of his nurseries. Anyhow, he had trees growing thereabouts through most of the next ten years.

In the meantime, back in 1828, his nursery plot on the Blanchard must have been a very lonely outpost indeed, even though it did mark the outer edge of Ohio's rapidly vanishing wilderness.

In 1828 also—to continue with tradition before turning to the records—he had trees sprouting vigorously, old-timers said, seventy-five miles down the Blanchard and the Auglaize on the Maumee. A nursery begun about this time stood for years at the mouth of the Tiffin River above Defiance.[11]

The town of Defiance was now the business center for the new region. Grown up around one of General Wayne's forts, it stood at the head of the state-long overland road that ran up over the earlier military route from the Ohio River at Cincinnati to the Maumee. Emigrants were streaming toward Defiance, the key post, from which they could scatter to land claims east or west on the hundred miles of the Maumee, or north on the Tiffin, or south on the Auglaize whose long branches—the Blanchard, the Ottawa, and Town Creek—could carry pirogues and keelboats up into the new lands of the swamp country and the sand ridges of the divide.

Just now, furthermore, there was talk of two canals which would bring progress sweeping into this region and make it soon the very crossroads of the lower Lakes. For both, the routes had already been surveyed. From the south, one canal would connect the Ohio River with the Maumee and Lake Erie. From the west, the other would unite the Mississippi and the Great Lakes through the Fort Wayne summit.

Given a set of determining factors such as these, it is not difficult to calculate a certainty beneath the abundance of Johnny Appleseed traditions around Defiance. His largest plot was a mile above the town, it is said, between Shawnee Glen, or Sulphur Hollow, and the mouth of the Tiffin River. Here he started several thousand seedlings that were ready to plant within a year or two after 1828.[12]

While attending this nursery, he may have lived in a giant hollow sycamore, thirteen feet across, in Shawnee Glen.[13]

From this nursery he is said to have transplanted a thousand seedlings to ground that he cleared at Snaketown, now called Florida, ten miles down the south side of the Maumee from Defiance. There they were left to be sold by a resident agent. Thomas Warren, Nathan Shirley, Lewis Platter, and Samuel Hughes of Delaware Township in Defiance County all set out orchards from this Snaketown plantation.[14]

A large orchard of transplants from the main Defiance nursery is said to have stood for many years below the river near present-day Kingsbury Park in the eastern part of the city. Various other trees in the neighborhood also were reputed to have survived with typical Johnny Appleseed tenacity. One on Horace Street was a large tree eighty years ago and in 1941 measured forty-two inches in diameter. Twin trees in Pontiac Park, on the north side of the river along U.S. Route 24, reputedly sprang from a stump of a Chapman tree. Whether of John's stock or not, the parent tree was a worthy veteran surely, for its stump measured fifty-four inches in diameter. A large native boulder has been set up along the River Drive to point out these trees and memorialize

Chapman's work.[15] His labors here probably continued through most of his last years, for John's trail down the north bank of the Maumee from Fort Wayne to his later land holdings on the river continued on to Defiance, and his tradition has haunted the entire distance.

In public fancy, here in the Maumee Country, John Chapman's fame has sometimes reached out in late years to gather in some earlier orcharding not his own. Here in the portage locality there were already ancient appletrees growing in many places. French missionaries and traders had introduced the fruit to what is now northeastern Indiana and northwestern Ohio long before, and the trees had been cared for through many years by Indians and trappers. Several of these tree pioneers lasted till very great age and to gigantic size. The fruit was said to be superior to most natural apples, being larger and of pleasanter taste. The trees grew taller than typical appletrees today, higher to the branches and longer in limb, like forest trees. One specimen on the narrow bottom north of the Miami at Defiance, nearly opposite the old fort, stood till destroyed by a gale in 1886, with a diameter of nine feet at the base, a height of forty-five feet, and a spread of sixty feet. In 1879, it bore two hundred bushels of fruit. Its site inside the city corporation on Route 24 is marked now by a concrete replica of its gigantic base. Another of these fruit trees from the *ancien régime*, on up the Maumee at Fort Wayne, was long famous as a landmark in the Indian country. It was calculated to have been at least one hundred years old in 1867.

4

In April, 1828, the traditions hand the trail over to the guidance of specific courthouse records.

Sometime that month, Chapman had reached the busy settlements fifty-five miles south of Defiance up the headwaters of the Auglaize and St. Marys. This was the south edge of the Maumee region, and the river towns there were the principal gateway to it from the old Virginia Military District and Congress lands below. Towns like Wapakoneta, St. Marys, and Shanesville were just now very important names in the trading and travel logs. They had been trading posts since the earliest white men had come to these rivers, and this had been the heart of strategic country during all the major military campaigns. But just now they were busier than ever because all the main routes from Cincinnati and the Ohio River ran through them to join with the overland or river routes along the St. Marys to Fort Wayne or along the Auglaize to Defiance.

Furthermore, the Shawnee Indians had clustered in reservations here around these headwaters with the result that in addition to the emigrants streaming north and the usual border settlers, the towns had a hurly-burly of traders, trappers, government agents, soldiers, private speculators, and hoodlums whose concern was largely to prey upon the Indians and eventually oust them. In spite of the noble efforts of the Quaker missionaries among these particular reservations, unscrupulous encroachment had its usual way.

On the Auglaize, forty miles south of Defiance and fifteen north of Wapakoneta, John was signing a lease agreement for a piece of land with one Jacob Harter early in April, 1828. During the British war sixteen years before, Colonel Poague of Harrison's army had built Fort Amanda on the Auglaize and had established a shipyard where large scows were built for transporting troops and supplies down the river to the Maumee and Lake Erie. The fort had served only short use, but when the first settlers had come in 1817, they had taken over the buildings for temporary housing and started one of the first important farming communities on the new lands. Harter had settled on Section 4 east of the river in 1825.

John's written agreement with him in April, 1828, is so nearly typical of his various lease agreements at this time that it is worth quoting entire: [16]

"This Indenture made and Concluded between Jacob Harter of Allen County in the State of Ohio of the first part and John Chapman of Richland County of the State of Ohio of the second part witnesseth that the said Party of the first part for and in consideration of the sum of forty apple trees hath leased and to farm letten unto the said Party of the second part and his legal representatives one half acres of land in section four in Township four south of Range five East in the district of Piqua where the said John doth plant an Apple Nursery, to have and to hold this said lot of Land for the term of forty years from the date of these presents the said party of the first part is to receive after the expiration of five years from the said party of the second part, or out of his nursery on the above described half acre of land letten to the Said Chapman for a nursery the above mentioned forty apple trees in witness whereof we have hereunto set our hands and seals this _____ day of April eighteen hundred and twenty eight.

his

Jacob X Harter

mark

John Chapman"

The document was witnessed by Ferdinand Miller and William Stewart, two well-known pioneers in the community.

"Where the said John doth plant"—was Chapman just establishing the Harter nursery now in 1828, or was he merely getting formal protection for a crop of trees started some time before? A "term of forty years from the date"— and John was now going on fifty-four.

If he was sowing seeds here in the Fort Amanda settlement now in April, 1828, he saved part of his stock for two more plantings a few days later. On April 6, he concluded an identically worded agreement with Picket Doute at St. Marys on the St. Marys River ten miles southeast of the Harter lease. Again he bargained for a half acre, promising forty trees in payment, the plot being in the southeast half of section 10, township 6, of range 4 east, "where the said John doth plant an apple nursery." The lease was attested to by William Lattimer and John Logan.[17] The site was south of the village of St. Marys, later on the land of Richard R. Barrington, between the end of Main Street and the canal feeder.[18]

Twenty-three days later, on April 29, Chapman was signing a third lease with William B. Hedges thirty miles down the winding St. Marys River in the northwesterly direction of Fort Wayne. This was at the trading post known as Shanesville (now Rockford). It was a particularly important spot in the early period. The reservations of Indians Anthony Shane, Chief Charlie, Peter Labadie, the Godfreys and others were located close by. Wayne's army had crossed the St. Marys here. It had been the seat of county justice till 1824, and would long be one of the most important shipping points to Fort Wayne both by road and by river.

Hedges had come in early as a clerk in Frenchman Anthony Madore's trading establishment and was in 1828 the best fixed white landholder in the community, a power in the county.

He drove a stiff bargain with nurseryman Chapman, or so portions of the lease suggest.[19]

Hedges leased to Chapman "*a certain enclosed lot or piece of ground lying below the little Branch, below Shanesville, between the little lane and the river . . . for the purpose of sowing appleseeds on.*" It was to be cultivated in a nursery "*for the space of ten years, more or less, as the case may require for the present year's sowing seed to come suitable for transplanting or setting out.*" For this privilege, Chapman was to pay to Hedges "*one thousand apple trees, to be taken as they average, suitable for market or transplanting on equal proportion for the space of ten years, so soon as they become fit for market. That is to say on an average of one hundred apple trees per year, or in the proportion when they are fit to set out.*" It was further understood that Chapman was "*not to be obliged to take or remove the remainder of the apple trees off the lot at the expiration of the ten years.*" He was, however, to "*pay one hundred apple trees a year rent that they may stand, or in that proportion, for what time they may stand, until taken off.*"

The lease was witnessed by John Greave and A. R. Hunter.

Chapman's route, this April, 1828, appears to have been down the St. Marys in the direction of Indiana and Fort Wayne. It was only thirty-eight miles. There was a good road along the right bank, or one could float leisurely in a canoe. There is no documentary proof of Chapman's presence in Fort Wayne until six years later, but traditions have him there long before that, and logic favors the traditions. This April, his easiest course of travel would have been down the St. Marys with the current to Fort Wayne, then by way of another downstream ride on the Maumee back into Ohio to

Defiance, then from there up the Auglaize and the Blanchard on his return trip east into central Ohio.

There was plenty of time for this journey before he turned up back in Mansfield on August 22 to take care of six years' interest due on his Madison Township lease. Though he had assigned to others his rights to the larger part of this quarter, he still held sixteen acres, the land office account was carried in his name, and he was responsible for payment of the interest. In 1828, he paid an accumulated obligation of $115. Thereafter, he took care of the payment regularly each year until his death.

Also in the same year of 1828, on October 30, he sold to Jesse B. Thomas one of the two town lots, the first land he had ever owned, purchased in Mount Vernon on Owl Creek in 1809. The original deed as reported by historian N. N. Hill is unusually interesting:

"I, John Chapman, (by occupation a gatherer and planter of apple seeds), residing in Richland County, for the sum of thirty dollars, honest money, do hereby grant to said Jesse B. Thomas, late Senator from Illinois, his heirs and assigns forever, lot No. 145, in the corporation bounds of the village of Mt. Vernon, State of Ohio." [20]

His other lot on the edge of Owl Creek was never sold.

John in 1828 still considered Richland County his legal home.

Of his occupation as a "gatherer and planter of apple seeds," the rivers a hundred miles to the northwest had seen much that year.

11

TO THE FORT WAYNE SUMMIT

More clearly than ever before, the seasons now called the beat in John Chapman's routine. If he was going west, he was usually skirting the Sandusky marshes in the spring, even before the first mallards and coot had returned; if he was going east, it was normally in late summer before the first wedges of canvasback and Canada geese were winging south. Year after year, there was scarcely a twelve month that did not leave some record of the regular east-west, west-east travels.

Mansfield and vicinity in central Ohio would be his home terminal until about 1834, and he was back there at the end of each year's round to attend to necessary business, to shelter for the winter, and to replenish his stock of seed. Of thirty-one specific date entries to be found now on documents relating to John's business between 1827 and 1840, all that are concerned with the Ohio end of his affairs fall in the late summer or autumn or winter.

On the other hand, of those dates that chronicle dealings among the new settlements of western Ohio and eastern Indiana, all but one fall in spring months. March, April, and

May were the season for new plans, more land, additional links to the nursery chain, another exploratory journey.

It was as if his life had been caught in a pulsing not his own. The following sampling of records and general hearsay for the years 1829-1836 will suggest the year-by-year swing that people saw back and forth across the land.

1 8 2 9

Having been west during the spring and early summer to care for his plantings in the Maumee Country, on July 16 John stopped in Amanda Township on the Auglaize to have the Harter lease of the year before sworn to before William Stewart, local justice of the peace.[1]

Thirty-one days later he was back east in central Ohio placing on record at the Mansfield courthouse his lease signed with John Oliver in 1826 for a half acre on the Black Fork. Four days afterward he paid the annual interest on his Madison township school lands.

1 8 3 0

West on the St. Marys River in May, he stopped at the county offices in the town of St. Marys on the seventeenth, to enter for public record both the Harter lease from the Auglaize and the Doute lease from the St. Marys. Harter's lease had taken three separate yearly rounds for the legal steps of signing, acknowledging, and recording. Today the parties to a lease or deed are glad to rush the papers to a registry in a matter of hours. Even the formalities of John Chapman's business were adjusted to the leisurely seasonal cycle. The Doute lease had been witnessed only two days before recording.

In August, back in Ohio, the school-land interest was paid as usual.

This is the year also when, a none-too-accurate memoir says, John first visited the little Indiana post of Fort Wayne. In October, 1871, John W. Dawson, Fort Wayne lawyer, former territorial governor of Utah, newspaper man, and writer of local history sketches, read as did many other old acquaintances of John Chapman the extended and spectacular account of him in the November issue of *Harper's New Monthly Magazine*. Dawson could remember Chapman from 1838 till 1845; so he sat down immediately and dashed off for the local *Sentinel* an account of Chapman's life around Fort Wayne. Though the resulting sketch has been oft-reprinted and quoted, it was done with hurried pen and was a patchwork of hearsay rather than careful investigation.

John had certainly come to Fort Wayne long before 1838, the date that *Harper's* assigned to him. One pioneer even fixed his first visit as early as 1825.[2] Traditions up the St. Joseph River above Fort Wayne, practically the only part of the immediate vicinity that had shown any substantial signs of clearing away the wilderness by 1828, said that Chapman had reached there that year, introduced himself as "John Appleseeds," and planted a nursery. Both Jacob Notestein of Cedar Creek Township farther upriver and William Caster of Lake Township to the west set out orchards in 1836, it was said, from the trees started on the St. Joseph.[3]

Dawson said that John first arrived with a boatload of seed "one autumn day" in 1830. "He kept the seed wet for preservation. His boat was daubed with mud and tree-moss, and looked quite in comport with his rough garb, untidy appearance and eccentric habits . . ."

The general picture is possible. Dugouts were the most

common type of canoe then faring on the Maumee, some of the larger ones carrying loads of two or three tons. John was an old hand at managing a pirogue. He was definitely interested in Fort Wayne, though he would have been there normally in the spring rather than in the autumn in the early thirties.

The town was still only a frontier settlement, with a big promise and little fulfillment. Its enviable location on the summit between the Lakes and the Mississippi waterways, however, together with the long talk of canals and roads had started a roaring boom town in the 1820's. So far, there had been little else. A city had been platted. Traders, shopkeepers, artisans, and riff-raff had crowded in for quick profits. Then the canal projects had dwindled into long talk. Indian trade continued to dominate affairs and tended to keep business at the characteristic border-town level of rough barter, bilking, intemperance, and brothels. When Henry Rudisill of Pennsylvania arrived in 1829 to look after the interests of John T. Barr of Baltimore, one of the town's proprietors, he found about 150 residents, mostly French and Indians. Domestic economy had developed so little that it was nine months before he could procure a pound of butter, and poultry or stock could not be had at any price.[4]

They needed appletrees, of course. According to Dawson, Chapman on his arrival planted a nursery

on what was then called the Taylor farm, near the canal lock, just east of this city [there is no record elsewhere to verify this site]; another at that time perhaps on the Taber farm, now called, just below the city on the north side of the River Maumee [nor of this]; and then taking a quantity of apple-seed he journeyed to Elkhart prairie, near Goshen now [nor of this]; one on the south bank of the Maumee river, about ten miles from here, in

Milan township . . . it was long prior to 1838, for in the autumn of that year, I passed down that river in company with Col. John Spencer, now deceased, crossing that stream at its bend and was shown by Col. S., the orchard which Johnny Appleseed before that time had planted [it was on the north bank, not the south, and was probably started about 1834]; another orchard he planted somewhat later on the St. Mary's, about nine miles up from this city, south side [no other record]; another on the land of David Archer [probably the St. Joseph nursery associated with the traditions of 1828]; and I have an indistinct recollection of having seen another about 1840, just below the village of Shanesville, where, or near where, Fort Adams once stood [the Hedges lease of 1828].

Dawson was near enough right about the Milan Township, the Archer, and the Shanesville sites that one suspects at least partial accuracy in the rest of his list. But there are no other clues to them. They may have existed but probably not all at one time. It is also true that Chapman in this later period rarely planted without a recorded lease or deed to the land he used.

Dawson's 1830 date for his arrival was probably an approximation.

1831

Chapman's plantings on the Auglaize and St. Marys were given the usual spring and early summer care this year, as the available trees from them would soon show.

Back east in August, the school-land interest was paid promptly.

1832

At Fort Wayne, it is interesting to note that Henry Rudisill, thrifty German that he was, was becoming thoroughly disgusted and disheartened with the shiftless, unprogressive border conditions that prevailed. To his employer, he had written on February 26, 1831,

The Country must improve before the Town, the Town is now to large for the Country around it and I am in hopes that since the Canal bill had been lost we will rid of a Class of Citizens who are no benefit to the Country at all, the Soil is good and Produce will if they were not to confounded lazy to improve it they would rather hunt and run after Indian Treatys and payments than to Cultivate their land.[5]

Now in 1832 the forces to dispel the inertia were already working, and though there are no specific records this year of Chapman's spring round in Fort Wayne, he knew what was going on. The first spadeful of earth for the Wabash and Erie Canal was turned at last on Washington's Birthday, and excitement began to run very high. Government lands to bear the cost of the waterway had been set aside in 1826 and 1827 but had not been specifically located by the federal commissioners until 1829. Sales had opened at the land office in Logansport on the Wabash end in 1830.

In Ohio that summer, John Chapman took care of his Mansfield interest as usual in August. Then on September 8, he sold the fourteen acres farther east in Wayne County that he had bought in 1825. He sold it to John H. Pile for a ten-dollar loss, but it must have been no longer useful and he was going to need the money for some of the cheap land going onto the market in Indiana.

1833

This year Brockman Brower, newly arrived in Greensburg Township of Putnam County, in western Ohio, saw John peddling trees down the Blanchard from his nursery near the headwaters. "Loading a canoe, he would descend the river, supplying all who were in need of fruit-trees. He thus devoted his time and means for the benefit of his fellow-men." [6]

John Barnd, who settled along the river that year, also planted some of Chapman's trees, and a good many other persons along the Blanchard remembered his trips back and forth along this river route through the Black Swamp.[7]

1834

On April 28, he was west in Fort Wayne, and this time he was applying at the newly established land office for 42.11 acres of the canal lands that had gone on sale while he was east the October before. The parcel lay in present-day Milan Township along the north side of the Maumee, about three miles down from Fort Wayne. He paid cash at the rate of two and a half dollars per acre.

Twenty-four days later, still in Fort Wayne, he applied for 99.03 acres more of the canal lands on the Maumee, this time at the rate of a dollar and a half. The tract was three miles farther down the north bank almost at the Ohio boundary.

That was in April and May. In August, he was attending to affairs back in Mansfield as usual. But that fall, he switched the poles of his axis and, apparently on his way west, on the day before Christmas stopped in the newly-laid-out town of Mount Blanchard to buy of Asa M. Lake three town lots for fifteen dollars.

1835

In April he was west attending to his Doute and Harter leases on the St. Marys and the Auglaize. He had begun his round from the Fort Wayne end, the order of dates suggests, and was headed east. On April 2, five years after signing the lease with Doute, he was paying the lessor in full the forty appletrees promised in the contract. Grown law-wary in his later years, Yankee Chapman promptly took the receipt over to the courthouse on the same day and entered it for public record.

Eleven days later, he had passed over to the Auglaize and was paying off in similar fashion the forty trees to Jacob Harter. Two days later, he was back in St. Marys to record this receipt also.

That August he was in Ohio as always, paying the Mansfield interest. But in October he was returning west and on his passage down the Blanchard stopped on the eighth at the Hancock County courthouse in Findlay to register his deeds to the Mount Blanchard lots bought the December before.

1836

In the spring, at the age of sixty-two, he was still briskly expanding his real estate enterprises in Indiana. On March 10, he paid cash at the Fort Wayne office for 18.70 acres at the rate of a dollar and twenty-five cents per acre in Maumee Township a quarter of a mile west of his first Maumee tract, along the east side of the big ox-bow loop in the river.

The next day he put down cash again for 74.04 more acres at the same rate, this tract forty-five miles south on the Wabash River in Wabash Township of Jay County. It was east of the present village of New Corydon in the extreme northeast corner of the county, just over the state line from Mercer County, Ohio, and fifteen miles as a crow flew from his nursery on Hedges' land at Shanesville.[8]

Two years later, on May 16, 1838, he bought forty more acres several miles northwest of Fort Wayne almost in the center of Eel River Township. This, too, was government land at a dollar and a quarter per acre.

Indiana now became his home base, but the summer trips to central Ohio seem to have continued to the year of his death.[9] How many nurseries he retained back in his familiar central Ohio valleys is no longer clear. There may have been one in his favorite Huron County neighborhood of New Haven above Plymouth, on the edge of the huge cranberry marsh above the town.[10] He may have continued his nursery in Sandusky Township, and seemingly he had one or more at some time in the settlements that began developing in the "New Purchase" territory of Crawford County around Bucyrus.[11]

12

LAST JOURNEYS

PEOPLE who knew John Chapman in Indiana and northwest Ohio during his closing years preserved much less about him than did the central Ohioans. Few came to know him as a personality at all. He never became an intimate part of their lives. He had not saved their cabins from the Indians. His missionary zeal did not burn so memorably here. And besides, he was a quarter century older now than when he had first reached Ohio, and he looked older than he was. He was seamier and more wind-beaten. He lived less and looked less like other people than ever before. He was queer, and few new acquaintances ever got much beyond the thick bark of that queerness. He left a vivid impression, but what folks remembered was less a portrait than a symbol, something less personal than elemental.

Down in Jay County, Indiana, M. W. Montgomery caught some of these recollections for a county history in 1864.[1] The 74.04 acres that Chapman had bought there on the Wabash in 1836 he worked more or less regularly from 1837 till 1845, so that people formed at least a general idea of him. Folk talk grew, as usual, but it lacked the exuberance it had shown on French Creek and the Mohican. It had settled down to the stiff, quietly wondering recollections of a queer old man with an unusual business, who had led an abnormally hard life.

"Among the pioneers of Jay was an oddity called Johnny Appleseed," Montgomery wrote. ". . . Many years ago he brought from Central Ohio, two bushels of apple-seed, on the back of an ox, and cleared small patches of ground on the headwaters of the Loramie, Auglaize, St. Marys, and Wabash rivers, besides various other places and planted apple-seeds."

No nursery on the Loramie, inside Ohio, is now on record.

"In the early settlement of this county, he was wandering about from one nursery to another, camping wherever night overtook him, selling trees. He had a nursery on the Wabash one mile east of New Corydon. He never carried a gun or wore a sound piece of clothing, though he possessed considerable property; never slept in a bed, or ate at a table; had no place he called home; was a devoted Swedenborgian in religion, and died near Fort Wayne in 1845."

That Chapman had owned a good-sized acreage on the Wabash about his nursery, the Jay County residents seemed already to have forgotten.

"He had once been a fine business man," the account concluded, "but an accident had caused a partial derangement of his mind. The trees from his nursery are bearing fruit in a dozen different counties in Indiana, and thousands are enjoying the fruit who never saw or heard of Johnny Appleseed."

The theory that old John's eccentric career had been started by a mental derangement due to an accident had trailed him all the way from the Allegheny. Curtis, who remembered him on French Creek, reported that he "had a deep scar on his face that disfigured his countenance very much. I forget how he obtained it, though he must have told me." No one else ever mentioned this scar. Curtis recalled no mental queerness in his early acquaintance, however, except to say that "his benevolence was unbounded" and that "he never resented any injury."

"I once saw him most outrageously abused by a man much smaller than himself," said Curtis, "for some offense he had unwittingly committed. After reviling him in the hardest language, he kicked him, all which John bore with great meekness, and totally unruffled, and if he had been struck on one cheek, he would have turned the other."

The late Glines memoir also caught an echo of the accident theory from members of the Chapman family. John was a very smart, intelligent young man, Glines reported, until about the age of twenty-one when "he received a kick from a horse that fractured his skull, which was trepaned at the time. From that time forth he manifested that singular character attributed to him."

The story reappeared in Jay County, Indiana, in 1860 through family channels again. John's half-sister, Persis Broom, and her family had followed him to Indiana from Perrysville, Ohio, about 1834. He was their chief support. The Perrysville tradition says that the Brooms were poor, that the Rices gave them five dollars to help them on their way, and that John on his next visit to Ohio repaid the money. Broom continued to be employed by John on his land holdings here in Jay County and elsewhere.[2]

There must have been some basis for the story of an early accident. But whether or not it started John Chapman on his strange path to glory is certainly not established by the fact that the story was handed down by much younger members of his family who felt a strong need to rationalize their kinsman's abnormalities.

2

John's chief labors during the last ten years of his life seem to have gone into developing his Indiana real estate. Partial record of the improvements suggests that his brother-in-law was his chief helper.

The 42.11 acres above the Maumee that John bought in 1834 lay in a wilderness that had yet known only Indians and squatters. Chapman's work there did not change the unsettled condition immediately, and later local historians do not bring the first permanent settler to the region until two years after that. But some time before his death, John established on this ground one of his most extensive nursery plantings. In 1845 fifteen thousand seedlings were growing there, of a size worth inventorying in his estate. Some of the trees, it is said, were still alive in 1935.[3] His work on the two other Maumee parcels has left no record, except for a tradition of another nursery on the Ox-bow Bend. These lands were all a sound investment of accumulated cash, however, whether he improved them or not, for the new canal was soon running down the south side of the river just across from his land, and there would be an inevitable enhancement of value as the region developed.

What he did with his forty acres in Eel River Township is also a blank page now. It was in the middle of a first-rate farming development, and its sale at a good price after Chapman's death suggests that it had undergone some development.

Of the Jay County tract, however, there is a fairly continuous record. These acres, applied for in March, 1836, had been patented to him with full title one year later. Sometime

during the year he spent twelve weeks in the neighborhood,
boarding at two dollars per week with Joseph Hill just over
the line in Adams County. Presumably he was working on
his newly acquired tract. The next year, he was back for
eighteen weeks, and again in 1839 for ten weeks. In 1840,
he returned for four weeks, in 1841 for two weeks, in 1842
for three, in 1843 for two (the board rate dropped to one
dollar), and in 1844 for two. The record of these annual
visits happened to be saved only because Chapman never settled the board bill and the entire account was presented as a
claim upon his estate in 1845.

The more or less periodic visits recorded for Jay County
apparently represent the times of Chapman's attendance on
his land—the longer stays being required in the beginning for
clearing and planting, the shorter for the maintenance of the
nursery stock that he had started there. Broom, who was
living in Wabash Township when John died, had work at
some time on John's Wabash tract, for he charged the estate
with the clearing and fencing of eleven and three quarter
acres there and the building of one log house. The date of
the work was not noted. In a second bill, Broom asked re-
muneration for clearing four more acres in 1843 and 1844,
for fencing them, for building one log house, eighteen by
twenty-one feet in size, and for scoring and hewing 1,834
feet of timber for a frame barn, thirty by forty feet. The
site of this labor is not made clear. Presumably it was on some
other of John's farms.

In addition to the improvements indicated in Broom's accounts, the appraisers of the Wabash property found one gray
mare and a nursery containing 2,000 appletrees worth on an
average of two cents apiece. Remains of a cabin and some
venerable fruit trees marked this site down till late years.

One tree definitely within the true Johnny Appleseed tradition is said to have reached a circumference of ninety-two inches.[4]

Chapman's annual stops here at the Hill home during the last seven years of his life show the itinerant existence he had come to lead. Other cabins sheltered him similarly in other portions of his range. North of Fort Wayne near the nursery on the St. Joseph he stayed at the home of a family named Worth. John was there when his last illness came upon him in 1845. The Worths charged the estate with a total of five weeks' board at "sundry times" between 1840 and 1845. He had come there first, they said, about 1836.

Along the north bank of the Maumee, the trail through his own acres led down the river to Defiance. Either by shore or by water, it was a normal route through a rapidly developing region. Most of the nearby orchards in the river counties of Paulding, Henry, and Defiance were attributed to his enterprise.

"When I was quite young, he stayed at my father's house clothed in rags and shoes bound on his feet with strings," wrote Judge D. C. Carey of Paulding County in 1891. Isaac Carey, his father, had lived in Carryal Township on the Maumee. "He seemed happy and was full of exhortation and good words . . . He did not believe in fire and brimstone as a punishment for the wicked. He said he thought that the worst part of Hades would not be worse than smoky houses and scolding women." [5]

To the south, his years of visits to nurseries on the Auglaize and the St. Marys left a long trail of local recollections. S. C. McCullough, who visited the Amanda nursery on the Auglaize in 1835, was told of an old man who appeared some years before, along the Auglaize and Ottawa rivers, hunting out alluvial lands on which to start his appletree stock.[6] Many orchards in Allen and neighboring counties were believed to have come from his seeds. One such orchard stood till quite late on the McHenry corner, at the intersection of North and Main streets in the city of Lima.[7]

Just south of the Harter nursery in Amanda Township, it was said, he started another over the line in what is now Logan Township of Auglaize. William Berryman who owned the land built his commodious log house along the river immediately below the plot. Many Logan Township pioneers planted from it. Some of the trees were still bearing in 1905. It was Chapman's practice, the tradition went, to stop by each nursery once a year to care for it.[8]

St. Marys people recalled him well. "I have often seen Johnny," Samuel Scott said in 1900, and like every one else he described John's singular dress and manners but regarded him as anything but a fool. John stopped at the Scott home on an average of twice a year. He was believed by early residents to be caring for a great number of plantings between the St. Marys and Lake Erie.[9]

The Hedges nursery at Shanesville, by Dawson's statement, was still in operation in 1840. The town kept close commerce with Fort Wayne by road and by river, and was only a short distance from Chapman's Jay County property. That he was in the neighborhood at least on occasional business is shown by his efforts to collect on debts there shortly before his death.

Other visits took him frequently over the Ohio line along the sand ridges of the divide into Van Wert County. One of Broom's daughters had married William Johns and settled here on 160 acres near the town of Van Wert. That was in 1837. Lucy Jane being a favorite niece, Chapman was often there and, as elsewhere, left traditions of business in the neighborhood.[10] There was a nursery near Delphos from which Bill Thorn once toted trees on his back. And in 1839, Chapman asked Alexander McCoy for a piece of ground, but since none was cleared he was sent to Daniel M. Beard, on whose place he planted, fenced with logs and brush, but never returned to care for it. Beard grafted many of the seedlings later and supplied stock to the neighbors. Orchards of his trees were pointed out for many years on the Johns, King, Evers, Gilbert, Brough Johnson, Samuel S. Brown, and John G. Morse farms. On William L. Martin's land along Dry Creek, east of where the infirmary was later built, some trees happened to be planted, appropriately, at a spot romantically famous for a duel fought by two Indians over a sweetheart.[11]

John's last trip to his niece's home was shortly before his death, it was said. He was leading a black ox—perhaps the animal that became part of the Jay County picture of him.[12]

Around Fort Wayne, reams of so-called reminiscences and family traditions concerning John have been written down in the past seventy-five years; but much of it has all too obviously been inspired first by the *Harper's* article of 1871 that made Johnny Appleseed a national hero, then by the growing realization of his value as a civic asset, and finally in recent decades by long controversies locally over the site of his grave and the promotion of related park developments.

Dawson stated in 1871 that Chapman commonly worked for local farmers during corn harvest. Captain James Barnett said he was the best husker he had ever hired. He always gave him a place to stay too. John Rogers and Absalom Halcomb also used to put him up for the night.

He was a temperate man, Dawson said (a fact that surely

THE APPLESEED TRAIL IN OHIO:
ASHLAND MEMORIAL, 1915

Photo courtesy of
Ashland Chamber of Commerce

HE FIRST CABIN IN RICHLAND COUNTY
From J. F. M'Gaw, Philip Seymour, *1883*

JOHNNY APPLESEED MEMORIAL BRIDGE AND
TRADITIONAL GRAVE SITE OF JOHN CHAPMAN

*Spanning the St. Joseph River near Fort Wayne, the
bridge was dedicated in 1949. Just below it, in Johnny
Appleseed Memorial Park, is a tombstone marking the supposed burial place of Chapman
in Archer Cemetery.*

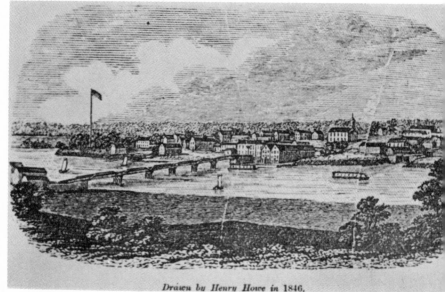

Drawn by Henry Howe in 1846.

THE MAUMEE AND DEFIANCE IN THE 1840'S

Henry Howe, Historical Collections of Ohio, *1847*

made him stand out singularly in early Fort Wayne) but took a dram of spirits now and then to give himself a little warmth.

Contrary to certain tales, Dawson said that John was always orderly in religious meetings, no matter what the faith. He remembered seeing him at a camp meeting in 1841: ". . . it was on the site of Lindenwood Cemetery, near a spring of water, on the north side,—I saw him lying on the ground near a large tree in good hearing of the pulpit, and I now have a vivid recollection of the earnest attention he gave to the the eloquent words of the clergyman, who discoursed of that New Jerusalem, which our hero hoped to reach, and there carry on his now earthly occupation among the sacramental hosts around the throne of God."

A few other Indiana recollections of John were caught in print from time to time in years after 1871, but all of them slipped too easily into the established pattern of the published stories, or else strayed so irreconcilably from known fact as to appear wholly unacceptable as biography. Down to Iven Richey of Tocsin, Indiana, who died in 1940 at the age of one hundred and three, there was someone who claimed to remember Johnny Appleseed.[13]

One tiny item of fact was recently found in an account book preserved by the Allen County-Fort Wayne Historical Society. On Washington's Birthday, 1840, the account shows, Chapman purchased of Hamilton, Taber, and Company, merchants in Fort Wayne, one pocket knife for seventy-five cents. Fortunately for the record, John did not have the cash in hand, and the item had to be charged. The bill, which he settled in full on the following April 4, was entered in the ledger not under his rightful name, nor under the "Johnny

Appleseed" of the legend, but under the title by which he was very likely better known in his lifetime, "John Appleseed." [14]

3

True to his life pattern, Chapman was a far traveler and an explorer of new ranges to the end.

"Silas Mitchell informs us . . ." wrote Norton, historian of Knox County, Ohio, in 1862, "that in the fall of 1843, when living in Whitesides County, Illinois, Johnny Appleseed passed through that county on foot, and stopped all night with Aaron Jackson, son of Ziba, and left in the morning, stating that he was then from the Iowa prairies on his way to a Swedenborgian Convention in Philadelphia." [15]

There is no reason for doubting this report of an expedition to Iowa even though the twenty-fifth General Convention of the Swedenborgians had been held in Philadelphia the June before. Perhaps, since time never pushed John with a hasty hand, he was heading for the next convention six months hence. Whatever his intent, he attended neither meeting, the records show. Whitesides County, Illinois, on the Mississippi directly across from Clinton, Iowa, would have been in a direct line with northern Indiana.

Although such a trip to the trans-Mississippi West has been suggested also by a very lively extension of the Appleseed story in Missouri and Arkansas during recent decades, the stimulus for these later tales from the St. Charles country and Ozarks is clearly literary and belongs to the legend only.

Other distant travels have been reported from time to time— into Kentucky, Arkansas, Minnesota, even across the plains to the foothills of the Rockies—but only the Iowa expedition has a tiny hint of verification in the record.

Closer to his accustomed haunts, one popular tradition takes him up the St. Joseph Valley north of Fort Wayne into southern Michigan. Cassopolis, Centerville, Coldwater, Jackson, and Holland all had him as a visitor and a planter, it is said. There is logic for the claims, but no proof.[16]

As in Ohio, so in Indiana, scarcely a county today is without a tree or a tradition. He was on the Elkhart River, it is claimed, in Elkhart, St. Joseph, La Porte, and Lake counties. He was down the White River Valley through Henry and Hancock and Marion, and down Salt Creek to Bartholomew. He visited old friends in Wayne, saw the Lincolns in Spencer, and the Poseys in Posey. Trees have been claimed to his credit at Goshen, South Bend, Trevlac, Windfall, Sauktown, Richmond, North Manchester, Winchester and elsewhere. None of these traditions can be scorned—nor can they be claimed as fact.

Back in central Ohio, he had faded so gradually from common view that no one remembered exactly when he had first gone west. People that historian Howe interviewed in 1845 said it was "about twenty years ago." [17] An article by T. S. Humerickhouse of Coshocton in *Hovey's Magazine of Horticulture* said in 1846 that it was "about fifteen years ago." Hill, the central Ohio historian, placed it in 1836.[18]

The Reverend John Mitchell traveling the Plymouth circuit north of Mansfield met Chapman in 1837, journeying along the road afoot, in his shirtsleeves, "as contentedly as a prince." He now lived "out West," he told Mitchell.[19]

In Mansfield, Samuel C. Coffinbury saw him last in 1840. He told Coffinbury his home was near Fort Wayne and that he had a sister living near there also.[20]

The Baughmans of Mansfield saw him last in 1843.[21]

On these last circuits through former haunts on Mohican waters, people told Hill that old Chapman usually passed down the Black Fork among the Copus, Irwin, Coulter, Tannehill, Rice, Oliver, and Priest families, thence to Finley's on Lake Fork till he reached Jacob Young's, Patrick Murray's, the Fasts, Masons, and the site of his old nursery near Leidigh's Mill. It was his custom to sleep on barroom floors.[22]

The Rices of Perrysville said he was back to see them "two or three times" after 1838, the last time in 1845, the year of his death.[23] If the latter date is correct, the visit must have been in the winter, for John died in March.

From Rosella Rice's romantic pen came several accounts of the venerable traveler and of the saintly impression he made on these concluding rounds. Her descriptions were to have a powerful effect upon the legend that was already growing.

"Almost the first thing he would do when he entered a house and was weary," she wrote, "was to lie down on the floor, with his knapsack for a pillow, and his head toward the light of a door or window, when he would say, 'Will you have some fresh news right from Heaven?' and carefully take out his old worn books, a Testament, and two or three others, the exponents of the beautiful religion that Johnny so zealously lived out—the Swedenborgian doctrines." [24]

"The last time we saw Johnny was one summer day when we were quilting upstairs. A door opened out upon the ground, and he stood his little bundle on the sill and lay down upon the floor resting his head on the parcel. Then he drew out of his bosom one of his old dingy books and read aloud to us." [25]

"We can hear him read now, just as he did that summer day when we were busy quilting up stairs, and he lay near the door, his voice rising denunciatory and thrilling—strong and loud as the roar of waves and winds, then soft and soothing as the balmy airs that stirred and quivered the morning glory leaves about his gray head." [26]

A more realistic picture comes from 1842, when John extended his Ohio trip down to the lower Muskingum Valley to see his family. His half brothers, Nathaniel and Parley, and his half sister, Mrs. Sally Whitney, still lived there.

W. M. Glines, thirty-two-year-old neighbor of Nathaniel Chapman, met John at this time. His recollections both from this meeting and from the Chapman family stories, set down thirty years afterward, have been referred to frequently in this book. Though highly inaccurate in detail, Glines' stories all seem to have the ghost of a likelihood behind them. At least his account of John's visit in 1842, coming from direct contact with the man himself, is worthy of consideration. It is unglossed and rugged, closely in keeping with the reality before the folk idealization began to prevail in the Appleseed stories. According to Glines, the last visit to Ohio was in October, 1842.

"Mr. Nathaniel Chapman was a neighbor to me at the time and a very warm friend with all. Johnny made his home with him while on his visit to his friends."

John Whitney, who had married Sally Chapman, was farming close by.

During the summer the lightning had struck a very large black oak tree on Whitney's land, and knocked it to pieces from the top to the roots, and some of the fragments were converted into very comfortable sized rails, and such lengths as made them convenient for that purpose. Johnny having heard of the circumstance and that Whitney had laid them up in his fence, he and Nathaniel came to my house and would have me go with them to see the rails that were made by lightning; when we got ready to start, I proposed taking my gun along to kill some squirrels or rabbits; to this Johnny demurred; he read me a severe lecture upon the subject of taking life from any living creature; he maintained that God was the Author of all life, hence it belonged to Him whenever he was ready to demand it, and in as much as we could not give life to any creature, we were not at liberty to destroy life with impunity; after his lecture and to please him, I put up the gun and we moved on.

We soon came to a creek that was necessary for us to cross; his brother and myself managed to cross over by stepping from one stone to another, but Johnny having been compelled to accept of a pair of old shoes while he was amongst his friends and had them on, very carefully removed them from his feet and waded over where there was more water; after getting over he rolled up the shoes and stuck them under his arm and plodded on barefoot through the woods and briars until we arrived at the fence in question.

He at once commenced an examination, he measured them, counted them and viewed the roots from whence they came; he then turned to Mr. Whitney and read him a sermon upon the wonderful Providence of God to man. Said he, God has given you a large family of boys, they have cleared you a large farm in the woods, and have worked hard to do it. Making rails is hard and heavy work. God pitied the boys, hence he sent the lightning to make your rails and he selected that hard old burley tree close by where you most needed them; now said the old man, can't you see it? Whitney hung his head for a moment, then replied that he always tried to feel thankful to God for His kind care over him and his family, but that he never heard of His making rails for anybody before.

Glines said that he heard Chapman tell several of the typical adventure yarns. One related how John had saved himself from freezing to death by burrowing into a huge snowdrift that Providence had prepared for him.

His account closed with a characteristic note on the old man's garb:

While on his last visit to Ohio in 1842, his niece, Miss Rebecka Chapman made him a shirt, one half of calico, the other muslin. On the one of the muslin, were two large letters, perhaps A.D. These he had so arranged that one was on either side of the bosom. That seemed to please him.[27]

4

Midway between the Indiana and Ohio ends of these journeys people along the Blanchard used to see him going through year after year, following his regular route. Daniel B. Beardsley, later historian of Hancock County, remembered him passing his boyhood home in the 1830's on the north side of the stream, three miles above Findlay. "He did not appear to have a very great quantity of this world's goods," Beardsley said. People found him "at all times sociable, but eccentric, full of pleasant story and good advice." They saw him last in 1839–40.[28]

In 1839, Chapman stopped at the village of Mount Blanchard to sell to Michael Shafer at a profit of twenty-five dollars his three town lots along the river. In a later day when monuments have sprung up to mark many parts of Johnny Appleseed's long peregrinations, one should by all means be set up somewhere on the headwaters of the Blanchard River, that marked for almost a quarter of a century the regular point on his yearly passages from east to west along the land bridge of northern Ohio.

Few people at one end of these later travels seem ever to have learned much about his business affairs at the other. Nobody beside himself ever knew the full extent of his property. When he died, even his administrators never managed to list all the real estate he still held. And along the trails between his chief centers of visitation, people found out far less. Not letting the right hand know what the left was doing was only Yankee caution. And permitting great numbers of people along his paths to feel that he was an innocent eccentric to whom money was a rarity was sensible perhaps, considering the sums that he transported from time to time and the lonely ways he traveled.

As to the impression of pennilessness that Chapman managed consistently to leave, his appearance certainly obscured the facts. During the last six years of his life, it is interesting to note that he possessed in land: one town lot in Mount Vernon, Ohio; seven parcels of farm ground in Ohio and Indiana totaling 353.88 acres; one 99-year lease for seventy acres in Richland County, Ohio, and at least four known leases for varying long terms on small tracts in several Ohio counties. Altogether, in the course of his long wanderings, he had owned either by deed outright or on long-time lease no less than twenty-two properties totaling nearly twelve hundred acres. These holdings never represented great wealth, but they were considerably better than those of the average settler in the Middle West.

The dusty records of John Chapman's real estate have little to do with the legend of Johnny Appleseed, of course, except for the proof they supply that the man behind the idealization was anything but a feeble-minded vagrant or the impractical fanatic that fancied versions of his life sometimes suggest. True, Chapman did not, as has been claimed, give all his substance to philanthropy along the trails, but he helped people freely when the need arose, gave gladly to the extension of his faith, and would have given more if ways had been devised to utilize the land he offered. He was scrupulously honest. Though his life had veered quite early into a tangent and never got back toward the center of normal living, he did not become a miser, hermit, or complete crank. He was a social being to the end, and he had a sense of humor that must frequently in these later years have enjoyed the thought that, in spite of his rolling-stone life, he had belied the adage and gathered enough moss to keep him a comfortable distance from the county house when his working days would be over.

The national concept of John Chapman came, of course, out of these final years. In it, he was always old, venerable, queer. People who first wrote down his story in the 1840's and '50's disregarded almost completely the fact that a man could not have been the same grayheaded, eccentric, gently dignified and even saintly individual for the whole last fifty years of his life. No matter whether they were telling about his breath-taking river adventures when he was twenty-three, or about his seed-planting in the Ohio wilderness when he was twenty-seven, or about his heroic services to the border during the Indian terrors when he was thirty-eight—they made him the same aged, grizzled, oddly dressed, quaint, and kindly messenger of God that lingered vividly in their imaginations from John Chapman's last visits back to Ohio when he was sixty-eight or seventy. Evidences of the growing mind, the developing personality, the expanding soul were not preserved, and for the most part have never been recovered since.

As the years passed, the highlights in the portrait would shine ever brighter, while the romantic shadows would grow more pleasantly impenetrable. Johnny Appleseed would become less and less real and would be pushed back farther and farther into the long-ago until, as Vachel Lindsay said,

> He ran with the rabbit and slept with the stream
>
> .   .   .   .
>
> In the days of President Washington.

And indeed to the twentieth century it has come to pass that John Chapman does seem as far back as George Washington in American time, although when he was only beginning his western adventures in Pennsylvania the days of President John Adams had already started. He was planting his first seeds in central Ohio in the days of Thomas Jefferson at the time the Louisiana territory was being purchased and Burr killed Hamilton. He was warning the towns of Indian raids in the days of James Madison and the War of 1812. He was taking up large acreages of Ohio land and winning his first fame as a Swedenborgian missionary in the days of James Monroe and the Missouri Compromise. He was extending his operations into Indiana in the days of John Quincy Adams, the first railroad, the completion of the Erie Canal, and the protective tariff bill. He would invest his life-savings at last in Maumee-Wabash canal lands in the days of Andrew Jackson, the Carolina nullification, and the battle of the Alamo. Not until the days of Presidents Van Buren, William Henry Harrison, and John Tyler did he grow old and make his last visits to Ohio. And the telegraph would have been invented, Texas annexed, the anti-slavery movement well under way, and James K. Polk inaugurated before Chapman's death in 1845.

During this time, all over the north-central Ohio counties that eventually shaped his legend, thriving cities and towns sprang up. The frontier had been swept away in 1812; now every acre was settled, even up into the marginal chestnut and oak groves along the ridges. Highways were everywhere, and by the time of John's last visits there were even canals and railroads. The cabins were falling into ruin or had already been replaced by up-to-date abodes of frame or brick. The real frontier—which, Frederick Jackson Turner once said, follows the hither edge of free land—had long since moved away from the cornland belt east of the Mississippi and had sent tongues of settlement far up the Missouri and the Platte into the foothills of the western mountains. The old first West, just over the Appalachians, that had been an absorbent for populations overflowing from the Atlantic coast when John Chapman paddled his pirogue down the Ohio, had grown up into a political unit so powerful that it was beginning to change the meaning of democracy in America.

People forgot, as they normally do with their heroes, that John Chapman had been no more of a fixed entity during this time than the land he lived on. It is a price that folk characters must always pay for glorification.

PART   FIVE

IN THE SUMMER of 1847, when his labors had literally borne fruit over a hundred thousand square miles of territory, at the close of a warm day, after traveling twenty miles, he entered the house of a settler in Allen County, Indiana, and was, as usual, warmly welcomed. He declined to eat with the family, but accepted some bread and milk, which he partook of sitting on the door-step and gazing on the setting sun. Later in the evening he delivered his "news right fresh from heaven" by reading the Beatitudes. Declining other accommodation, he slept, as usual, on the floor, and in the early morning he was found with his features all aglow with a supernal light, and his body so near death that his tongue refused its office. The physician, who was hastily summoned, pronounced him dying, but added that he had never seen a man in so placid a state at the approach of death. At seventy-

●

From Man to Myth

two years of age, forty-six of which had been devoted to his self-imposed mission, he ripened into death as naturally and beautifully as the seeds of his own planting had grown into fibre and bud and blossom and the matured fruit.

Harper's New Monthly Magazine, November, 1871

So he kept on traveling far and wide,
Till his old limbs failed him, and he died.
And he said at the last: " 'Tis a comfort to feel
I've done good in the world, though not a great deal."

Weary travelers, journeying west,
In the shade of his trees find pleasant rest;
And they often start, with glad surprise,
At the rosy fruit that round them lies.

And if they inquire whence came such trees,
Where not a bough once swayed in the breeze,
The answer still comes, as they travel on:
"These trees were planted by Apple-Seed John."

LYDIA MARIA CHILD

'Apple-Seed John," *Saint Nicholas,* 1880

13

A TIME TO DIE

N ORTH of Fort Wayne, March of 1845 came in cloudy and fair by turns, with light showers. The temperature ranged from 27° in the morning to 47° in the evening, and the wind was in the southeast. So says the diary of Rapin Andrews, weather hobbyist of Perry Township, whose meteorological jottings give the only details we have now of the day-by-day setting in Allen County, Indiana, for the last month of John Chapman's life.[1] Of the first eighteen days in March, nine had either rain or snow, and the mercury fluctuated between 12° and 57° with the average just above freezing.

For several years, Chapman had been stopping for short periods at the cabin of a Mr. and Mrs. Worth, believed to have been William Worth, along the St. Joseph River about three miles up from Fort Wayne. Richard Worth, a son, when interviewed twelve years after Chapman's death, said that his father had been one of the old nurseryman's first acquaintances in the neighborhood. "Mr. and Mrs. Worth were his friends," wrote Dawson summing up the local tradition in 1871, "and had, long years before, given him a place in their cabin when he sought it. They too have long since died, leaving a name for hospitality and goodness."

In 1857, twelve years later, the Reverend T. N. M'Gaw of Mansfield hunted up Richard Worth, the son, in De Kalb County, Indiana, for some facts concerning their friend's last years. Richard had been living either with or near his father at the time of Chapman's visits, and after his death had presented the claims for board, nursing, and funeral expenses in behalf of his father—or so the estate papers seem to indicate. With all respect for what a dozen years can do to a man's memory, Worth's few statements—the earliest and most nearly contemporary now available—are invaluable for their account of Chapman's death and burial.[2]

"Johnny Appleseed made his appearance in this region about the year 1836," M'Gaw reported Worth as saying, "and commenced planting nurseries along different streams of this then wild and uncultivated region. Among the first of his acquaintances was the father of Mr. Worth, who was then residing near Fort Wayne, in Allen County . . . The residence of Mr. Worth was upon the banks of the St. Joseph where Johnny had planted a nursery, which at the time of his death was in a thrifty condition."

This nursery, county tradition has placed on the west side of the river about three miles up, on land originally owned by David Archer.[3] As late at 1929, Miss Eliza Rudisill, then eighty-nine years old, said she could remember it. In 1916 Hiram Porter of St. Joseph Township, then ninety, claimed that he once helped his father transplant about fifteen or twenty trees from it.[4] No lease, or other authentic record of this nursery, however, has ever turned up. The Worth cabin, according to the son's statement, was near the nursery.[5]

Worth related to M'Gaw a number of the usual stories

Sculpture by Edmond Amateis, for American folklore group, New York World's Fair, 1939. (World Wide Photos.)

The Johnny Appleseed theme in commercial advertising. Drawing by David Hendrickson, 1940. (Reproduced by permission of the Travelers Insurance Company, Hartford, Conn.)

Drawn by Henry Howe on a pleasant day in June, 1846.

NORTHWESTERN OHIO, 1846

JOHNNY APPLESEED'S LAST HAUNTS
(Henry Howe, Historical Collections of Ohio, *1847)*

ASHLAND, OHIO *(Drawn by Henry Howe in 1846)*

Chapman had left behind—about bare feet, rattlesnakes and the "primitive Christian" episode from Mansfield. Several of the yarns are new to the Appleseed canon:

"Johnny at one time was invited to a house raising, to which he went, hoping to be of some use on this as well as other occasions. In the act of carrying a log, he espied a house on fire in the distance. 'Fire!' said he and dropped the log; he started off at full speed, his companions (about forty of them) followed suit. Johnny was then sixty-eight years old and yet he outran the whole of them, arriving at the burning building first."

There was the inevitable bear, of course, but one that was unaware of Johnny's previous courtesies to the ursine tribe:

"One time while on the banks of the Maumee, he was attacked by a bear, which he killed with a pole while swimming towards him."

The last of the Worth stories is one of the most delightful Johnny Appleseed tales ever spun. Like all the best Chapman yarns through the years it had come first from his own telling and reveals the chuckle that must have been present in a goodly number of his autobiographical narratives that, ever since the first exhilarating capers along the Allegheny, he had been planting across the Middle West.

On one occasion while conversing with Mr. Worth, [M'Gaw wrote] John related an anecdote which he said took place in Richland County, Ohio.

He stated that he took a job of deadening several acres of timber for a gentleman living there. He went out one fine morning and worked hard until about half past eleven o'clock, when he lay down to rest until his dinner would be brought to him.

Shortly after he lay down, his employer came with his dinner, and on approaching the place where he lay saw chips falling all around Johnny and he asleep. The wind was blowing briskly at the time. The man thought Johnny was a supernatural being, took fright, and ran back to his cabin leaving Johnny to enjoy his slumber unmolested while the work of deadening was going on.

There is no reason for supposing that Chapman thought of the Worth cabin in any special way as home, or that he would have preferred it as a place to die. The board bill that Richard Worth presented to Chapman's administrator shortly after his death, shows that Chapman had boarded there five weeks and about five days out of five years. Worth's cabin was no more home than other places where he was in the habit of stopping on his rounds. But it was one where he felt free to stay and where he found the friendship and the simple hospitality he required. When chance ended his journeys in their home, the Worths were the sort of people who gave him the care and courtesy that are due a man's greatest moment.

Sometime during the cold, wet first half of this March, Chapman had been "some fifteen miles from where Mr. Worth resided."

Information was conveyed to him that some cattle had broken into his nursery on the St. Joseph, and he immediately started for the nursery. When he arrived, he was very much fatigued, having exhausted his strength in the journey, which, being performed without intermission, and on foot, was too great a task for the poor old man. Johnny lay down that night never to rise again.

This may have been on March 10, since the Worth claims for board terminated on that day.

A fever settled on his lungs, which baffled the physician's skill, and in a day or two after taking sick, he passed to the spirit land.

Dawson said in 1871 that Chapman died "with a disease then prevalent here, and commonly called the winter plague. . . . His illness lasted about two weeks."

He could not have been bedfast for more than a few days, for the Fort Wayne *Sentinel* of Saturday, March 22, reported his death as of "Tuesday last"—that would have been on March 18.[6]

Two other dates have been also advanced for his death. Dawson said March 11—he had glanced over the Chapman estate papers in the Allen County courthouse before writing his article and may have noticed the termination of the Worth board bill on the tenth. He was very likely wrong. The other date appeared in Richard Worth's claim for care and funeral expenses:

> "*Expence of sickness ten dollars*
> *Expence for laying him out three dol-*
>   *lars fourty four cts*
> *Expence of coffin to Samuel Flutter Six Dolar*
> *March the 17, 1845.*" [7]

"Our townsman, Samuel C. Fletter" (Flutter) upon whom Dawson relied for some of his data, claimed not only to have built the coffin but to have attended Chapman's dying hours, dressed his body, buried him, and erected a stone marker. The estate papers confirm only that he collected on the coffin. Fletter told Dawson, too, that Chapman had on, when he died, next his body "a coarse coffee-sack, with a hole cut in the centre through which he passed his head. He had on the waists of four pairs of pants. These were cut off at the forks, ripped up at the sides and the fronts thrown away, saving the waistband attached to the hinder part. These hinder parts were buttoned around him, lapping like shingles so as to cover the whole lower part of his body, and over all these were drawn a pair of what was once pantaloons." Fletter was talking in 1871, more than a quarter century after the events and after people's imaginations, including his own, had been pretty well colored by the growing tradition.

"We buried him respectably," said Richard Worth in 1858, "in David Archer's grave yard, two and a half miles north of Fort Wayne."

The Archer family burial lot was located on a sandy knoll a few rods west of the river a short distance south of the general locations attributed to the Chapman nursery and Worth's cabin. The feeder to the Wabash and Erie Canal, constructed in 1835, ran along the east base of the cemetery mound, paralleling the river. A beautiful little elevation over-looking the St. Joseph, it was used for many years as a grave-yard by pioneer families. Now, though most of its burials are no longer identifiable, the plot has been fortunately preserved and falls within Fort Wayne's municipal park developments up the St. Joseph River. Parnell Avenue leads almost directly to the spot. The several-hundred-acre tract, now known as the Johnny Appleseed Memorial Park, together with the Johnny Appleseed Memorial Bridge over the St. Joseph, close by, was dedicated May 21, 1949, and now constitutes the most extensive single memorial to John Chapman.

Chapman was buried, Dawson understood from Fletter, "at the east side of this mound, near its foot . . . and a stone was then put up to mark the spot." If such a stone ever existed —and it is doubtful—no one else remembered it. In 1900, John H. Archer, grandson of David, reported of the cemetery and Chapman's burial place:

I find that there are quite a number of persons yet living here that remember him well, and enjoy relating reminiscences and pecularities of his habits and life. The historical accounts of his death and burial by the Worths and their neighbors . . . in David Archer's private burial grounds, is substantially correct. The grave, more especially the common head-boards used in those days, have long since decayed and become entirely obliterated and at this time I do not think that any person could, with any degree of certainty come within fifty feet of pointing out the location of his grave.[8]

In 1916, the Indiana Horticultural Society selected an appropriate spot to memorialize Chapman near the top of the knoll, and erected around it an iron fence. Within it in 1935, the Optimist Club of Fort Wayne erected a natural granite boulder brought from the Milan Township nursery site on the Maumee where John had fifteen thousand seedlings growing when he died. "HE LIVED FOR OTHERS," says the inscription.

In recent years, certain local investigators have advanced the belief that the Worth cabin and Chapman's burial place were on the other side of the river, a little farther up. Although much hearsay and circumstantial evidence purporting to have been passed on from generations now dead have been summoned to the argument, not a single fact has been brought to light that shakes the statement of Richard Worth recorded in 1858 that John Chapman was buried in David Archer's cemetery.[9] The exact spot of the burial is no longer known, however, and never will be again.

No particular place can adequately memorialize John Chapman, anyhow. Precisely defined spots in graveyards are for mere people, not for a man whose memory had become a working principle even before he died. Johnny Appleseed is no disconsolate ghost hanging around a forgotten burial site. He still strides up and down the St. Joseph above Fort Wayne, but he now is staking out miles of parkway and trails to lead residents of a busy modern city into the open air where they may enjoy many acres of natural beauty at their front doors.

Back in March, 1845, however, the notice of Chapman's death in the Fort Wayne *Sentinel* on the following Saturday did little to clear up any mistaken impressions local people had of him. No death notice of similar length ever exemplified more poignantly how little a neighborhood can know about a long and familiar resident.

After noting the death of a local stonecutter "on Tuesday last," the item continued:

On the same day, to this neighborhood, at an advanced age, MR. JOHN CHAPMAN—(better known by the name of Johnny Appleseed).

The deceased was well known through this region by his eccentricity and the strange garb he usually wore. He followed the occupation of a nurseryman, and has been a regular visitor here for upwards of 20 years. He was a native of Pennsylvania, but we understand his home—if home he had—for some years past was in the neighborhood of Cleveland, Ohio, where he has relatives living. He is supposed to have owned considerable property, yet he denied himself almost the common necessaries of life—not so much perhaps from avarice as from his peculiar notions on religious subjects. He was a follower of Swedenbourgh, and devoutly believing that the more he endured in this world the less he would have to suffer and the greater would be his happiness hereafter—he submitted to every privation with cheerfulness and content, believing that by so doing he was securing snug quarters hereafter.

In the most inclement weather he might be seen barefooted and almost naked, except when by chance he picked up articles of old clothing. Notwithstanding the privations and exposure he endured, he lived to an extreme old age, being probably not less than 80 years old at the time of his death—though no person would have judged from his appearance that he was 60. [He was approaching 71.] He always carried with him some works of the doctrine of Swedenbourgh, with which he was perfectly familiar, and would readily converse and argue on his tenets, evincing much shrewdness and penetration.

His death was quite sudden. We saw him in our streets only a day or two previous.

Within twenty years, elaborate accounts of John Chapman's last beautiful hours in a wilderness cabin on the banks of the St. Joseph began to appear variously in print and eventually crept into the legend—his last supper, the reading of the Beatitudes, an eloquent prayer, the glow of sunset through the falling petals of the appletrees. Even though at variance with known facts, there is no more worthy monument to a noble life than a beautiful story.[10]

Except for the passing pageantry of the weather, the few simple items reviewed above are all that has been saved of John Chapman's end. March 18 is usually given now as John Chapman's final day, but the definiteness is far more a matter of convenience than of significance. One March day more or less in 1845 means little now and meant less to John Chapman. He was beyond calendaring.

Besides, as the Andrews diary shows, the days were much alike. On the seventeenth: "Cloudy. Snow showers" with the mercury just above the freezing mark. On the eighteenth, the same, except that the temperature dropped from 29° at noon to 19° in the evening. For both the nineteenth and the twentieth, identical entries: "Snow Showers all day."

Some time amid the March snows John Chapman died and his body was placed back into the earth to which, more than most of his fellows, he had always remained peculiarly close. There is no evidence that a single relative or long-time friend was present to keep the usual precious tryst with times past.

But spring would come on the twenty-first, and eighteen days afterward the Andrews weather entry would read:

"*In the night thunder showers—then fair—first apple blossoms.*"

14

THE VANITY OF RICHES

IF John Chapman had conned the book of *Ecclesiastes* as carefully as he had the doctrines of Emanuel Swedenborg—and doubtless he had—he was familiar with some of the bitterest questions ever asked about the profit of man's labor under the sun. He also knew the correct answers.

Nevertheless, the eternal Yankee in him would surely have squirmed a bit if he could have known how fittingly the disposition of his own estate was to illustrate that irony, pointed out by the Preacher of old, when a man wins property or honor, but cannot enjoy it himself. Instead, "a stranger eateth it."

A few days after Chapman's death, John Harold who had married a daughter of Persis Chapman Broom, and who was probably living in Jay County, made a trip up to Fort Wayne to inquire about his uncle's estate.[1] His investigation took a week, at the end of which with Elza A. McMahon of Fort Wayne retained as counsel, he applied to the Allen County Circuit Court on April 2 for authority to administer the property.

"There are persons who are unlawfully intermeddling with the Estate of John Chapman deceased late of said County," his sworn statement read, "whereby the same will be lessened in value to the injury of said Estate." He was duly appointed, with Lysander Williams of Fort Wayne sharing the $300 bond.

Harold appears to have done a good job of rounding up items to be inventoried. Chapman's gray mare was for some reason over in Van Wert County, Ohio, and it was necessary for Harold to spend four days gaining possession of her on a writ of replevin. In Jay County, John L. Waterman and Sherburn A. Lewis, proprietor of the new town of New Corydon, appraised the mare at $17.50 and the two thousand seedlings on Chapman's Wabash Township land at two cents apiece. They also appraised the improvements that William Broom, Harold's father-in-law, had been making for Chapman on the tract, at $155. Up in Milan Township at the nursery on the Maumee, Thomas McDugal, William Harper and John Nuttle, the first settler in the township and a neighbor whom Chapman had often visited, appraised 15,000 more trees at three cents apiece and listed a due bill on McDugal for $6.

By August 12, when he submitted a report of the findings, Harold had listed assets totaling $588.18 which included in addition to the property mentioned above a judgment in Mercer County, Ohio, for $60 against Archibald McIntyr and a receipt of judgment in the same county for $12.18. There was also a note on Nathan Bronson for $3. The McIntyr note was dated August 3, 1841. The suit to collect on it had been instituted by Chapman himself on February 10, 1844. In a trial the following August, he had been awarded full payment with $9.20 interest. Collection was still pending in 1849.[2]

Harold had also sold four hundred appletrees to Charles Muldoon for $24, collecting fourteen of it, and forty more to James Hutchinson for $2.40. He had paid a debt of $3.50 to Benjamin Saunders in appletrees.

He continued as administrator till the next April when he had accumulated the following claims against the estate:

> Broom's first bill for improvements appraised at $155.
> A second bill by Broom submitted in November, for $127.68.
> Joseph Hill's board bill for $104.
> William Worth's board bill for $8.75.
> Richard Worth's bill for funeral expenses, $19.44.
> Harold's own expense account of $67.62, including the ten dollars he had paid his attorney.

He credited himself with the gray mare valued at $17 and five hundred appletrees at $15. In the accounting, the mare and the trees appear to be all he ever received for his services.

In the estate that was now turned over to the administratorship of Franklin P. Randall, Fort Wayne lawyer, and for many years the town's most notable jurist, politician, and public servant, the rest of the personal property inventoried by Harold was ignored. If anyone ever sold more appletrees or collected on the several notes, no record was kept and no accounting made.

Randall listed as assets only the five parcels of real estate owned by Chapman in Allen and Jay counties. Of the claims previously submitted he allowed during the next ten years the Worths' bills in full and those portions of Broom's claims that had been assigned to two creditors, Theophilus Wilson, well-to-do Jay County merchant, and Moses Jenkinson, John W. Dawson's law partner just then interested in Jay County land. He also charged the new inventory with the fee already credited to Harold in the gray mare and the five hundred appletrees. None of the other earlier claims against the estate was ever paid.

On January 5, 1847, Randall bid in for himself, through the formality of sheriff's sale for taxes, both the 99.03 acres in Maumee Township that Chapman had bought in 1834 and the 18.70 in the same township bought in 1836. The total bid for the two was $5.83, the amount of taxes due. The next day he bid in similarly for $2.84 five acres of the forty that Chapman had bought in Eel River Township in 1838. Under the law Randall as administrator could have redeemed these tracts within two years by settling the taxes in full. The 99.03 acres in Maumee Township were never redeemed.

Later the 42.11 acres in Milan Township were sold in 1849 to Peter Schlinck for $30; the 40 acres in Eel River Township in 1851 to John Hathaway for $120; the 18.70 acres on the Ox-bow Bend in Maumee Township in 1854 to William W. Carson, Fort Wayne lawyer, for $37.60; and the 74.04 acres in Jay County in 1854 to Moses Jenkinson for $222, who paid for it chiefly through assignments of the Broom claims. Administration costs absorbed the proceeds from all these sales.

The administrators never listed, probably because they did not know of them, Chapman's one remaining town lot in Mount Vernon, Ohio; his three acres in Mohican Township, Richland County, Ohio; his leasehold of seventy acres of school land in Madison Township, Richland County, or any other leases in Ohio.[3]

Among more than six hundred dollars' worth of claims against the estate that remained unhonored were two mementoes of long-vanished years, the promissory notes given by John in Franklin, Pennsylvania, in February, 1804, to Nathaniel Chapman for "one hundred dollars in land or apple trees with interest till paid," and to the children of Nathaniel and

Elizabeth Rudd for "one hundred dollars to be paid and interest till they become of age." The sums had never been paid. Nor were they now. Who presented them through the law firm of Dawson and Jenkinson is not now known.

Dawson, referring to these notes in his article of 1871, was puzzled as to the location of the "Franklin" in the headings of the notes. His bad guess was that it must have been the village of Franklin on the Miami River in western Ohio. Shades of forgotten and happy adventures in Pennsylvania's beautiful Allegheny Valley when the West and John Chapman were young!

15

THE LEGEND FLOWERS

I

THE red-blooded folk talk that had leaped the Atlantic to break into print in England twenty-eight years before John Chapman's death had never lost any of its growing power and soon was to show that the passing of the earthly form was merely the unshackling of the Johnny Appleseed who had already become the reality.

The first harvest of stories, as the previous chapters have shown, had been a motley growth. Being the immediate result of Chapman's impact upon hundreds of frontier people in dozens of communities across Pennsylvania, Ohio, and Indiana, they were as diverse as folks themselves. Anything about him that caught attention had been good for a yarn. To readers familiar only with the standard twentieth century idealization, the foregoing pages must have revealed many odds and ends of folk talk that have now dropped by the wayside as the more dignified and gently fashioned apotheosis has taken form. The heterogeneous tales, already very active as a result of the first Pennsylvania and Ohio years, had been well established by 1817, as the Manchester report has shown. Thereafter, they multiplied and grew in wild diversity as long as any one lived who remembered him. Many of the stories were written down—the politer ones at least—during the big wave of pioneer reminiscing and county history making that hit the east part of the Middle West between 1850 and 1890. In old families of the Mohican country and around Fort Wayne, some of these crudely turned tales are still being passed down by parents who heard them directly from their grandfathers.

But the process of idealization had also begun years before Chapman's death. Although his personal eccentricities continued to be enhanced, largely because of the innocent quaintness they gave to the stories, other aspects of his life very early began to take on an orderly and selective development, particularly his religious mission, his pioneering in horticulture, his heroism on the Indian border, and his personal benevolences. By the time of his death, these had already melded, in central Ohio at least, into the outlines of the present-day Johnny Appleseed.

Although the story has always had a consistent oral growth, several printed items have been very important in giving the idealization impulse and direction. Two of these date from the year after John Chapman's death.

The April, 1846, issue of *Hovey's Magazine of Horticulture* printed a sketch of John's career as a pioneer horticulturist in the West, written by T. S. Humerickhouse of Coshocton in the Muskingum Valley portion of the Appleseed country. The author did not know that John had died the year before, nor could he remember his true name, but he felt that his significance in Middle Western fruit culture should be emphasized. The result was a brief, laudatory sketch of Chapman's mission, methods, and importance as a pioneer nurseryman. "He has continued occasionally to return in the

autumn to his beloved orchards hereabouts," the author concluded, "for the double purpose of contemplating and rumi-
nating upon the results of his labors, and of gathering seeds
from his own seedling trees. . . . Recently, his visits have been
altogether intermitted. Our hope is, that he may yet live in
the enjoyment of a green old age, happy in the multitude of
its pleasing reminiscences." [1]

This oversimplification of Chapman as a pioneer pomologist was soon reprinted in various agricultural papers and set
the pattern that has been kept intact through the years as he
has evolved from a primitive planter into a culture hero
responsible for all first orchards in America.

The other event was the visit the same year to Mansfield of
Mr. Henry Howe, recently arrived from the East to collect
materials for a history. His *Historical Collections of Ohio*
published the next year was a monumental work, and his two-
page account of John Chapman, expanded in the revised edition forty-two years later, was to be basic in nearly everything ever written about Johnny Appleseed since.

Howe was a journalistic historian, a master at the craft of
compiling local history, biography, tradition, topographical
description, and his own drawings into volumes that would
appeal to a large subscription trade. He had set out from New
England to do a series in the manner of John W. Barber's
historical collections of Connecticut (1836) and of Massachusetts (1839), and when he reached Marietta, Ohio, in
1846 had already published his works for New York, Pennsylvania, New Jersey, and Virginia. His Ohio volume was to be
his masterpiece. Notebook and sketchbook in hand, he set out
in January to visit every county in order to interview old settlers, copy records, visit graveyards and historic spots, and
make pencil sketches for woodcuts. He crossed the state four

times, gathering not only much authentic history, but hearsay, personal memoirs, curious bits of all sorts that resulted in a volume that is often anything but good history, but which did more than any other book to give the sons and grandsons of the frontier in Ohio a background of fact and tradition to be proud of and which is often now the only printed source, reliable or not, for much that is believed about the early days.

In Mansfield and Richland County, Howe heard of Johnny Appleseed. His informants seemingly did not know of the old man's recent death, and Howe was not able to record the event till his revision of 1889. But he read the Humerickhouse sketch and listened to stories of Chapman's nurseries, his New England ancestry, eccentric dress, primitive saintly life, Swedenborgian faith, humanitarianism, and similarity to John the Baptist. He recorded anecdotes about his kindnesses to mosquitoes, bears, and rattlesnakes. He dressed him in a coffee-sack cloak and a mushpot hat, and he set down the bare-footed Christian story.

For years, Howe's book was the most widely read history in Ohio and a powerful stimulus to other local history writing. Every neighborhood was soon busy gathering scraps of the past from records, from old men's memories, and often from imagination. Howe's Johnny Appleseed stories, like many others he told, were widely copied and augmented, and have been ever since. They are especially important for turning attention to Chapman's kindnesses to creatures of the wild, and to the eccentricities of his appearance. Johnny's similarity to both John the Baptist and St. Francis of Assisi has rarely escaped a writer since.

A third powerful literary influence on the tradition that was now shaping up rapidly in the central Ohio valleys was a local novel, *Philip Seymour*, published in 1858 by the Reverend James F. M'Gaw of Mansfield. M'Gaw used Johnny as a minor character in a thin, highly romantic plot in the Scott and Cooper tradition based upon the Copus-Zimmer-Ruffner massacres of 1812. In his treatment of Johnny, he followed Howe closely but added other local tales such as that of Johnny's two wives in the heaven to come. He also made Chapman a participant in the events of the Copus massacre and gave him a beautifully idyllic death near Fort Wayne. Before he finished his novel, M'Gaw had at hand his brother's letter, quoted earlier, giving Richard Worth's account of Chapman's death in the Worth cabin. These details M'Gaw enhanced into a thing of lingering beauty that soon became a standard part of biographical sketches and, needless to say, has never lost any of its saintly decoration in subsequent reworkings.

Another contributory literary force was Miss Rosella Rice, minor Ohio novelist of the 1850's whose accounts of John in the appendix to the 1883 edition of *Philip Seymour*, in the 1889 edition of Howe's *Collections*, and in several county histories have been largely responsible for the extreme sentimentalization that took over the story for many years. Born in Perrysville, Ohio, in 1827, Rosella remembered late visits of John to her home and vicinity. When she developed into a highly romantic novelist and contributor to *Arthur's Illustrated Home Magazine, Godey's Lady's Book,* and other feminine journals in the 1850's, it was not surprising that she should use the quaint figure of Johnny Appleseed for one of her themes. Her accounts were vivid, dramatic, and lush with feeling. They stressed particularly the spirituality and beauty in the venerable missionary-nurseryman. Even the cruder eccentricities she included seemed to drop away as dross to let the soul shine through.

"His bruised and bleeding feet now walk the gold-paved streets of the New Jerusalem," she would conclude, "while we so brokenly and crudely narrate the sketch of his life—a life full of labors and pain and unselfishness; humble unto self-abnegation; his memory glowing in our hearts, while his deeds live anew every springtime in the fragrance of the appleblossoms he loved so well." Johnny's feet, always due for more than their share of commiseration, are walking on no uncomfortable pavements of hard gold in his New Jerusalem, but on forest paths padded soft with ageless leaf-mold, or on new-turned earth sun-warmed for the reception of brown seeds.

W. D. Haley's article, "Johnny Appleseed; A Pioneer Hero," in the November, 1871, issue of *Harper's New Monthly Magazine*, has been in some ways the most influential piece ever written about Chapman, for it lifted a localized legend out of its Middle Western locale and gave it sudden coast-to-coast prominence before a public that accepted it immediately and warm-heartedly as a national possession to be cherished. Haley's account, consequently, has colored practically all writing on the subject ever since, especially that of a literary sort. Haley, who also came from the Muskingum Valley, built upon the accounts of Howe, M'Gaw and Rosella Rice, repeating the same anecdotes, adding a few others, but intensifying the eccentricities, the humanitarianism, the heroic deeds on the Indian border, and the primitive but far-extending nursery-chain that was carried on not for profit but as a divinely guided mission. He gave the story much beauty and drama. He quoted Rosella Rice's eloquent description of Chapman's readings from the scriptures and hinted strongly of blighted love. He chose only the colorful and quaintly charming anecdotes and left out practically everything that sounded harshly crude or coarsely suggestive. The resulting characterization has been the literary Johnny Appleseed ever since, and though cruder anecdotes continued to be told in Ohio and Indiana for many years, the folk talk gradually lined up with the printed versions.

2

Hero tales expand in certain natural ways. The first tendency, as the early Appleseed stories have richly shown, is to exaggerate salient peculiarities, personal traits, and special events. Simplification follows, and then if the story evolves long enough, an idealization that selects and reshapes many diversities into a logical whole.

Symbols soon appear. John Chapman's colorful nicknames are good examples—"John Appleseed (or Appleseeds)," "Appleseed John," "Johnny Appleseed," or just "Appleseed." Apples and appletrees were not just trademarks; they became life tokens. In the absence of records, appleblossoms attached themselves to Chapman's birth and inspired numerous charmingly sentimental stories about his childhood. Other orchards and blossoms decorated his youthful education and romances, and have even drifted soft petals down upon his dying body.

Similarly, Johnny has become the planter of all first orchards, not merely in the Middle West where the chances of his having supplied early seedlings are always good, but everywhere. Connecticut, Massachusetts, Vermont, New York, Pennsylvania, Maryland, Virginia, Kentucky, Tennessee, Missouri, Nebraska, Arkansas, Wisconsin, Iowa, the Rocky Mountain states and the Pacific coast have all claimed his labors. In the states where he really worked, scarcely a county is now without a tree or orchard said to be his. Similarly, all varieties of apples roll in his direction. The Rambo is said to have been his favorite. The Jonathan, the Chapman, the Baldwin, the Grimes Golden, the Ben Davis, and others have all been attributed to seedlings planted by him. It does not matter that not one of them can be traced authoritatively to his labors. In a sense he originated all new apples. He stands for everything good and progressive in American horticulture. Nurserymen now invoke the blessings of the Johnny Appleseed moon on their spring plantings and sing his praise during the fall harvest. He is the patron saint of the American orchards.

3

Episodic accretions to John's story have come from many directions; scarcely a year passes without a new one.

The love hints in the early talk have grown into especially lively chapters since the beginning of the twentieth century. The Reverend Newell Dwight Hillis's novel *The Quest of John Chapman* (1904) was the first to develop a full love plot, and his formula has stuck ever since. John, in his story, was a promising Harvard student, the son of a Massachusetts minister. He loved Dorothy Durand, daughter of his father's bitterest foe in the congregation. Because of the hostility they could not marry. The Durands went West with the first Ohio settlers and soon disappeared in the great wilderness. John's seed-planting mission was first just a device for seeking out his lost Dorothy. He found her in Kentucky, but too late, for she had died a short time before of a strange fever and a broken heart. Then, his planting turned into a life mission of service for humanity. Years later he returned to her grave to plant appleseeds that sprouted into the symbolic words, "Apple Blossoms."

The Reverend Mr. Hillis's formula has stuck in most of the other stories woven about John Chapman's loves. Sometimes the name is Sara Crawford, or Betty Stacey, or Alice something, but the long separation, the search, and death just when they are about to be united are firmly fixed in the pattern. The most popular of the fictional treatments has been Mrs. Eleanor Atkinson's *Johnny Appleseed: The Romance of the Sower* (1915). So convincing was her presentation of the imaginary Pittsburgh episode and others that they have been widely reprinted as biography in historical and horticultural publications.

A recent claim carries the love affair back to Clinton, Connecticut. There, the young lady of his choice gave him the mitten in the firmest New England manner, but her refusal was such as to set going the spiritual catharsis.

Folksier and more realistic versions of John's love longings have circulated to some extent in Middle Western communities. His old man's interest in young girls and his visions of connubial satisfaction in the world to come have stirred enough anecdotes to send a rampant libidotheorist into raptures. Fortunately for Johnny, however, the evidence now is only in folk talk. Some versions in Ohio and Indiana say that John finally found his beloved, that they were married, but that her death occurred soon afterward. Some of John's descendents are occasionally pointed out.[2]

Out in Missouri, it is said that he married an Indian girl and lived with her on Turkey Creek in Ralls County. One morning he walked into the tepee, gazed longingly at his baby, then walked away, never to be heard of again. No explanation for his desertion has been given. Certainly, there can be little doubt that if he had been as familiar a figure in Missouri during the last fifty years of his life as he was in Ohio and Indiana, his spouse could easily have trailed him.

A great many other episodic accretions have joined John Chapman's story. Typical is a newspaper account recently circulated of his meeting with the English actor, Wilbur Chapman, on the "Cotton Blossom Floating Palace Theater" showboat at Mt. Vernon, Indiana, in 1827. According to a story attributed to Vernon Posey, while the boat was tied up at Mt. Vernon, Johnny tramped into town and was persuaded by an old friend to visit the show. No one noticed him until in the midst of the merriment, his clear voice rang out asking divine pardon for the frivolities of the stage. The audience recognizing him flocked to greet him and the performance broke up. Actor Chapman, at first disgusted, sought out the other Chapman and in time came to know him well. The next season his handbills and river-port dodgers proclaimed the famous appletree man was a relative, and the showboat did a thriving business under the new name of Chapman's "Apple Blossom Theatre." [3]

This normal tendency of a folk hero to pick up friends among both local and national celebrities has led to a wide acquaintance for John. He knew George Washington, Daniel Boone, Simon Kenton, the Wetzels, John James Audubon, Robert Dale Owen, the "Lost Dauphin," and both Abraham Lincoln and his father. He did battlefront service under George Rogers Clark, Anthony Wayne, and Henry Harrison. He fought or scouted in battles from Tippecanoe to Lookout Mountain (twenty years after his death!). The list grows yearly.

The most significant of these episodic additions have been touched in earlier chapters.

4

The unpredictably diverse career that Johnny Appleseed has had in Missouri and neighboring states seems to have been due to specific literary stimuli.

In 1886, Denton J. Snider, a St. Louis litterateur and philosopher in the Hegelian tradition, published in his *Goethe's Faust, First Part—A Commentary*, thirty pages of poetry and discussion that he called "Johnny Appleseed's Ode to Goethe as Read at the Chicago Literary School." [4] Johnny was portrayed as a deeply discerning scholar and poet whose manuscripts Snider had somehow acquired. The eleven stanzas and 582 lines of Johnny's ode rambled through an elaborate apostrophe to Chicago and Goethe. "Were I to choose my occupation in Paradise," Johnny is quoted in a footnote, "I would sit down to read for all eternity Goethe's writings." Johnny Appleseed spending eternity with the volumes of Goethe is one of the most incongruous pictures ever imagined.

Three years later, Snider published *The Freeburgers*, a novel in the romantic German style built about the influence of a Johnny Appleseed tree upon the life of a young visionary. Johnny is presented as an itinerant nurseryman, fiddler, rhymer, singer, and philosopher. His fiddle "somewhat larger than the usual size" he played with amazing versatility. "He would thrum it, or pick it, like a guitar; he would place it between his knees like a violincello, and draw the bow upon its strings; finally he would put it against his shoulder and play it like the ordinary violin." His voice was "of the finest texture."

Five years later *Johnny Appleseed's Rhymes* appeared under the editing of "Theophilus Middling" (Snider). Middling in his capacity of "peripatetic lecturer and purveyor general to literary clubs" had run across the rhymes here and there in the Middle West. The poet had been in Ohio, Indiana, in the valley of the Illinois, in Kentucky, as far south as Tennessee, and as far west as the Rockies. "He seems to flit about the Mississippi Valley defiant of time and place, now here, now there, like a spirit disembodied." How true!

The rhymes are mostly aphoristic jingles such as:

> Tell me if you can
> Who is the man
> That is able to make
> The greatest mistake?—
> Well the answer scan:
> 'Tis the greatest man.
>
> .   .   .   .
>
> Even to the mule
> Man can sometimes go to school,
> If the man too be a mule.

Philosopher-poet Johnny had read not only his beloved Goethe, but all the German philosophers and Darwin. Middling's running comment is in the manner of *Sartor Resartus*, a ridiculous hodge-podge of references to Professor Reginald Brazenose and Colonel Godlove Himmelshine, comparisons of texts, references to ancients and moderns, and philological quibbling.

In the *St. Louis Movement* (1902) Snider admitted that he had first heard the Appleseed story when a youth around Mansfield, and that it had influenced him very deeply. He felt that it was the "only original American Mythus," a true "creative center," as indeed it has been. Snider's many writings, rarely read now except as curiosities, deserve this extended mention chiefly because of their role in turning Johnny into a rhymer-minstrel and because of the regional Missouri tales that seem to have resulted from them. These have found their way into various local papers and historical reports and seem to reflect a vigorous oral circulation. The Indian wife tale has been already mentioned. His appletrees are said to have lingered for many years in the St. Charles country, along the old Howell's Ferry road.

Up Salt River at Spalding Springs, Johnny is said to have appeared at Frenchman Bouvet's fort one night chanting:

> I sow while others reap,
> Be sure my warning keep,
> Indians will come by break of day,
> Indians hunting scalps, I say.

The union of the Ohio border hero with Snider's rhymer is obvious.

He planted widely in Missouri, Kansas, and Arkansas, go the tales. A narrative printed by Fred W. Allsopp in *Folklore of Romantic Arkansas* (1931) uses episodes from Mrs. Atkinson's novel, along with Snider's poetry, and a dash of the Arkansas traveler, with whom Johnny's shade seems to be combining, just as in Missouri, it is said to have merged with a ribald Johnny Applejack, and in Pennsylvania with the historic Coal Oil Johnny.

As a literary device, John Chapman is now standard equipment whenever the stage must be set on the Middle border. Local history pageants are never without him. In novels, plays, and poetry he steps accommodatingly out of the shadows to assist at any opportune time. In addition to the older fiction, already mentioned, he has had a part in such recent novels as Merle Colby's *All Ye People,* Howard Fast's *The Tall Hunter,* Robert Harper's *Trumpet in the Wilderness,* Clark McMeekin's *Reckon with the River,* Ethel Hull Miller's *Out of the Roaring Loom,* Mary Schumann's *My Blood and My Treasure,* Vachel Lindsay's *The Golden Book of Springfield,* and Ross Lockridge's *Raintree County.*

The poets find him a perennial theme that freshens every spring and fall with blossom time and apple harvest. Lydia Maria Child, Carl Sandburg, Rosemary and Stephen Vincent Benét, Frances Frost, Vachel Lindsay, Edgar Lee Masters, Nancy Byrd Turner, William Henry Venable, and many more have sung his praise.

Lydia Maria Child's "Apple-Seed John" has long been the favorite. Published first in *St. Nicholas* (1880), it has been reprinted many times. It tells a simple story of a kindly unspectacular man who spent his life doing things for others:

> He said at the last: "Tis a comfort to feel
> I've done good in the world, though not a great deal."

A recent favorite has been the little ballad, "Johnny Appleseed," that the Benéts included in their *Book of Americans* (1933). It is trimly turned and unpretentious. Since no true folk ballad on Johnny has yet been found, the musical setting of this piece by Elie Siegmeister for the American Ballad Singers serves as a charming substitute.

Vachel Lindsay came nearer than any other poet to catching the epic quality in Chapman's legend and giving it poetical form. To him, Johnny Appleseed was the embodiment of Walt Whitman's common man living for and with his fellows and symbolizing the spirit of the new American democracy. In his novel, *The Golden Book of Springfield* (1920) Chapman becomes a canonized saint. His seeds produce the world's first orchards of the "Apple Amaranth," a mystic fruit that engenders heroes and imparts to all who eat of it a love of eternal beauty; pilgrims follow his trails eastward and westward planting America and eventually all the world with the sacred amaranth. The boughs even mount to the doorsteps of heaven and clamber over the walls to adorn the highest towers.

He was a New England kind of saint, [Lindsay wrote in *The Litany of Washington Street* (1909)] much like a Hindu saint, akin to Thoreau and Emerson . . . He kept moving for a lifetime toward the sunset, on what we would call "The Mystical Johnny Appleseed Highway," leaving in his wake orchards bursting and foaming with rich fruit, gifts for mankind to find long after . . . Johnny Appleseed's appletrees marched straight west, past his grave at Fort Wayne, Indiana, through the best apple country of Illinois to the Pacific, and stands there singing Whitman's "Passage to India."

The Appleseed story itself Lindsay embodied in the long three-part "In Praise of Johnny Appleseed" (1921, 1927, 1928), which he is said to have called his greatest work. Its rambling method, free-verse form, and vivid frontier imagery tell the story of John's trip over the Appalachian barricade, his life with the Indians and settlers, and his beatification in old age. It remains the greatest of the Appleseed poems. Eunice Lea Kettering has recently given it a beautiful choral setting.

Lindsay never dropped the Appleseed theme. Lyric after lyric was added to the saga: "The Apple-Barrel of Johnny Appleseed" and "Johnny Appleseed Still Further West" in *Going to the Sun* (1923); "How Johnny Appleseed Walked Alone in the Jungle of Heaven," "How Johnny Appleseed Speaks of the Appleblossom Amaranth That Will Come to

This City," "Johnny Appleseed Speaks of Great Cities in the Future," "Johnny Appleseed's Hymn to the Sun," "Johnny Appleseed's Ship Comes In," "Johnny Appleseed's Wife from the Palace of Eve," "Johnny Appleseed's Wife of the Mind," and "The Fairy from the Appleseed" in the *Collected Poems* of 1927.

A comparison of editions shows that Lindsay even transferred to this Appleseed category certain lyrics that had been written originally under other titles on other themes. He had for years been seeking a story and poetical device with which he could attain an integration that would express the soul of America. His continuing interest in the story of John Chapman, his additions to it, and his eager search for information as late as 1929 suggest that he contemplated a further longer work. Even in their present form, the various lyrics on Johnny Appleseed fit together in one extended work of dignity and power.

5

During recent decades, as conservation and reclamation began to emerge during major national worries, it was inevitable that the shade of Chapman should soon appear to direct the new work.

As early as 1929, a delightful folklore play by Henry Bailey Stevens pitted the tree-planting Johnny Appleseed against the tree-slaughtering Paul Bunyan.

When the boys of the Civilian Conservation Corps began reforesting barren slopes, fighting insect pests, and planting trees along bare roads, Lewis Mumford described them in *Faith for Living* (1940) as pushing the Johnny Appleseed trail just a little farther toward its ultimate goal.

Robert West Howard in his *Two Billion Acre Farm* (1945) looked back to John as the "American saint who saw the vision of a settled agriculture that would ensure the 'God's country' he preached and believed."

And Louis Bromfield finds him always somewhere close in his Pleasant Valley, the patron saint "of the earth and stream and forests."

A fine dramatic tribute to Johnny's interest in everything good and fruitful appeared in Marc Connelly's and Arnold Sungaard's play, *Everywhere I Roam*, that opened for a short run at the National Theatre, New York, in December, 1938. In it Chapman became the symbol of all wholesomeness that centers in the land and in simple living as opposed to the standardization and destruction of values that must arise from modern tendencies toward industrialization.

Among John Chapman's beneficent pursuits, it used to be said, was the distribution of medicinal herbs and plants. Now in a later century he has added all flowers and trees to his catalogue and has become the patron of floriculture too. All beauty and fruitfulness are in his keeping.

In Richmond, Indiana, it is said that flowers were a passion with him and that he made several trips to Pennsylvania for the express purpose of bringing bulbs and seeds.

In Mr. Bromfield's Ohio, John is even credited with introduction of the wild day lilies and graceful old Norway spruces that mark early dooryards.

It is not surprising, therefore, that organized garden clubs long ago came under his kindly direction, and that in 1940 the Men's Garden Clubs of America established a national annual Johnny Appleseed Award for the most meritorious service in gardening and horticulture performed by one of their members. In 1950, stimulated by the garden clubs of

Ohio, the Ohio state department of highways officially designated state routes 33, 31, and 25 a "Johnny Appleseed Highway" north and south across the state, though it does not follow specific John Chapman trails.

The current vitality of the Appleseed tradition is apparent everywhere. A chain of memorials now reaches from Massachusetts to Illinois. Every year sees his name recurring in editorials, articles, books, poetry, ballet, music, and drama.

And the folk tales sprout as healthily as ever. Even as these last paragraphs have been in the writing, a letter from Kentucky says that John once traveled the mountains of that state paying his board by giving his hosts appleseeds, and an informant from Oregon insists that he started the early orchards in her state. He has been out in Arkansas and Missouri again and reappears, robust and rollicking, in an Ozark yarn related by Vance Randolph in *Who Blowed Up the Church House?* The tale will doubtless have a large and happy following, for it has already been reprinted, as the single sampling of American folklore, in a popular anthology, *The World of History*, edited by Courtlandt Canby and Nancy E. Gross for the Society of American Historians.[5]

Where the Chapmans settled in 1804 on Duck Creek, in Washington County, Ohio, says a newspaper feature,[6] Johnny returns ever autumn to the old family cemetery atop a hill south of Dexter City, in which a half-brother and other relatives lie buried. He is usually seen swinging his legs happily from the branch of a gnarled appletree near the gravestones, munching an apple, and reading a New Church tract. Only specially favored persons may be aware of him, of course—a woman on her way to do a neighborly deed, or a small boy off to the woods with eyes that have not yet become blinded to the magic that lurks in September haze.

It is quite true that Johnny Appleseed is there, happy and vigorous, and his dreams as he stretches his sturdy feet to the autumn sun are not so much of adventures past as of work to come.

He'll be out your way next.

APPENDIX A · John Chapman's Ancestry

APPENDIX B · John Chapman's Nurseries

APPENDIX C · John Chapman's Land Holdings

John Chapman's Ancestry

For the documented reconstruction of the Chapman-Simons family lines, see Florence E. Wheeler's "John Chapman's Line of Descent from Edward Chapman of Ipswich," *Ohio Archaeological and Historical Quarterly*, XLVIII (Jan., 1939), 28-33, from which the following summary has been derived.

I. CHAPMAN LINE

1. Edward Chapman
   b. England _____
   d. Ipswich, Mass., 1678
   married Mary Symonds
2. John Chapman
   b. Ipswich _____
   d. Ipswich, 1677
   married Rebecca Smith, 1675
3. John Chapman, Sr.
   b. Ipswich, 1676
   d. Tewksbury, 1739
   married Elizabeth Davis, 1702
4. John Chapman, Jr.
   baptised, Ipswich, 1714
   d. Tewksbury, 1760
   married Martha (Perley) Boardman, 1738/39
5. Nathaniel Chapman
   b. Tewksbury, 1746
   d. Salem, or Lower Salem, Washington County, Ohio, 1807
   married (1st) Elizabeth Simons (or Simonds) of Leominster, Mass., August 9, 1769
   CHILDREN: Elizabeth, b. November 18, 1770

John, b. September 26, 1774 ("Johnny Appleseed")
Nathaniel, b. June 26, 1776
married (2nd) Lucy Cooley of Longmeadow, July 24, 1780
CHILDREN: Nathaniel, b. December, 1781
Abner, b. July 16, 1783
Pierly, b. March 6, 1785
Lucy, b. July 21, 1787
Patty, b. February 26, 1790
Persis, b. November 15, 1793
Mary, b. January 19, 1796
Jonathan Cooley, b. February 2, 1798
Davis, b. April 25, 1800
Sally, b. April 23, 1803

II. SIMONDS (SIMONS) LINE

1. William Simonds, Sr.
b. England _____
d. Woburn, Mass., 1672
married Judith (Phippen) Hayward, 1643/4
2. James Simonds
b. Woburn, 1658
d. Woburn, 1717
married Susanna Blodgett, 1685
3. James Simonds
b. Woburn, 1686
d. Woburn, 1775
married Mary Fowle, 1714
4. James Simons
b. Woburn, 1717
d. Leominster _____
married Anna Lawrence, 1740
5. Elizabeth Simons
b. Leominster, 1748/9
d. Leominster, 1776
married Nathaniel Chapman, February 8, 1770

John Chapman's Nurseries

Traditional as well as documentable nurseries have been listed, but only those for which there is at least one early printed reference.

PENNSYLVANIA

WARREN COUNTY   On Big Brokenstraw Creek, "near's White's," *c.* 1797–1804. (Lansing Wetmore in Warren, Pa., *Ledger*, March 29, 1853: J. S. Schenck and W. S. Rann, eds., *History of Warren County, Pennsylvania*, 1887, 153-4.)

VENANGO COUNTY   Near Franklin on French Creek, *c.* 1798–1804. (Wetmore, *loc. cit.;* R. I. Curtis in *Ohio Pomological Society Transactions*, 1859, 68-9.)

OHIO

CARROLL COUNTY   One mile southwest of Carrollton on "the old Ward farm," *c.* 1801. (H. J. Eckley, ed., *History of Carroll and Harrison Counties, Ohio*, 1921, I, 15; *Carroll Republican*, February, 1887.)

BELMONT COUNTY   On headwaters of the Big Stillwater, between Morristown and Freeport, *c.* 1801. (J. A. Caldwell, *History of Belmont and Jefferson Counties*, 1880, 191-3.)

JEFFERSON COUNTY   Near the mouth of George's Run, four miles below Steubenville, opposite Wellsburg, W. Va., *c.* 1801. (*Ibid.*)

LICKING COUNTY   On "Scotland farm, about three miles in a northeasterly direction from Newark," *c.* 1812. (Isaac Smucker, *Our Pioneers*, 1872, 15.)

COSHOCTON COUNTY   In New Castle Township, near the blockhouse "at the northwest corner of the Giffin section, on the farm now owned by Daniel McKee," *c.* 1807–1812. (N. N. Hill, *History of Coshocton County, Ohio,* 1881, 567.)

In Tiverton Township, "near the north line of lot 36, Section 3, a short distance from the Mohican River," *c.* 1807–1817. (*Ibid.,* 595.)

On "Nursery Island" in the Mohican River, a short distance from the line between Butler Township, Knox County, and Coshocton County, *c.* 1807–1812. (N. N. Hill, *History of Knox County, Ohio,* 1881, 433.)

KNOX COUNTY   On the North bank of Owl Creek, in the "Indian Fields" directly west of Center Run, *c.* 1807–1812. (A. Banning Norton, *A History of Knox County, Ohio,* 1862, xi.)

At Mount Vernon, "on the ground where James W. Forrest established his pottery," *c.* 1807–1812. (*Ibid.*)

RICHLAND COUNTY   On the west bank of Rocky Fork, "on the flats, within the present limits of Mansfield, near where once stood the Pittsburgh, Fort Wayne and Chicago Railway Depot," *c.* 1812–1820. (H. S. Knapp, *History of the Pioneer and Modern Times of Ashland County,* 1863, 28; A. A. Graham, *History of Richland County, Ohio,* 1880, 269-71; E. Bonar McLaughlin, *Pioneer Directory and Scrap Book . . . of Richland County, Ohio,* 1887, 15.)

Between Charles Mills and Mansfield, "on the farm now owned by Mr. Pittinger," no date suggested. (Knapp, *loc. cit.*)

In Sandusky Township, S. W. Quarter, Section 24, Township 20 N., Range 21 E., *c.* 1818. (Appendix C.)

ASHLAND COUNTY   On the Black Fork, "on the Ruffner quarter section," *c.* 1812. (Knapp, 535.)

In Green Township, S. E. Quarter of Section 27, Township 20, Range 16, "near the southeast corner," *c.* 1829. (See John Oliver lease, Appendix C.)

On the Black Fork in Green Township, "on the farm now owned by Michael Hogan," N. W. Quarter, Section 20, Township 20 N., Range 16 E, *c.* 1815–1818. (Knapp, *loc. cit.,* Mansfield *Ohio Liberal,* August 13, 1873; Appendix C.)

On the Black Fork "near Petersburg" (now Mifflinville), no date suggested. (*Ohio Liberal,* August 13, 1873.)

In Orange Township, "where Leidigh's Mill now stands," *c.* 1818. (Knapp, *loc. cit.*)

In Mohican Township, on Jerome Fork, in S. W. Quarter, Section 26, Range 15, Township 31, *c.* 1823. (Appendix C; Knapp, 397.)

In Green Township, "on the John Murphy place northeast of the farm owned by the late James Rowland," no date suggested. (Knapp, 308.)

HANCOCK COUNTY   On the Blanchard River "near the headwaters," *c.* 1828 (*Putnam County Pioneer Reminiscences,* No. 1, 1878, 60; No. 2, 1887, 45; *History of Defiance County, Ohio,* 1883, 109.)

DEFIANCE COUNTY   At the mouth of Tiffin River, about one mile above Defiance, "on lands now owned by Charles Krotz," *c.* 1828. (*History of Defiance County,* 1883, 109.)

On the Maumee River "opposite Snaketown" (now Florida, *c.* 1829–1830. (*Ibid.*)

ALLEN COUNTY   Along the Auglaize River, Amanda Township, on land leased of Jacob Harter, 1828. (Appendix C.)

In Amanda Township on Dye Sutherland farm in Section 15, *c.* 1828. (*History of Allen County, Ohio,* 1885, 237.)

AUGLAIZE COUNTY   Along the St. Marys River, south of the city of St. Marys, on land leased of Picket Doute, 1828. (Appendix C.)

In Logan Township on the William Berryman farm in N. E. Quarter, Section 27, *c.* 1828. (C. W. Williamson, *History of Western Ohio and Auglaize County,* 1905, 705.)

MERCER COUNTY   On the St. Marys River below Shanesville (now Rockford) on land leased of William B. Hedges, 1828. (*History of Van Wert and Mercer Counties, Ohio,* 1882, 121-2; Appendix C.)

HURON COUNTY   In New Haven Township, Section 4, "on the lands now owned by George Ganung, on the east side of the marsh," *c.* 1825. (*Fire Lands Pioneer,* V, 61-3.)

LOGAN COUNTY   On Mill Branch, "on the farm now owned by

Alonzo and Allen West," *c.* 1828 (Joshua Antrim, *History of Champaign and Logan Counties*, 1872, 148-60.)
"Somewhere on Stony Creek," *c.* 1828. (Ibid.)

INDIANA

ALLEN COUNTY   Along the north bank of the Maumee River in Milan Township on land purchased in 1834. (Appendix C.)
West of the St. Joseph River in Washington Township, about three miles north of Fort Wayne, *c.* 1828 or 1845. (*Ohio Liberal*, Aug. 20, 27, 1873; John W. Dawson, letter in Fort Wayne *Sentinel*, Oct. 21, 1871.)

JAY COUNTY   North of the Wabash River in Wabash Township on land purchased in 1836. (Appendix C.)

John Chapman's Land Holdings

1797–1804. French Creek Township, Venango County, Pennsylvania. "He took up land several times, but would soon find himself without any, by reason of some other person 'jumping' his claim." (J. H. Newton, *History of Venango County, Pennsylvania*, 1879, 595.)

1809. Mount Vernon, Knox County, Ohio. Lots 145 and 147 purchased of Joseph Walker for $50, Sept. 14, 1809 (Knox County Deeds A, 116). Lot 145 sold to Jesse B. Thomas, Nov. 3, 1828, for $30. Entered for record, Nov. 5, 1828. (*Ibid.*, G, 504.)

1814. Washington Township, Richland County, Ohio. N. E. Quarter, Section 1, Township 20, Range 18. 160 acres in Virginia Military District School Lands, value $320. 99-year lease, May 31, 1814, to John Chapman and Jane Cunningham. Contingent expenses $10. One interest payment, 1820, $19.20. Forfeited 1823. (Virginia Military School Land Ledger, Auditor of State, 196.)

1814. Madison Township, Richland County, Ohio, S. E. Quarter, Section 15, Township 21, Range 18. 160 acres, in Virginia Military District School Lands, value $320. 99-year lease, Aug. 22, 1814. Contingent expenses $10. Interest payments, 1822, $57; 1828, $115; 1829–36, $19.20 yearly; 1837, $7.38 on 70 acres from Aug. 22, 1836; 1838–44, $8.40 yearly. 70 acres forfeited May 28, 1853. (Virginia Military School Land Ledger, 275.) Recorded June 17, 1818, (Richland County Deeds, I, 493.) 90 acres assigned to Alexander Curran and John C. Gilkison, June, 1818 (*Ibid.*, I, 493.) 34 acres assigned to Henry H. Wilcoxen, June 1, 1818 (*Ibid.*, I, 493). 20 acres assigned to Mathias Day, Nov. 20, 1818 (*Ibid.*, II, 26.)

1815. Wooster Township, Wayne County, Ohio. N. E. Quarter,

Section 21, Township 15, Range 13. 160 acres, in Virginia Military District School Lands, value $320. 99-year lease to Richard Whaley, Oct. 13, 1814; assigned to John Chapman, Feb. 28, 1815, for $100. No further record. (Wayne County Deeds, I, 355.)

1815. Green Township, Ashland County, Ohio. N. W. Quarter, Section 20, Township 20, Range 16. 160 acres, in Virginia Military District School Lands, value $320. 99-year lease, April 10, 1815. Contingent expenses $10. Recorded, Richland County Deeds, I, 521; Virginia Military School Land Ledger B, 73.)

1818. Mansfield, Richland County, Ohio. Lot 265, purchased of Henry Wilcoxen for $120, June 1, 1818, recorded Aug. 6, 1818 (Richland County Deeds, I, 523). Sold to Jesse Edgington, Oct. 30, 1818. (*Ibid.*, I, 614.)

1818. Sandusky Township, Richland County, Ohio. S. W. Quarter, Section 24, Township 20, Range 20. 160 acres, in Virginia Military District School Lands, value $320. 99-year lease to Moses Modie, June 7, 1815, assigned to William Huff, then to John Chapman, April 27, 1818. No further record. (Richland County Deeds, I, 482.)

1823. Mohican Township, Ashland County, Ohio. Two and one half acres in S. W. Quarter, Section 26, Township 21, Range 15, purchased of Alexander Finley June 25, 1823, for $40. Recorded July 26, 1826 (Wayne County Deeds, IV, 396). Abandoned.

1825. Plain Township, Wayne County, Ohio. 14 acres in S. W. Quarter, Section 29, Township 19, Range 14, purchased of Isaac and Minerva Hatch, Dec. 21, 1825, for $60. Recorded July 26, 1826. (Wayne County Deeds, IV, 397.) Sold to John H. Pile, Sept. 8, 1832, for $50 (*Ibid.*, XXXII, 46.)

1826. Orange Township, Ashland County, Ohio. One half acre in S. E. Quarter, Section 27, Township 20, Range 16. Leased April 22, 1826, by John Oliver, landlord, to John Chapman, tenant, a piece of ground "where the said John Chapman plants fruit." Term 40 years. Payment 20 appletrees Recorded Aug. 18, 1829 (Richland County Deeds, VI, 220).

1828. Amanda Township, Allen County, Ohio. One half acre in Section 4, Township 4 South, Range 5 East, "where the said John doth plant an Apple Nursery." Leased of Jacob Harter, __ day of April, 1828. Term 40 years. Payment 40 apple-trees at the end of five years. Acknowledged by Jacob Harter, July 16, 1829. Recorded May 17, 1830 (Mercer County Deeds, B, 15). Payment received, April 13, 1835, and recorded April 14, 1835 (*Ibid.*, C, 188-89.)

1828. St. Marys Township, Auglaize County, Ohio. One half acre in Section 10, Township 6, Range 4, East, "where the said John doth plant an Apple nursery." Leased of Picket Doute, April 6, 1828. Term 40 years. Payment 40 appletrees at the end of five years. Acknowledged by Picket Doute, May 15, 1830. Recorded May 17, 1830 (*Ibid.*, B, 14). Payment received April 2, 1835, and recorded April 2, 1835 (*Ibid.*, C, 177).

1828. Dublin Township, Mercer County, Ohio. "A certain enclosed lot or piece of ground lying below the Little Branch, below Shanesville, between the Little Lane and the River, to John Chapman for the purpose of sowing apple-seeds on, and is to be cultivated in a nursery for the space of ten years, more or less. . . ." Leased of William B. Hedges, April 29, 1828. Payment, 1,000 apple trees "to be taken as they average suitable for the market or transplanting on equal proportion for the space of ten years . . . on an average of One Hundred Apple Trees per year. . . ." Not recorded. (*History of Van Wert and Mercer Counties*, 1882, pp. 121-2.)

1834. Milan Township, Allen County, Indiana. Fraction of S. E. Quarter, Section 28, Township 31 North, Range 14 East. 42.11 acres of canal land, north of the Maumee River at $2.50. Entered at the Fort Wayne Land Office, April 28, 1834 (Entry Book, County Auditor; Descriptive Tract Book, Register of Installments, Wabash and Erie Canal, Auditor of State, 127). Final payment, April 28, 1834. (Register of Final Payments, Wabash and Erie Canal, Auditor of State, 19).

1834. Maumee Township, Allen County, Indiana. Fraction of S. E. Quarter, Section 3, Township 31 North, Range 15 East. 99.03 acres of canal land at $1.50. Entered at the Fort Wayne Land Office, May 23, 1834 (Entry Book; Descriptive Tract Book). Final Payment, Sept. 21, 1853, in name of John F. Swift, purchaser (Register of Final Payments, 191).

1834. Mt. Blanchard Village, Hancock County, Ohio. Lots 51, 52, 53. Purchased of A. M. Lake, Dec. 24, 1834. Recorded Oct. 8, 1835 (Hancock County Deeds, I, 380). Sold to Michael Shafer, May 20, 1839 (Ibid., III, 118).

1836. Maumee Township, Allen County, Indiana. East fraction of S. E. Quarter, Section 4, Township 31 North of Range 15 East. 18.70 acres at $1.25. Total $23.38. Entered at the Fort Wayne Land Office, March 10, 1836 (Entry Book). Application, Receipt, and Certificate, March 11, 1836; Patent March 20, 1837 (General Land Office Records, National Archives, and U. S. Department of the Interior).

1836. Wabash Township, Jay County, Indiana. S. E. fraction of N. W. Quarter, Section 3, Township 24 North, Range 15 East. 74.04 acres at $1.25. Total $92.55. Entered at the Fort Wayne Land Office March 11, 1836 (Tract Book, Jay County Recorder's Office, 86). Application, Receipt, and Certificate, March 11, 1836; Patent March 20, 1837 (General Land Office Records, National Archives and U. S. Department of the Interior).

1838. Eel River Township, Allen County, Indiana, S. E. Quarter of N. W. Quarter, Section 22, Township 32 North, Range 11 East. 40 acres at $1.25. Total $50. Entered at the Fort Wayne Land Office, May 16, 1838 (Entry Book); Deed Register, State Archives (Indiana State Library); Application, Receipt, and Certificate, May 16, 1838; Patent, September 20, 1839 (General Land Office Records, National Archives and U. S. Department of The Interior).

Bibliography, Notes, and Index

Notes

CHAPTER ONE

1. The account appeared first on March 29, 1853, in a series of historical sketches for the Warren (Pa.), *Ledger*. It was copied with a few minor changes in J. S. Schenck and W. S. Rann (eds.), *History of Warren County, Pennsylvania* (Syracuse, 1887), 153-54. It has been completely overlooked in the development of the popular myth.

2. Charles Peirce, *A Meteorological Account of the Weather in Philadelphia from January 1, 1790, to January 1, 1847* (Phila., 1847), 214.

3. Usually credited to Mrs. Ernestine Perry, Springfield, Mass. The bulk of the important genealogical detective work, however, has been done by Miss Florence E. Wheeler, Leominster public librarian.

4. Leominster, Mass., *Vital Records . . .* (Worcester, 1911), 36-7; *Leominster 200th Anniversary* (Leominster, 1940), 14. The original birth entry in the City Clerk's office reads:

> John Chapman Sun of
> Nathanael and Elizabeth
> Chapman Born at Leominster
> September ye 26th 1774

5. Florence E. Wheeler, "John Chapman's Line of Descent from Edward Chapman of Ipswich," *Ohio Archaeological and Historical Quarterly* (OAHQ), XLVIII (1939), 28-33; Jacob Chapman, *A Genealogy, Edward Chapman of Ipswich, Mass., 1642-1678 and His Descendents* (Concord, N. H., 1893); Leominster, Mass., First Congregational Church Records; Rufus P. Stebbins, *A Centennial Discourse Delivered to the First Congregational Church and Society in Leominster, September 24, 1843;* David Wilder, *History of Leominster . . .* (Fitchburg, 1853).

6. Destroyed by fire in August, 1896. Reproduced in Mary A. Tolman, *Old Landmarks in Leominster* (Leominster, 1896), Plate 6.

7. Miss Fannie P. Gates, local historian of Leominster, is the ac-

cepted authority for identification of John Chapman's birth site. In her family, who have owned the land for more than 125 years, the tract was long referred to as the "Nathaniel Chapman lot." The present Whiting Gates farm includes all three tracts formerly occupied by the Johnson brothers. The present residence is on the Asa Johnson place just south of, and across the road from, the Jonathan Johnson lot where the Chapmans lived. (Miss Gates, letter, Feb. 10, 1938.)

8. Wilder, *op. cit.*, 41; Henry S. Nourse, *The Military Annals of Lancaster, Massachusetts* (Lancaster, 1889), 112-13; records, Adjutant General's Office, War Department, Wash., D. C.

There is one brief glimpse of the Chapman family in the records of the First Congregational Church, June 25, 1775, when Nathaniel and Elizabeth together with their two children, Elizabeth and John, were established in full membership under the pastorate of the Reverend Francis Gardner. (*Records*, 32, 59)

An original company return preserved in Leominster public library shows that Nathaniel Chapman, then serving under Captain Wilder, was 28 years old, and was 5 feet 9 inches tall.

9. Original in the possession of Mrs. Kitty Dix Humphrey, Detroit, Mich., a great-granddaughter of Elizabeth Chapman, sister of John. First published by the Johnny Appleseed Memorial Commission, Fort Wayne, Ind., in a mimeographed booklet edited by Robert C. Harris (1936).

10. Zebedee Simons, Elizabeth's brother, had enlisted along with Chapman in the original company of Minute Men from Leominster.

11. *Vital Records*, 36-7, 301.

12. *Massachusetts Soldiers and Sailors of the Revolutionary War* (Boston, 1896–1908), III, 333; miscellaneous records, Adjutant General's Office, War Department; *Journals of the Continental Congress, 1774–1789* (Wash., 1910), XI, 472; XVII, 670-72, 793.

13. Richard Salter Storrs, *Proceedings at the Centennial Celebration . . . of Longmeadow* (Hartford, 1883), 228, and Genealogical Appendix, 51; Springfield, Mass., Marriage Records, 174; Dr. Stephen Williams' *Records of Baptisms, Admissions into and Dismissions from the Church . . . in the Town of Longmeadow.*

For the most important clue to the Chapmans during this period, however, modern investigators are obliged to old Jabez Colton, town clerk in Longmeadow about the beginning of the 1800's. He was the community's chief scholar for many years and general master of the inkpot. He had a bent for neighborhood genealogy and scrupulously gleaned names and dates from gravestones, Bibles, town records, and memories. From his collections to a large degree Storrs compiled his genealogical appendix. Nathaniel Chapman's second marriage and the births of their large family as recorded by Colton are printed in Storrs.

14. *Heads of Families, First Census of the United States: 1790, State of Massachusetts* (Washington, 1908), 116. The identity of the Nathaniel Chapman house in Longmeadow has been established chiefly through the labors of Miss Annie Emerson, local historian of early houses. Formerly the house stood at 135 Bliss Road. The remodeled structure has been moved around the corner to 14 Fairfield Terrace.

CHAPTER TWO

1. J. H. Newton, *History of Venango County, Pennsylvania* (Columbus, 1879), 120, 451.
2. *Op. cit.*
3. General historical background from Paul Demund Evans, *The Holland Land Company* (Buffalo, 1924); Schenck and Rann, *op. cit.;* various state and county histories and related studies.

   Dr. Evans has never noted Chapman's name among the Holland Land Company records. Messrs. Van Eeghen of Amsterdam searched the company's archives for the present study in 1938 without finding any clues.
4. Newton, *op. cit.*, 595.
5. Newton had apparently examined the original ledgers in 1879 and copied from them a sampling of names that happened to include the Chapmans. The ledgers cannot be located today.
6. Census 1800, National Archives.
7. R. I. Curtis, "John Chapman, alias 'Johnny Appleseed,'" *Ohio Pomological Society Transactions* (Columbus, 1859), 68-9.
8. Newton, 595.
9. W. M. Glines, *Johnny Appleseed by One Who Knew Him* (Columbus, 1922).

CHAPTER THREE

1. John Chapman estate papers, Allen County, Indiana; reprinted in Robert C. Harris (ed.), "Johnny Appleseed Source Book," *Old Fort News*, IX (March-June, 1945), 11.

2. Charlemont, Mass., *Vital Records* (Boston, 1917), 196.

3. Curtis, *op. cit.*

4. Background data can be studied in S. A. Beach, *The Apples of New York* (Albany, 1905); W. J. Green, Paul Thayer, and J. B. Keil, *Varieties of Apples in Ohio* (Ohio Agricultural Experiment Station Bull. No. 290); S. P. Hildreth, *Pioneer History . . . of the Ohio Valley* (Cincinnati, 1848); and in a great variety of local histories.

5. Writers' Program, W.P.A., *Tales of Pioneer Pittsburgh* (Phila., 1937); Henry A. Pershing, *Johnny Appleseed and His Time* (Strasburg, Va., 1930); James Lattimore Himrod, *Johnny Appleseed . . . by the Grandson of One Who Knew Him Well* (Chicago, 1926); Daniel Rasneck, "Patron Saint of All Orchards Spent Life Fulfilling New Year's Resolution to Become Apple Missionary," Indianapolis *Sunday Star*, Jan. 10, 1937; E. John Long, "Johnny Appleseed in Pittsburgh," *Western Pennsylvania Historical Magazine*, XIII, 256-260; Clarence Edward MacCartney, *Right Here in Pittsburgh* (Pittsburgh, 1937); and Henry Chapin, *The Adventures of Johnny Appleseed* (New York, 1930).

6. Letters, Eleanor Atkinson to author, 1937–1940.

7. Van Wyck Brooks, *The World of Washington Irving* (New York, 1944), 119; Pershing, *op. cit.;* letters to the author from numerous persons in Butler, Crawford, Erie, and Washington counties, and LeRaysville, Pa.; Kinzua, Quaker Bridge, Rochester, and Wilson, N. Y.; various newspaper clippings. In 1937 a W.P.A. writer collected from Frank G. Ellsworth, 87, of Turk Hill Road, Perinton, N. Y., a tradition that his great-grandfather's Baldwin orchard was planted by Johnny (letter, John A. Lowe to author, Feb. 5, 1937.) A tree supposedly his was reported at Eagle Rock, Venango County, in 1915 (*Green's Fruit Grower*, XXXV, 37).

8. Dr. E. W. E. Schear, Westerville, O., great-grandson of Frederick Medsger.

9. Carroll (Ohio) *Republican*, February, 1887; reprinted in H. J. Eckley (ed.), *History of Carroll and Harrison Counties, Ohio* (Chicago, 1921), I, 15. Chapman's traditional planting in Carroll County was identified as on the Ward or James Huston farm.

10. J. A. Caldwell, *History of Belmont and Jefferson Counties, Ohio* (Wheeling, 1880), 191-93; J. B. Doyle, *20th Century History of Steubenville and Jefferson County, Ohio* (Chicago, 1910), 198-99.

11. Caldwell, *op. cit.* A planting of trees on the Neff or Helpbringer farm on a hill above Glencoe has also been attributed to him.

12. MS. notes of John H. James, Urbana, O., Jan. 23, 1857. from conversation with William Stanvery (photostat in Ohio Arch. and Hist. Soc. Library); letter from James quoted in H. S. Knapp, *History of the Pioneer and Modern Times of Ashland County, Ohio* (Phila., 1863), 27-38; Isaac Smucker, *Our Pioneers* (Newark, O., 1872), 15. The Writers' Program, W.P.A., *Ohio Guide* (N. Y., 1940), 498, incorrectly locates this planting on the south fork of the Licking near Etna. There seems to be no basis for the statement in Writers' Program, W.P.A., *Berkshire Hills* (N.Y., 1939), 218, that about 1801 Chapman was trudging along the old Walker Brook trail to the topmost point of Jacob's Ladder near Becket, Mass. Nor do any facts support the story that in 1800, Chapman planted orchards down both banks of the Ohio as far as Cincinnati and Louisville (Missouri State Board of Horticulture, *Annual Report*, 1907).

CHAPTER FOUR

1. Erected by the school children of Ashland County: dedicated July 28, 1915, to "an Ohio hero, patron saint of American orchards, and soldier of peace."

2. Inscription: "Johnny Appleseed. An eccentric pauper-philanthropist who followed the advancing fringe of civilization was John Chapman. Barefooted and in rags, this kindly man carried appleseeds from the cider presses of Pennsylvania and planted them in small spots he cleared throughout Ohio. So was begun Ohio's great apple industry."

3. In Sherman-Heineman Park, dedicated by Richland Horticultural Society, Nov. 8, 1890; rededicated at new location Sept. 26, 1953.

4. Copus massacre monument, Mifflin Township, Ashland County, erected 1882.

5. Louis Bromfield, *Pleasant Valley* (N. Y., 1945) and *Malabar Farm* (N. Y., 1948). See also *The Farm* (N. Y., 1933) and "Johnny Appleseed and the Dauphin," *Saturday Review of Literature,* XXVIII (Jan. 6, 1945), 14-16.

6. A. Banning Norton, *A History of Knox County, Ohio* (Columbus, O., 1862), 50-51.

7. *Ibid.,* 133, "on the ground where James W. Forrest established his pottery, and known more recently as Rich's pottery." Cf.

N. N. Hill, *History of Knox County, Ohio* (Mount Vernon, 1881), 224.

8. Copy in Mount Vernon public library.

9. Hill, *Knox County*, 540.

10. Norton, 50

11. Howe, *op. cit.*, II, 485.

12. Caldwell, 192; Doyle, 198.

13. Storrs, Gen. Ap., 26.

14. See statements of Rosella Rice in appendix to M'Gaw, *op. cit.*, and in Howe, II, 485. Cf. *History of Washington County, Ohio* (Cleveland, 1881), 552.

15. Glines, *op. cit.*; Storrs, Gen. Ap., 26; typescript of censuses 1800, 1803, Ohio Arch. and Hist. Soc. Library; and original 1810 census report, Marietta College Library.

16. Dedicated Sept. 27, 1942, by the Johnny Appleseed Memorial Commission and the Washington County Pioneer Association Inscription:

> Without a hope of recompense
>   Without a thought of pride
> John Chapman planted appletrees,
>   And preached, and lived, and died.

17. Much of the lower Muskingum extension of the myth is traceable to the novels, *The Quest of John Chapman* by Newell Dwight Hillis (N. Y., 1904) and Mrs. Atkinson's *Romance of the Sower*.

18. N. N. Hill, *History of Coshocton County, Ohio* (Newark, O., 1881), 567.

19. Norton, 128.

20. Hill, *Coshocton County*, 567.

21. Hill, *Knox County*, 489.

22. Hill, *Coshocton County*, 595.

23. *Ibid.*

24. Original in Boy Scout headquarters, Mansfield, O.

25. Hill, *Knox County*, 433.

26. Knox County Deed Book A, 221. See Appendix C.

27. Purchased by Cecil Knerr in 1943.

28. Never sold by Chapman and overlooked by the executors of his estate in 1845.

29. According to Ben Jones, Licking County local historian, many trees planted by settlers in the Welsh Hills northeast of Granville came from Chapman's nursery on the Wilson tract north-

east of Newark. A man born in 1803 told Jones that such trees were planted in the White settlement of the Welsh Hills; other claimed were growing on the Jones farm but had been grafted with better fruit.

Other Licking Valley claims include: an orchard on the Rufus Enyart farm, three miles east of Hanover; an orchard on the Bert S. Everett farm west of Granville (the trees were given in return for hospitality); an orchard on the Willis A. Chamberlin farm south of Granville; an orchard on the Paul Lyons farm, Worthington road; an orchard near Fallsburg; a nursery on the Leonard Nichols farm along Mootz Run and a tree on the Pendleton farm, St. Albans Township; and old trees attributed to him around Buckeye Lake.

30. Smucker, *loc. cit.*
31. Smucker, 15.
32. On "Scotland Farm," *Ibid.*
33. The late Charles V. Critchfield, Mount Vernon, told the writer that his father remembered trees in the Owl Creek nursery still growing in 1840. See Hill, *Knox County*, 540.
34. Hill, *Coshocton County*, 595.
35. *Ibid.*, 567.
36. Numerous horticultural reports, newspaper stories, etc. The value of seeding trees on the Cincinnati market in May, 1806, was seven cents each (in July, six cents) for trees that would be ready to transplant the following fall or spring. Cincinnati *Liberty Hall*, May 5, 1806.

CHAPTER FIVE

1. The Tippecanoe extension of the myth is due chiefly to the Himrod and Pershing works, *op. cit.*
2. S. C. Coffinbury, letter to Mansfield *Shield and Banner*, Nov. 23, 1871, reprinted in Mansfield *Ohio Liberal*, Aug. 27, 1873; Henry Newman, letter, March, 1873, in A. A. Graham, *History of Richland County, Ohio* (Mansfield, 1880), 450; E. Bonar McLaughlin, *Pioneer Directory and Scrap Book . . . of Richland County, Ohio* (Mansfield, 1870), 15.
3. H. S. Knapp, *History of the Pioneer and Modern Times of Ashland County, Ohio* (Phila., 1863), 535.
4. *Ibid.*, 397; George William Hill, *History of Ashland County, Ohio* (Cleveland, 1880), 409.
5. W. W. Williams, *History of the Fire-Lands Comprising Huron*

and Erie Counties, Ohio (Cleveland, 1879), 298-300; *Fire Lands Pioneer,* I, 9, 11-12, 15; XV, 1080-81.

6. *Fire Lands Pioneer,* n.s., V, 126.

7. Aug. 25, 1812, quoted by Luther Coe in *Fire Lands Pioneer,* I, 46-47.

8. *Fire Lands Pioneer,* I, 14, 44-45; II, 30; *Western Reserve Historical Society Tract* No. 92, 44-45; Captain John Robison, *Journal* (typescript in Ohio Arch. and Hist. Soc. Library); various local histories of the area.

9. McLaughlin, 18.

10. Hill, *Ashland County,* 54; Howe, II, 475; J. P. Henderson, MS. letters, June 24, July 2, 1873, in *Brinkerhoff Scrapbook* (Ohio Arch. and Hist. Soc. Library); McLaughlin, 15; Mansfield *Ohio Liberal,* June 25, 1873.

11. Norton, 140; Mansfield *Ohio Liberal,* June 25, 1873; M'Gaw, Appendix, xvii; and various undated clippings in *Brinkerhoff Scrapbook.*

12. Norton, 140.

13. John Weldon, letter, undated clipping in *Brinkerhoff Scrapbook,* 1873.

14. *Ibid.*

15. *Western Reserve Historical Society Tract* No. 12, 3.

16. Worthington, O., Sept. 18, 1812.

17. *Western Reserve Historical Society Tract* No. 92, 64-68.

18. M'Gaw, Appendix; *OAHQ,* XXI, 379-95; Samuel Riddle, *History of Ashland County Pioneer Historical Society* (Ashland, 1888), 57-99; Howe, I, 257; Norton, Chap. XII; various local histories. Cf. Mansfield *Ohio Liberal,* Oct. 15, 22, 29, and Nov. 5, 1873.

19. *Western Reserve Historical Society Tract* No. 92, 69-70.

20. Hill, *Coshocton County,* 567.

21. *Ohio Liberal,* Oct. 15 to Nov. 5, 1873.

22. Chapman's name was included at the suggestion of Rosella Rice, local historian and free-lance writer.

23. Norton, 132, said that he traveled from settlement to settlement along "the Mohican, Owl Creek, the White Woman, the Muskingum, the Tuscarawas, and other water courses." A Morrow County *History* (1880) says he carried news of the Zimmer and Copus murders to Perry and Franklin townships. See also William J. Bahmer's *Centennial History of Coshocton County* (Chicago, 1909), I, 62-63.

CHAPTER SIX

1. *Fire Lands Pioneer*, V, 29.

2. *Ohio Liberal*, Aug. 13, 1873; Knapp, 535; Pershing, 128-29; *Fire Lands Pioneer*, I, 15.

   In Morrow County several nurseries and many early orchards were attributed to him, though none has substantiation. Orchards have been claimed for the Edwin M. Conklin farm in Westfield Township, the W. Smith Irwin farm northeast of Mt. Gilead, and the "school lands" in Gilead Township. He also visited Chester, Washington, and Franklin townships. Trees have been pointed out near Shelby. A Roxbury russet on the B. C. Ramey farm near Centerburg is said to memorialize seeds and seedlings brought by Peter Kile from his plantings near S. Woodbury and Fulton. *History of Morrow County, Ohio* (Chicago, 1880), 219-23, 292, 373; Ruth Winslow Gordon, *A Spray of Apple Blossoms* (Georgetown, O., 1935).

3. See Appendix C for the documents and other references for this and each of the following leases and purchases.

4. Martin Kellogg, letter from Norwalk *Reflector*, 1883, quoted in *Fire Lands Pioneer*, n.s., III (Jan., 1886), 77-78.

5. Charles Robertson, *History of Morgan County, Ohio* (Chicago, 1886), 485.

6. C. S. Coffinbury, *op. cit.*

7. Glines, *op. cit.*

8. *Ohio Liberal*, August 13, 1873.

9. Coffinbury, *op. cit.*

10. Glines, *op. cit.*; *Fire Lands Pioneer*, XI, 89; *History of Morrow County*, 292.

11. M'Gaw, Chap. III, and 1873 clipping in *Brinkerhoff Scrapbook*, Howe, II, 486.

12. *Ohio Liberal*, Aug. 13, 20, 1873.

    In addition to the fuller quoted sections of the Vandorn letter, all incidental dialogue is reproduced verbatim from the letter.

13. W. D. Haley, "Johnny Appleseed—A Pioneer Hero," *Harper's Monthly Magazine*, XLIII (Nov., 1871), 830-36.

CHAPTER SEVEN

1. *Report of the Society for Printing, Publishing and Circulating the Writings of Emanuel Swedenborg*, Manchester, England, Jan. 14, 1817.

2. See below. New Church background for this chapter depends heavily upon Carl Theophilus Odhner's *Annals of the New Church* (Bryn Athyn, Pa., 1904).

3. *Ibid.*, 451.

4. Coffinbury, *op. cit.*; *History of Defiance County, Ohio* (Chicago, 1883), 302.

5. *Some Letters of William Schlatter 1814 to 1825* (typescript from letter books), New Church Theological School Library, Cambridge, Mass.

6. *Ibid.*, April 16, 1821.

7. *Ibid.*, Nov. 18, 1822.

8. *Ibid.*, March 20, 1820.

9. *Ibid.*, April 16, 1821.

10. Quoted in Ophia D. Smith's "The Story of 'Johnny Appleseed,'" *Johnny Appleseed: A Voice in the Wilderness . . . Centennial Tribute*, 3rd edition (Paterson, N.J., 1947), 50.

11. Schlatter, Sept. 18, 1817, Dec. 20, 1818.

12. *Ibid.*, Nov., 1822.

13. *Ibid.*, Nov. 18, 1822. A list of "Readers and Receivers" for 1820, among Schlatter's letters for 1822, includes "John Chapman, Richland County."

14. *Journal of the Proceedings of the Fifth General Convention of the Receivers of the Doctrines of the New Jerusalem*, Philadelphia, June 3, 1822, 7.

15. MS. notes of John James, Jan. 23, 1857, photostat in Ohio Arch. and Hist. Soc. Library.

16. Mrs. Helen V. Austin, "Johnny Appleseed, the Pioneer Pomologist of the West," *Missouri State Horticultural Society Annual Report*, XXXIII, 13-18.

17. Norton, *op. cit.*, 132-33.

18. Letter in *Indiana Horticultural Society Transactions*, XXII, 35-40.

19. C. C. Palmer in Chicago (Ohio) *Times*, Aug. 25, 1910; W. W. Williams, *History of the Fire Lands* (Cleveland, 1879), 303-4.

20. *The New Jerusalem and Its Heavenly Doctrines*, Sec. 36-37. Other Swedenborg quotations below are from *Divine Love and Wisdom, Doctrines of the Holy Scriptures,* and *Heaven and Hell.*

21. James MS.

22. Graham, *op. cit.*, 539, 542, 545.

23. Schlatter, Nov. 18, 1822.

24. Chapman was never an ordained minister; all his missionary efforts were voluntary and unofficial. Nevertheless, a strong tradition

has it that he held a license to preach, and Pershing even cites specific time and place of his ordination! This much quoted tradition stems from the statement of Coffinbury that he had seen Chapman's New Church credentials and that Chapman had served as a missionary for two or three successive years as early as the fall of 1780 along the Potomac banks in northeastern Virginia. John would have been six years old in 1780. Since Coffinbury seems to have been a fairly reliable reporter, he must have misinterpreted some New Church correspondence he had seen in Chapman's possession. In Abingdon, Virginia, where a New Church group once thrived, there is a late tradition that Chapman once passed through the town. (Fannie Wethers, letter, March 20, 1939.)

25. John H. James, letter, March 26, 1938.
26. *New Jerusalem Messenger*, XXIV, 108.
27. Ednah C. Silver, *Sketches of the New Church in American on a Background of Civic and Social Life* (Boston, 1920), 50; Marguerite Beck Block, *The New Church in the New World* (N. Y., 1932), 122.
28. *New Church Journal*, March 26, 1890.
29. Family traditions reported in letters and interviews.
30. Silver, 50.

CHAPTER EIGHT

1. Hill, *Ashland County*, 183-85.
2. Estate papers.
3. William Cheesebrough, Stonington, Conn., "Journal of a Journey to the Westward," *American Historical Review*, XXXVII, 65-88.
4. Surveyed in 1807.
5. *OAHQ*, IX, 315.
6. *Ohio Liberal*, Feb. 24, 1874, says that in 1816 John Coulter and David Hill brought five hundred trees in a small boat to supply the neighbors round. Hill's *Ashland County*, 148, sets the date in the spring of 1815. Coulter and Edward Haley had set out some fruit trees, presumably Chapman's, when they first came in the fall of 1810.
7. On the farm "now owned by Michael Hogan," *Ohio Liberal*, Aug. 13, 1873.
8. Original owned by Mrs. Grace Culler, Shiloh, O.
9. Knapp, 28, 118, 514; Hill, *Ashland County*, 184.
10. Original owned by Mrs. Rose Zimmerman, Perrysville.

11. Glines, *op. cit.*
12. Hill, *Ashland County*, 184; Cf. Knapp, 409.
13. Benjamin Douglass, *History of Wayne County, Ohio* (Indianapolis, 1878), 196-207.
14. Cleveland *Plain Dealer*, Oct. 13, 1940; Ashland *Times-Gazette*, April 5, 1941.
15. Douglass, 198-99; Lucy Lilian Notestein, *Wooster of the Middle West* (New Haven, 1937), 11.
16. Knapp, 355.
17. Howe, II, 486. Knapp says also that Conrad Castor who arrived from Pennsylvania in the fall of 1817 set out an orchard from a Chapman nursery on the John Murphy place northeast of the farm owned by the late James Rowland.
18. *Indiana Horticultural Society, Transactions*, XXII, 35-40. The first orchard in Blooming Grove Township, Richland, was planted by William Trucks, Daniel and James Ayres from Chapman stock. They came to the county in 1815. (Graham, 394, 400). The first orchards in Jefferson Township were set out from his trees about 1818 by Jonathan Oldfield and George Aungst (*Ibid.*, 435).
19. *Op. cit.*

CHAPTER NINE

1. Howe, II, 486.
2. McLaughlin, 22-25.
3. *Ohio Liberal*, undated clipping in *Brinkerhoff Scrapbook*.
4. Howe, II, 486.
5. Letter, April 22, 1881.
6. *Ohio Liberal*, Aug. 13, 1873.
7. From the author's interviews in northern Ohio.
8. Howe, I, 260.
9. Knapp, 32; Howe, II, 486.
10. *Ohio Liberal, Brinkerhoff Scrapbook*.
11. *Ibid.*
12. *Ibid.*, Aug. 13, 1873.
13. Norton, 130-31.
14. *Ibid.*
15. Howe, II, 485.
16. Haley, *op. cit.*
17. David Ayres, *op. cit.*
18. Himrod, 16.

19. *Fire Lands Pioneer,* V, 99.
20. Knapp, 38.
21. *Ibid.,* 333
22. Norton, 130.
23. *Ohio Liberal,* July 30, 1873.
24. Haley, *op. cit.*
25. Glines, *op. cit.*
26. Himrod, 16.
27. Hill, *Ashland County,* 183-85.
28. *Op. cit.*
29. Himrod, 16.
30. Norton, 130.
31. Graham, 839.
32. Howe, I, 260; Hill, *Richland County,* 239-40; John W. Dawson, letter, Fort Wayne *Daily Sentinel,* Oct. 21, 23, 1871.
33. Knapp, 37.
34. *Ibid.*
35. *Op. cit.*
36. Glines.
37. *Op. cit.*
38. Himrod, 19.
39. Knapp, 36.
40. Coffinbury, *op. cit.*
41. Knapp, 327-28.
42. Hill, Ashland County, 186.
43. *Ohio Liberal, Brinkerhoff Scrapbook.*
44. *Ibid.,* April 15, 1874.
45. *Op. cit.*
46. Dawson, *op. cit.*
47. Howe, II, 485.
48. *Op. cit.*

CHAPTER TEN

1. *Putnam County Pioneer Reminiscences* No. 1 (Ottawa, O., 1878), 60.
2. *Op. cit.*
3. Knapp, 28-31.
4. Joshua Antrim, *History of Champaign and Logan Counties* (Bellefontaine, O., 1872), 148-60; J. W. Ogden, *History of Champaign County, Ohio* (Chicago, 1881), 292-98.
5. *History of Logan County* (Chicago, 1880), 234-48.

6. Marie Dickore in Cincinnati *Times-Star*, Sept. 25, 1942; Florence Murdoch in *OAHQ*, LIV, 113-26.

7. Howe, II, 469.

8. *Putnam County Pioneer Reminiscences* No. 2 (Ottawa, O., 1887), 45.

9. *History of Defiance County, Ohio* (Chicago, 1883), 109.

10. Hancock County Deeds, I, 380.

11. *Defiance County* (1883), 109.

12. *Ibid.*, Defiance *Crescent-News*, Sept. 26, 1941.

13. *Crescent-News, loc. cit.*

14. *Defiance County* (1883), 109.

15. *Crescent-News, loc. cit.*

16. Mercer County Deed Book B, 15. Mrs. Jacob Harter was Rebecca Copus. As many central Ohio families were now moving into northwestern Ohio, it is possible that Chapman had many old acquaintances there. Nearly every new county has a "Richland" township.

17. Mercer County Deed Book B, 14.

18. C. W. Williamson, *History of Western Ohio and Auglaize County* (Columbus, O., 1905), 696-99.

19. *History of Van Wert and Mercer Counties, Ohio* (Wapokoneta, O., 1882), 122.

20. Hill, *Coshocton County*, 267. Cf. H. Kenneth Dirlam, *John Chapman . . .* (Mansfield, O., 1954), 26. The recorded version in the new Knox County Deed Book is slightly different. Norton reported that Chapman once pointed out to Joseph Mahaffey two lots "about where Morey's soap factory was carried on" and said he might come back to them. The tail-race of the Clinton Mill Co. washed away some of the ground. The Mt. Vernon Woolen Factory later stood on another portion. Chapman was not seen in Mt. Vernon after 1829 (*op. cit.*, 133).

CHAPTER ELEVEN

1. See Appendix C for this and all other references to leases and real estate in this chapter.

2. Glines reporting the Chapman family version said: "About 1822 or 23, he turned up at Fort Wayne . . . where it is said he obtained a piece of land . . . where he planted a large nursery . . . He made several visits to Ohio in order to obtain more apple seeds. When he could manage to descend a stream in the direction he wished to travel, he would dig out a rude canoe or roll a

log into the stream and straddle it, so that he might float in the right direction."

3. T. B. Helm, *History of Allen County, Indiana* (Chicago, 1880), 147, 155, 178.

4. H. G. Sauer, *Geschichte der deutschen even.-luth. St. Pauls-Gemeinde zu Fort Wayne, Ind., vom Jahre 1837 bis 1887.* (St. Louis, 1887), 9.

5. Letter, Feb. 26, 1831, Indiana State Library.

6. *Putnam County Pioneer Reminiscences* No. 1, 60.

7. D. B. Beardsley, *History of Hancock County* (Springfield, O., 1881), 185.

8. J. F. Snow, *History of Adams County, Indiana* (Indianapolis, 1907), 57, 209; Appendix C.

9. Various undated visits to central Ohio homes seem to belong to the 1820's and -30's. Rosella Rice could remember falling over a leather bag of seeds left during the night for safekeeping (M'Gaw, Appendix). Louis Bromfield says that Chapman paid many visits to his great-grandfather, Jacob Barr, near Mansfield (letter, Dec. 7, 1937). A. J. Baughman said the man who knew and understood Chapman best was Dr. William Bushnell of Mansfield. Baughman's parents planted two orchards from Chapman's trees between 1827 and 1835. His grandfather, Capt. James Cunningham, told many tales of Chapman (Baughman, *Richland County*, I, 218). E. B. McLaughlin said that Chapman often visited his uncle Andrew Thompson on the school quarter half a mile south of Mansfield and on Section 27, farther south. He also visited John Stewart (McLaughlin, 22), and Lawrence Easterly (*Missouri State Hort. Report*, I, 208-9) south of Mansfield, and John A. Halter on Spring Mill Road (Mrs. Mary Pauley, 1945). Hiram R. Smith of Mansfield recalled that Chapman stored seeds in their barn (W. A. Duff in *Stories of Old Sandusky*, 1911.) Mrs. E. J. Howard told Pershing (*op. cit.*) that she remembered him at her father's home, near Cuyahoga Falls, Ohio. She was ten when Chapman died. Mrs. Jessie Louise Smith, Independence, Iowa, reports that Chapman visited her grandfather's cider press south of Big Prairie Station near Wooster, and that her mother, born in 1834, remembered him (Indianapolis *Star*, May 11, 1936). The Hedges, Hossinger and Jacob Parker families all had lively traditions of his visits to Mansfield. (Dirlam, *op. cit.*)

10. *Fire Lands Pioneer*, I, 15; V. 61-63. According to the reference,

trees were transplanted from the New Haven nursery in 1825, "He was accustomed to travel around with an old dilapidated horse and wagon, peddling cranberries which he picked in the Great Marsh." Cf. Columbus, O., *Dispatch*, Oct. 22, 1939.

11. Norton, 135: "He concluded to migrate farther west, and managing to get an old mare or two loaded with seeds, he left this part of the country for Sandusky prairie; and from thence made his way west, planting nurseries and living after the manner he did here, till finally the old fruit ripened, and was gathered near Fort Wayne, Indiana leaving nothing save the fragrance of good deeds and charitable acts to teach to the future that such a being as Johnny Appleseed had ever been and passed like an exhalation— the moisture of the morning's dew dried up by the heat of the sun at meridian!"

Many nurseries, orchards, and individual trees have been attributed to Chapman in Crawford County. According to John E. Hopley, *History of Crawford County* (Chicago, 1912), 551, he had a nursery on the Whetstone near the present city of Galion and planted orchards along the Sandusky. A large spring in front of Memorial Hospital in Bucyrus was said to be a favorite resort. A tree on the McMichael farm near Bucyrus, said to have been a century and a quarter old in 1946, is supposed to have been planted by John in payment for a night's shelter. W. L. Bloomer, in the Galion *Inquirer*, Sept. 25, 1945, located orchards on the Jonathan Fellows farm where the junior high school now stands and on the Hetter farm north of the Whetstone. Judge Stanbery saw Chapman in Crawford County in 1832.

Many unverifiable and dubious rumors of Chapman's visits to other Ohio neighborhoods spring from this period. Down the Scioto Valley, his trees have been pointed out north of Dublin and at Powell near O'Shaughnessy Dam. He is said to have slept on the floor of the Griswold tavern in Worthington and planted trees near the town. Others were planted near Camp Chase, Canal Winchester, and Buckeye Lake. Chapman Creek in Clark County has been associated with him. In 1918 an eighty-year-old tree near Chillicothe was claimed for him. Highland County says he visited the Leonard Butler cabin on Zane's trace and planted trees at the site of Etnah, historic Indian village in the woods overlooking Seven Caves. Other stories place him in Fayette, Butler, and Hamilton counties.

CHAPTER TWELVE

1. *History of Jay County, Indiana* (Chicago, 1864), 209.
2. McLaughlin, 25; Howe, II, 486.
3. Estate papers. A tree in this nursery was thriving in 1889, 93 inches in diameter (Robert S. Robertson, *Valley of the Upper Maumee River*, Madison, Wis., 1889, I, 392). For the estate papers see selected documents in Robert G. Harris, "Johnny Appleseed Source Book," *Old Fort News*, IX (March-June, 1945), Nos. 1-2.
4. J. F. Snow, *History of Adams County, Indiana* (Indianapolis, 1907), 57. In 1838, George W. Hall, Portland, current owner, reported that the site had become an island in the Wabash, but that trees and the cabin site were still to be seen. Family tradition says that Chapman stopped at the home of Joseph Braner, nurseryman, in the northwest corner of Jay County.
5. O. Morrow and D. W. Bashore, *Historical Atlas of Paulding County, Ohio* (Madison, Wis., 1892), 17.
6. *History of Allen County, Ohio* (Chicago, 1885), 237.
7. Mrs. Julia E. Meily, Lima, O., interview, 1946; memoirs preserved in Allen County Historical Society.
8. C. W. Williamson, *History of Western Ohio and Auglaize County* (Columbus, 1905), 696-99, 705.
9. J. D. Simkins, *Early History of Auglaize County* (St. Marys, O., 1901), 71.
10. Thaddeus S. Gilliland, *History of Van Wert County, Ohio* (Chicago, 1906), 143-46, 184. Lucy Jane Broom was born near Marietta, Aug. 2, 1816.
11. Community traditions collected in typescript, Van Wert public library; Gilliland, 83, 141, 143.
12. Van Wert library typescript; Van Wert *Times-Bulletin*, Oct. 8, 1941. There is an interesting reflection of a Richland County folk tale in the Van Wert tradition that Chapman once told Mrs. Gordon Gilliland to bring up her twelve-year-old daughter well as he intended to come back and marry her later. Mrs. Gilliland, very angry, told him never to come to the house again, and he never did.
13. Letter, July 18, 1938. Richey, who was born in 1837, remembered Chapman's staying over night two or three times at their farm two miles south of Fort Wayne, he claimed.
14. Harris, 15.
15. Norton, 135.

16. *Michigan History Magazine*, XII, 156; Fort Wayne *Journal-Gazette*, Sept. 20, 1936.

17. Howe, II, 484.

18. *Ashland County*, 184-85.

19. Norton, 133.

20. *Op. cit.*

21. A. J. Baughman, *History of Richland County* (Chicago, 1908), I, 218.

22. Hill, *Ashland County*, 184-85.

23. Howe, II, 486-87.

24. Knapp, 32-33.

25. M'Gaw, Appendix.

26. Knapp, 33.

27. *Op. cit.*; J. P. Henderson of Newville, Richland County, in a letter to the *Ohio Liberal*, Aug. 13, 1873, wrote: "Though Mr. Chapman may have been in this neighborhood after I came here late in the fall of 1830, it was never my good fortune to see him. From all I have heard, the description of him given by the late Dr. Fuller of Loudonville, I judge to have been correct, that 'he was a miserable looking old creature.'" Family tradition says that Chapman stayed two different nights at the Levi Sellers home halfway between Mount Vernon and Martinsburg (Miss Margaret McCormick, Mount Vernon, 1945).

28. D. B. Beardsley, *History of Hancock County* (Springfield, O., 1881), 131-35.

CHAPTER THIRTEEN

1. Rapin Andrews, *Diary*, typescript in Indiana State Library.

2. *Ohio Liberal*, Aug. 20, 27, 1873.

3. *Op. cit.* Sold to Emanuel Rudisill in 1843 and later associated with the name of Bleke. Dawson located the nursery on the northwest corner of the Rudisill land, on the St. Joseph road.

4. Fort Wayne *News-Sentinel*, Nov. 6, 1929.

5. Dawson said that the Worths lived on land then owned by Jesse Cole on the Feeder Canal in St. Joseph Township. In recent controversy, proponents of the traditional and historically supported belief that the Worth cabin, Chapman's nursery, and his burial place were on the west side of the river are the Johnny Appleseed Memorial Commission of Fort Wayne, the Johnny Appleseed Memorial Association, and the permanent Johnny Appleseed Committee of the Allen County Fort Wayne Historical Society.

The argument that these sites were across the river on the land now owned by Wesley S. Roebuck has been supported by Mr. Roebuck, the Three Rivers Forum, and a commission appointed in 1935 by the American Pomological Society. The Roebuck view is based largely upon the sworn statements in 1934 of one Eben Miles Chapman, age 76, who claimed to be the grandson of "Andrew Chapman, who was a brother of John Chapman." Cf. *OAHQ*, LII, 181-87, 276-84; H. A. S. Levering, "A Discussion of the Dawson Letter, and the Claims of Richard Worth against the Estate of John Chapman," July 28, 1939, typescript in Indiana State Library; Lizzie Roebuck, *Genealogy of the Chapman Family: Relatives of John Chapman (Johnny Appleseed)* (Fort Wayne, 1947).

6. Harris, 15-16.

7. *Ibid.*, Plate C.

8. Baughman, *Richland County*, I, 217.

9. Cf. report of the American Pomological Society Commission, *OAHQ*, LII, 181-87.

10. M'Gaw's *Philip Seymour* (1857–1883), was apparently the chief stimulus for these details.

CHAPTER FOURTEEN

1. Unless otherwise noted, the data of this chapter may be found in the estate papers, the most important of which are reprinted in Harris' *Johnny Appleseed Source Book* previously cited. The accounting reported throughout the administration appears confused and incomplete. The present author is responsible for the interpretation given here.

2. *Mercer County Judgment Index*, Book I, Case 270; Journal D, p. 215; Final Record D, p. 320; Col. 2, p. 245; Fee Book 7, p. 11. Still pending April 28, 1849.

3. The seeming apathy of the family in the dissolution of the estate may have been due to ignorance of John Chapman's holdings. Randall in 1848 issued the usual legal notice that the names and ages of heirs were not known.

CHAPTER FIFTEEN

1. For the numerous literary references related to this chapter see the author's *John Chapman: A Bibliography* (1944) and "Johnny Appleseed in American Folklore and Literature" in *Johnny Ap-*

pleseed: A Voice in the Wilderness, a centennial tribute by Harlan Hatcher, Robert Price, *et al* (1945).

2. From personal letters and interviews.

3. Monte M. Katterjohn in Indianapolis *Sunday Star* March 3, 1940.

4. (St. Louis, 1886), 377-407.

5. Randolph, New York, 1952; Canby and Gross (eds.), Mentor Books, 1954. Cf. *Missouri Historical Review,* XIX (1928), 622-629; Earl A. Collins, *Folk Tales of Missouri,* Boston, 1935, 47-51; *Arcadian Life* (Caddo Gap, Ark.), Jan., 1936; *Ozark Guide* (Winter, 1949), 22.

6. Columbus (O.) *Citizen,* Sept. 26, 1943.

A Selected Bibliography

From the hundreds of constantly multiplying printed allusions to Johnny Appleseed, the following items have been chosen because they represent either recent scholarship, important sources of biographical fact, major records of the popular tradition, books useful for children, or outstanding reflections in the arts. The list of memorials will be of service to the public visitor.

BIBLIOGRAPHY

Robert Price. *John Chapman: A Bibliography of "Johnny Appleseed" in American History, Literature and Folklore*, Paterson, N.J., 1944.

BIOGRAPHY

H. Kenneth Dirlam, *John Chapman, by Occupation a Gatherer and Planter of Appleseeds*, Mansfield, O., 1954.

Robert C. Harris (ed.). "Johnny Appleseed Source Book," Fort Wayne, Indiana, *Old Fort News*, IX (March-June, 1945), 3rd edition, May, 1949.

Journal of the Proceedings of the Fifth General Convention of the New Jerusalem. . . . Philadelphia, June 3-5, 1822.

Carl Theophilus Odhner, *Annals of the New Church*, I, *passim*, Bryn Athyn, Pa., 1904.

Robert Price. "A Boyhood for Johnny Appleseed," *New England Quarterly*, XVII (Sept., 1944), 381-393; "The New England Origins of Johnny Appleseed," *Ibid.*, XII (Sept., 1939), 454-469; "Johnny Appleseed: Yankee Peddler," *Farm Quarterly*, V (Summer, 1950), 80-81.

Report of the Society for Printing, Publishing and Circulating the Writings of Emanuel Swedenborg, Manchester, England, Jan. 14, 1817.

Florence E. Wheeler. "John Chapman" in *Leominster 200th Anniversary*, Leominster, Mass., June 2-8, 1940, pp. 15-17; "John Chapman's Line of Descent from Edward Chapman of Ipswich," *OAHQ*, XLVIII (Jan., 1939), 28-33.

FOLKLORE AND IMPORTANT REPORTS OF POPULAR TRADITION

B. A. Botkin (ed.). *A Treasury of American Folklore*, N.Y., 1944, 255-6, 261-70; *A Treasury of New England Folklore*, N.Y., 1947, 558-560.

Louis Bromfield, *Pleasant Valley*, N. Y., 1945, 26-35, 90-91.

Frances Frost. "Johnny Appleseed" in *Legends of the United Nations*, N.Y., 1943, 154-161.

W. M. Glines. *Johnny Appleseed by One Who Knew Him*, Columbus, O., 1922.

Harlan Hatcher. *The Buckeye Country*, N.Y., 1940, 166-73.

W. D. Haley. "Johnny Appleseed—A Pioneer Hero," *Harper's Monthly Magazine*, XLIII (Nov., 1871), 830-36.

Henry Howe, *Historical Collections of Ohio*, Cincinnati, 1847, 1889-91, 1896. In the last edition, I, 260; II, 484-7, 673.

H. S. Knapp, *History of the Pioneer and Modern Times of Ashland County, Ohio*, Philadelphia, 1863, 27-38.

Vachel Lindsay, *The Litany of Washington Street*, N.Y., 1929, 69-93.

James F. M'Gaw, *Philip Seymour; or, Pioneer Life in Richland County, Ohio*, Mansfield, O., 1857, 1883, 1902, 1908.

A. Banning Norton, *A History of Knox County, Ohio, from 1779 to 1862 Inclusive*, Columbus, O., 1862, 50.

Robert Price, "Johnny Appleseed in American Folklore and Literature" in *Johnny Appleseed: A Voice in the Wilderness* by Harlan Hatcher, Robert Price *et al.*, Paterson, N.J., 3rd edition, 1947, 1-21.

Charles Allen Smart, "The Return of Johnny Appleseed," *Harper's Monthly Magazine*, CLXXIX (Aug., 1939), 225-34.

Dixon Wecter, *The Hero in America*, N.Y., 1941, 193-98.

REFLECTIONS IN THE ARTS

1. *Poetry*

Rosemary and Stephen Vincent Benét, "Johnny Appleseed" in *A Book of Americans*, N.Y., 1933, 47-49.

Lydia Maria Child, "Apple-Seed John," *St. Nicholas*, VII (July, 1880), 604-5.

Frances Frost, "American Ghost," *New York Herald Tribune*, Aug. 21, 1943.

Ernest C. Leverenz, *Johnny Appleseed and Shorter Poems*, N.Y., 1951.

Vachel Lindsay, "In Praise of Johnny Appleseed" and eight other poems on the same theme in *Collected Poems*, N.Y., 1927; "The Apple-Barrel of Johnny Appleseed" and "Johnny Appleseed Still Farther West" in *Going to the Sun*, N.Y., 1923; and *Johnny Appleseed and Other Poems*, N.Y., 1928, 1930.

Edgar Lee Masters, "Johnny Appleseed" in *Toward the Gulf*, N.Y., 1918, 42-45.

Carl Sandburg, "Johnny Appleseed," *Chicago Daily News*, Oct. 20, 1926; *The People, Yes*, N.Y., 1936, 231.

Nancy Byrd Turner, "Rhyme of Johnny Appleseed," *Child Life*, Aug. 28, 1937.

2. *Novels*

Eleanor Atkinson. *Johnny Appleseed: The Romance of the Sower*, N.Y., 1915.

Louis Bromfield. *The Farm*, N.Y., 1933, 103-5.

Mary Hartwell Catherwood. *Lazarre*, Indianapolis, 1901.

Howard Fast. *The Tall Hunter*, N.Y., 1942.

Newell Dwight Hillis, *The Quest of John Chapman: The Story of a Forgotten Hero*, N.Y., 1904.

Vachel Lindsay. *The Golden Book of Springfield*, N.Y., 1920.

3. Children's Fiction

Emily Taft Douglas. *Appleseed Farm*, N.Y., 1948. 128 pp.

Ruth Langland Holberg. *Restless Johnny: The Story of Johnny Appleseed*, N.Y., 1950. 210 pp.

Meridel LeSueur, *Little Brother of the Wilderness: The Story of Johnny Appleseed*, N.Y., 1947. 68 pp.

Mabel Leigh Hunt. *Better Known as Johnny Appleseed*, Philadelphia, 1950. 212 pp.

Walt Disney's Johnny Appleseed, adapted by Ted Parmalee from the Walt Disney Picture "Melody Time," N.Y., 1948, 1949. "A Little Golden Book."

4. Music

Walt Disney, Johnny Appleseed songs from *Melody Time*, 1948.

Harvey B. Gaul. *Old Johnny Appleseed*, cantata for treble voices, C. C. Birchard & Co., Boston, 1926.

Harvey Worthington Loomis and David Stevens. *Johnny Appleseed*, operetta in one act for children, Willis Music Co., Cincinnati, 1925.

Elie Siegmeister. "Johnny Appleseed," lyric by Rosemary and Stephen Vincent Benét, in Olin Downes and Siegmeister (eds.), *Treasury of American Song*, Howell, Soskin, & Co., 1940.

Jacques Wolfe, "Johnny Appleseed," lyric by Merrick F. McCarthy, for chorus of mixed voices, with baritone solo; also for high or low voice with piano accompaniment, Carl Fischer, N.Y., 1946.

MEMORIALS

Ashland, Ohio. Monument erected by school children of Ashland County. Dedicated July 28, 1915.

Ashland, Ohio. Copus massacre monument, Mifflin Township, Ashland County. Erected 1882.

Dexter City, Ohio. Monument erected by the Johnny Appleseed Memorial Commission and the Washington County Pioneer Association. Dedicated Sept. 27, 1942.

Fort Wayne, Indiana. Johnny Appleseed Memorial Bridge over St. Joseph River. Dedicated May 21, 1949.

Fort Wayne, Indiana. Johnny Appleseed Memorial Park, including the Archer Burying Ground with the traditional site of John Chapman's grave. The site is marked by an iron fence, the gift of Hon. Stephen B. Fleming, 1916, and by a granite stone dedicated by the Optimist Club, May 26, 1935.

Fort Wayne, Indiana. Granite boulder in Swinney Park, gift of Hon. Stephen B. Fleming, erected by the Indiana Horticultural Society, 1916.

Leominster, Mass. Granite marker at traditional site of John Chapman's birthplace. Dedicated June 4, 1940.

Mansfield, Ohio. Monument in Sherman-Heineman Park, gift of Hon. M. B. Bushnell. Dedicated by Richland Horticultural Society, Nov. 8, 1890. Rededicated Sept. 26, 1953.

Pomeroy to Toledo, Ohio. Johnny Appleseed Memorial Highway, State Routes 33, 31, and 25. Dedicated Sept. 28, 1950.

Springfield, Mass. Monument in Stebbins Park, erected by Springfield Garden Club, 1936.

Index

305